Paternal Deprivation

Family, School, Sexuality, and Society

Henry B. Biller
University of Rhode Island

Lexington Books
D.C. Heath and Company
Lexington, Massachusetts
Toronto   London

Library of Congress Cataloging in Publication Data

Biller, Henry B.
　Paternal deprivation; family, school, sexuality, and society.

　Bibliography: p.
　1. Paternal deprivation. 2. Father and child. 3. Sex role. I. Title.
[DNLM: 1. Child development. 2. Father-child relations. 3. Paternal
deprivation. 4. Psychosexual development. WS105 B597p]

BF723.P33B54　　　155.9'2'4　　　74-928
ISBN 0-669-91694-3

To my wife, Lana
and
our sons
Jonathan, Kenneth,
Cameron, and Michael

Contents

Preface

This book can be considered a sequel to *Father, Child and Sex Role* (Biller 1971a). Although some of the sections are much the same, *Paternal Deprivation* offers an increased coverage of most of the topics covered in *Father, Child and Sex Role*. What distinguishes *Paternal Deprivation* as a new book, rather than as a revision, is a concentration on various forms of paternal deprivation, a strong focus on the father-infant and father-mother relationships, a detailed analysis of the influence of fathering on cognitive functioning and school adjustment, and much more emphasis on the ways in which inadequate fathering can contribute to the development of personal, sexual and social problems.

The preparation of this book was much facilitated by my participation in a number of invited speaking and writing endeavors during the last few years. An invitation to present a paper (Biller 1972a) at *The Medical Research Council of Ireland's Symposium on the Experimental Behavior Basis of Mental Disturbance* greatly stimulated my thinking concerning the concept of paternal deprivation. An invitation to present a paper (Biller 1974a) at *The 1973 Nebraska Symposium on Motivation* (Cole and Dienstbier 1974) and also an invitation to contribute a chapter (Biller 1974b) to Anthony Davids' (1974) *Child Personality and Psychopathology: Current Topics* helped me to bring together the material presented in Chapter 5 concerning fathering, cognitive and academic functioning. The last part of Chapter 9, a brief summary of guidelines for effective fathering, is based on an invited article (Biller 1973a) to *The London Sunday Times Magazine*.

I would like to take this opportunity to express my appreciation to my colleagues for their continuing interest in me and my work; I am especially grateful to Allan Berman, Anthony Davids, Barry L. Josephson, Dennis L. Meredith, Peter F. Merenda, Patricia Raymond, Mollie S. Smart, Russell C. Smart, and Carolyn Waller. The publication of this book also owes much to the consistent support of Michael McCarroll, Carolyn Hanson, and Elizabeth Patterson of Lexington Books.

Henry B. Biller

1 Paternal Deprivation and Sex Role Functioning

The thesis of this book is that paternal deprivation, including patterns of inadequate fathering as well as father absence, is a highly significant factor in the development of serious psychological and social problems. Much of the material in this book concerns the impact of variations in fathering on sex role development. Paternal deprivation can lead to conflicts and rigidities in the individual's sex role adjustment, which in turn are often related to deficits in emotional, cognitive, and interpersonal functioning.

This book is an attempt to review, analyze, and integrate a large body of diverse data concerning the possible linkage of variations in fathering to individual differences in children's behavior. Relevant data have come from many different fields including anthropology, child development and family relations, education, psychiatry, social work, and sociology as well as from several different areas of psychology. There is much emphasis on the methodological shortcomings of previous research and the need for more systematic investigations and theoretical integrations.

Preview

Chapter 1 serves as an introduction to many of the issues which are explored in much greater depth in ensuing chapters. Chapter 2 deals with several theories concerning a boy's identification with his father. An attempt is made to present an integrated view of the interaction of familial, constitutional, and sociocultural factors on a boy's relationship with his father and his masculine development. There is an emphasis throughout this book on the importance of realizing that a child's constitutional characteristics and a family's sociocultural background must be taken into account in trying to understand the dynamics of family interactions.

Chapter 3 describes data relating to father-infant attachment and considers the impact of different dimensions of paternal behavior on a boy's sex role functioning. Chapter 4 analyzes research concerning the effects of father absence, surrogate models, and sociocultural background on masculine development. Chapter 5 reviews evidence pertaining to the influence of adequate and inadequate fathering on various facets of personal and social adjustment. There is a concentration on the role of paternal deprivation in the development of psychopathology. The importance of the father-mother relationship and peer group factors are heavily stressed in Chapter 5 as well as in other chapters.

1

Chapter 6 concentrates on the influence of the mother-child relationship on the personality development of the paternally deprived boy. Chapter 7 is devoted to a vast array of data indicating the significance of the father-daughter relationship on a girl's emotional and interpersonal functioning. Chapter 8 integrates findings concerning the impact of the father-child relationship on cognitive functioning and academic adjustment. There is a focus on the way in which the effects of paternal deprivation and the feminized classroom can combine to negatively affect the personality development of children. Chapter 9 reviews some of the current ways our society is coping with paternal deprivation and presents some potential solutions to this debilitating problem.

Biological and Sociocultural Perspective

There is a tremendous range of adult male-infant interactions among different species (and even within species) of nonhuman primates (Jolly 1972). Such findings indicate that male primates at least have a capacity to be effective caretakers and socializers of the young. Except for nursing, the male marmoset takes over almost complete care of the young. Male baboons are often involved in grooming and infant-care activities and male chimpanzees have usually been found to be protective, nurturant, and permissive with infants. In general, males among New World monkeys (e.g., lemurs, marmosets) are much more active and positive in their attachment to their young than are those among Old World monkeys (e.g., pigtail macaques, rhesus).

A particularly unpredictable group are male rhesus monkeys. They sometimes appear very hostile towards infants, even killing them under crowded conditions. However, they have at other times been observed grooming and playing with the young (Mitchell 1969). Observations in laboratory situations indicate that the adult rhesus monkey is capable of rearing an infant monkey. The adult male monkey's initial hostile impulses can be controlled and an adult-infant attachment gradually develops. Situational factors appear to be very important in the quality of the adult rhesus monkey's responsivity toward infants and juveniles (Redican and Mitchell 1973).

Among humans as well as other primates, there may be biological predispositions involved in father-child attachments. Nonhuman primates sometimes are found in social groupings similar to the human family (La Barre 1954). In addition to the somewhat indirect support of the father-child attachment due to the father-mother sexual attachment, there may be the influence of other biologically-based factors. Man's curiosity, his sensitivity to tactile stimulation, and a basic nurturant instinct which emerges under certain conditions predisposes him, or at least allows him, to find fathering stimulating and gratifying. The ability to appreciate imitation by another is also a fundamental reinforcer of fathering and probably also has a biological basis (Biller and Meredith 1974).

However, human societies differ tremendously with respect to the usual amount of time the father is involved with his children. Mead (1957) noted that in some preliterate societies, fathers take much responsibility for the care of their infants. For example, among the Australian aborigines, the father after a successful morning hunt will carry and care for the young infant while the mother gathers vegetables. Among the Marquesans, men commonly engaged in many activities relating to infant and child care (Linton 1936). In contrast to such preliterate societies, Mead could find no complex society with a written tradition that ever bestowed any expectation or prestige upon fathers for caring for their infants.

Investigators making cross-cultural comparisons (on the basis of ethnographic accounts of preliterate societies) have presented data suggesting that the amount of father-child involvement in a society can influence the personality development of its children. Romney's (1965) reanalysis of Barry, Bacon, and Child's (1957) findings indicate that: in societies where there is relatively little father availability, emphasis on children being compliant prevails; whereas, in societies with high father availability, children are expected to be assertive. Romney's data can be interpreted as suggesting that the frequent availability of an active, involved father makes it more likely for individuals to actualize their potentialities. Bacon, Child, and Barry (1963) discovered that societies with relatively low father availability had high crime rates. Stephen's (1962) data suggest that intense, restrictive mother-child relationships are more likely to occur in societies in which there is relatively low father availability in childhood. Close binding mother-child relationships appear to be negatively related to sexual adjustment in adulthood. Children seem to develop much more adequately in societies in which the father is actively involved in childrearing (Biller 1971a).

In our society, men have been judged to be good fathers if they provide for their family economically, but the quality of father-child interactions has not been given enough attention. The maternal role has been seen as the key process by which children become socialized. It has been argued that childrearing is an essential dimension of the adult feminine role, but definitions of masculinity have seldom encompassed fathering activities. In contrast to the emphasis on the mother-child relationship, there has been relatively little attention given to the impact of the father-child relationship on personality development. Throughout most of the first half of the twentieth century, childrearing was seen mainly as the mother's responsibility, and the father was not expected to be an important person in the socialization process (Brenton 1966; Gorer 1948; Mitscherlich 1969; Nash 1965).

There was also a paucity of scientific inquiry into the nature and consequences of fathering until quite recently. For example, a review of American family research between 1929-1956 revealed only eleven publications pertaining to the father-child relationship but 160 concerned with the mother-child relationship (Peterson et al. 1959). A particularly dramatic example of the relative neglect of the father's role can be seen in the vast literature on the influence of maternal deprivation (Bowlby 1951; Goldfarb 1955). It has only been recently that most researchers have begun to realize that maternal deprivation is not necessarily equivalent to parental deprivation; and that the potential influence of paternal behavior must also be considered if the effects of parental deprivation are to be understood (Biller 1972a; Nash 1970; Rutter 1972; Yarrow 1964).

Father-absence in America is a widespread and profound problem—over 10 percent of the children in this country live in fatherless homes. In some ghettoes the figure is as high as 50 percent. These statistics give some indication of the scope of the problem, but they fail to spell out the serious consequences of the paternal deprivation found in even many so-called "father-present" American families. Research with both intact and "broken" families has revealed a widespread lack of the father-involvement necessary for the optimal personality development of children (Biller 1971a; Biller and Meredith 1974).

There are many situations in which the father lives with his family but has little contact with his children. A review of data concerning the amount of time fathers spend at work and with their children suggests a picture of general paternal deprivation, since a large number of fathers have only minimal contact with their children. An increasing number of middle class males, particularly business and professional men, work 55 hours or more a week. The executive-professional man is also often involved several hours a week in commuting to work. Of course, many men work at home as well as at the office, and this may further lessen their opportunities to interact with their children. Some research has suggested that the average family spends only about an hour a day together and most of this is during meal time (LeMasters 1970; Lynn 1974).

The pattern of low participation of the husband in the family is often evident even during the expectant father period. Liebenberg (1967), studying first-time expectant fathers, reported that the majority were relatively unavailable to their pregnant wives because of heavy work or educational commitments. Ban and Lewis (1971) interviewed fathers of one-year-olds and found, that on the average, they spent only about 15 to 20 minutes per day with their infants. Relative to the mother, the father usually spends much less time with his infant, particularly in early infancy. I have observed large individual differences among fathers with infants. Some fathers are spending two hours a day in direct interaction with their infants by the time the infants are nine months old, but the majority of fathers spend little more than 10 or 15 minutes a day during the week in one-to-one interaction with them (Biller 1974c).

Similarly, my research with kindergarten-age and elementary school children has suggested wide individual differences in degree of father-child interaction. Again, the average appears to be relatively low. In a study of predominantly lower-middle-class and middle-class kindergarten boys, I found that most fathers (94 of 159 families where father was at home) were away two or three evenings a week or were away on business trips several days a month (Biller 1968a). Some of our other research projects have also suggested that most fathers spend relatively little time in one to one interactions with their children (e.g., Blanchard and Biller 1971; Reuter and Biller 1973). Of course, the time the father spends with his family is only one indication of his involvement; and much of the material in this book indicates that the quality of the father-child relationship is particularly important.

The Concept of Paternal Deprivation

Paternal deprivation is a term that can be used to include various inadequacies in a child's experience with his father or father surrogate. Paternal deprivation can be in the context of total father absence or separation from the father for some extended period of time. But the child does not necessarily have to be separated from his father to suffer from paternal deprivation. Paternal deprivation can occur when the father is available but there is not a relatively meaningful father-child attachment.

An examination of the quality of the father's behavior when he is available and interacting with his child is needed. A child's attachment with an ineffectual and/or emotionally disturbed father can also be considered a particular form of paternal deprivation (Biller 1972a). Paternal deprivation does not take place in a vacuum. A thorough analysis must take into account such variables as the reason for paternal deprivation, the sex and developmental status of the child, the quality of the mother-child and mother-father relationships, the family's structure and sociocultural background, and the availability of surrogate models.

Much of the interest in the effects of paternal deprivation has evolved from growing concern with the psychological, social, and economic disadvantages often suffered by fatherless children. However, it is important to emphasize that father absence per se does not necessarily lead to developmental deficits and/or render the father-absent child inferior in psychological functioning relative to the father-present child. Fatherless children are far from a homogeneous group. To begin with, an almost infinite variety of patterns of father absence can be specified. Many factors need to be considered in evaluating the father-absent situation: type (constant, intermittent, temporary, etc.), length, cause, child's age and sex, child's constitutional characteristics, mother's reaction to husband-absence, quality of mother-child interactions, the family's socioeconomic status, and availability of surrogate models. The father-absent child may not be paternally deprived because he has a very adequate father-surrogate, or he may be less paternally deprived than are many father-present children.

The child who has an involved and competent mother *and* father is more likely to have generally adequate psychological functioning, and is less likely to suffer from developmental deficits and psychopathology, than is the child who is reared in a one-parent family. This generalization is not the same as assuming that all father-absent children are going to have more difficulties in their development than are all father-present children. For example, there is evidence that children with competent mothers are less likely to have certain types of developmental deficits than are children who have a dominating mother and a passive-ineffectual father. The father-absent child may develop a more flexible image of adult men, and at least may seek out some type of father surrogate, whereas the child with a passive-ineffectual and/or rejecting father may have a very negative image of adult males and avoid interacting with them (Biller 1971a).

The age of onset of paternal deprivation appears to be a very important factor. Infants often form strong attachments to their fathers as well as their mothers (Ban and Lewis 1971; Biller 1971a, 1974c; Pedersen and Robson 1969). A strong and positive attachment to a nurturant and competent father can much facilitate the infant and young child's development. Our observations have suggested that children who are able to form strong attachments to both their mothers and fathers during infancy have more positive self-concepts and success in interpersonal relations than children who have only an attachment to their mothers (Biller 1971a, 1974c; Biller and Meredith 1974).

On the other hand, the lack of an attachment to a father or father surrogate in the first few years of life, or a relatively permanent disruption of an ongoing fathering relationship, may have unfortunate consequences for the child. Father absence before the age of four or five appears to have more of a disruptive effect on the individual's personality development than does father absence beginning at a later-age period. For example, in our research, we have consistently found that boys who become father absent before the age of four or five have less masculine sex-role orientations (self-concepts) and more sex-role conflicts than either father-present boys or boys who become father-absent at a later time (Biller 1968b, 1969b, 1974a; Biller and Bahm 1971). Other data have indicated that early father absence is often associated with a low level of independence and assertiveness in peer relations (Hetherington 1966), feelings of inferiority and mistrust of others (Santrock 1970b), and antisocial behavior (Siegman 1966).

Findings from cross-cultural studies have suggested that very close and exclusive relationships with mothers in the first two or three years of life, and the relative unavailability of fathers, are frequently associated with sex-role conflicts and sexual anxiety in adolescence and adulthood (Burton 1972; Burton and Whiting 1961; Stephens 1962). Some research also points to a particularly high frequency of early father absence (before age four) among emotionally disturbed children (Holman 1953) and adults (Beck, Sehti, and Tuthill 1963). It, of course, may be that father absence at different age periods affects different dimensions of personality development (Biller 1971a; 1974a).

Serious criticisms can be directed towards much of the research that has been conducted concerning father-child relationships. For example, investigators have often ignored variations among father-absent families and also implicitly made the tenuous assumption that father presence ensures an active father-child relationship. Furthermore, the potential interactions of paternal influence with factors such as variations in mothering and the child's constitutional predispositions have generally not been taken into account.

The Concept of Sex Role

Much of the material in this book relates to the various ways in which paternal deprivation may affect the sex-role development process. Since the sex-role development process is very complex and involves many dimensions of personality functioning, it is important to examine some basic issues and definitions concerning the concept of sex role (Biller 1971a, 1972b; Biller and Borstelmann 1967).

Sex-role development encompasses an exceedingly large cluster of variables. In everyday conversations such terms as masculine, feminine, sissy, tomboy, and homosexual are often used to convey observations related to sex role. A difficulty is that these terms often mean different things to different people. An individual may be labeled as masculine or feminine on the basis of his behavior and appearance. When such statements are examined more carefully, it is often found that a person is called masculine when exhibiting aggressive or assertive behavior and called feminine when emitting more passive or dependent behavior. Such labels are not very precise but are frequently used and have a pervasive reality for many people (Biller 1972b).

Sex role preference refers to an individual's valuation of certain activities and objects. Males and females often differ tremendously in the kinds of things they do and the types of objects they prefer: for instance, boys and girls typically play with different types of toys and engage in different kinds of games. Men and women usually differ in their hobbies, in the books they read, and their preferences for occupational activities. There are many individual differences among members of a given sex, but the individual who has a wide range of interests may best maximize his or her potential.

A problem with much of the research on sex role development is that it has been restricted to measurement of sex role preference. In itself, an individual's sex-role preference does not appear to be a particularly valid indicator of his overall masculinity or femininity, and much more attention needs to be given to other aspects of sex role functioning. A related problem concerns the frequent confusion, or assumed isomorphism, of the awareness of social norms relating to sex role behavior with sex role preference. The knowledge of culturally expected sex role differences does not mean that the individual personally prefers or makes same-sex choices (Biller 1971a, 1972b).

Sex role adoption relates to the individual's functioning in social and environmental interaction. Aggressiveness, independence, and competence in physical activities, are generally perceived to be masculine characteristics. Certain types of intellectual expertise, particularly when they are enmeshed in a problem-solving context, are usually considered quite masculine. It is interesting to note that middle-class individuals are more likely to associate intellectual prowess with masculinity whereas working-class individuals emphasize physical competence (Biller 1966a).

Possibly because many societies put a higher value on "masculine behaviors," the task of defining femininity seems more difficult. Femininity has often been associated with the lack of masculine characteristics. Sometimes it is defined as the opposite of masculinity. More frequently than masculinity, it is defined in a negative manner. Passivity, dependency, and timidity are often considered feminine behaviors. However, femininity can be viewed as including various interpersonal skills and the ability to express a variety and intensity of emotions. Sensitivity, understanding, empathy, the ability to mediate, to verbally communicate feelings and attitudes, to soothe and to comfort are in the forefront in the description of the positively feminine woman (Biller 1971a; Biller and Weiss 1970).

Obviously such positive characteristics can also enhance the male's personality, as can the ability to be assertive and independent make for a more effective female. In fact, regardless of their sex, the most actualized individuals possess both positive masculine *and* feminine qualities. For example, to be viewed as masculine, a male can possess a high level of interpersonal sensitivity, as long as he also manifests a pattern of typically masculine behaviors. It does not make much sense to label a man as unmasculine because he occasionally cries or likes to openly express his affection to others. If he is also masculine in appearance, and assertive and aggressive, he may even be perceived as more masculine because of his sensitivity and gentleness.

I am emphasizing positive facets of sex role behavior. There are certain sex role-related behaviors that can be considered to be very meaningful in the sense of self-actualization while others are related to a lack of competency. For example, assertiveness and independence have been traditionally considered to be hallmarks of the masculine role and certainly in *most* contexts are indices of competency. On the other hand, masculinity has often been associated with aloofness and insensitivity to others' feelings. Such characteristics can be generally viewed as manifestations of interpersonal incompetency.

The feminine role has more consistently been equated with incompetency, such characteristics as timidity and dependency being seen as very salient dimensions. Nevertheless, one can extract such personality traits as nurturance and sensitivity from definitions of femininity. Again, the focus is on the development of positive masculine characteristics such as assertiveness and independence and positive feminine characteristics such as nurturance and sensitivity. A basic assumption is that, although there may be biological factors predisposing some degree of overall sex differences, both males and females can be judged as more competent if they possess both positive masculine and positive feminine characteristics (Biller 1972a).

There has been a consideration of how others perceive the individual's sex role behavior in social and environmental interactions (sex role adoption) and how the individual perceives sex-typed opportunities in his environment (sex role preference). However, the most important and perhaps the most stable component of sex role development appears to be related to the individual's self-perceptions. *Sex role orientation* refers to how the individual perceives himself in terms of his sex-role adequacy. A basic dimension of the individual's sex role orientation is how he views his body. Satisfaction with one's body and its related reproductive capacity is very important. The acceptance of one's biology is critical for positive self-concept development. Factors such as physical appearance and perceived attractiveness to the opposite sex can be extremely important in the individual's overall psychological adjustment (Biller 1971a).

Sex role orientation includes both the individual's perception of his relative masculinity and/or femininity and how he or she feels about himself in this regard. Such perceptions are not necessarily consistent with his sex role preference or sex role adoption. An individual may be very masculine in his preference and adoption but feel very uncomfortable about such behavior and merely be conforming to social pressures. On the other hand, he may be manifesting culturally inappropriate behavior and desire more self-congruence. There may also be a more subtle discrepancy in which anxiety or defensiveness is exhibited but the individual is not clearly aware of the source of his problem (Biller 1971a, 1972a).

Rigidities in Socialization

Two of the most basic problems in socialization are related to the rigidity of conventional sex role stereotypes. The first has to do with expected parental behaviors and the second with the typical "feminization" of preprimary and elementary school education. In a sense, these are very related issues in that in both the early socialization process in the family and in the beginning stages of our educational process, there is often marked paternal deprivation.

Sex role distinctions are very much linked with the way in which father and mother roles are defined. The mother in most societies is expected to be nurturant and sensitive, and to be an expert in family communications and in dealing with intra-familial tensions, while the father is to be most competent in dealing with environmental exigencies and in solving problems which require a knowledge of the nonsocial environment (Zelditch 1955). Aside from certain types of expected tutelage of the son by the father in some societies, there often seems to be little concern for the quality of father-child interactions, especially in infancy and early adulthood.

Given the way males and females have been socialized in our society, it is likely that, over and above constitutional predispositions, fathers and mothers will have different ranges of competencies and interests (Biller 1971a). For example, fathers are more apt to have assertive and independent characteristics whereas mothers are more likely to have a high level of interpersonal sensitivity and ability to communicate feelings. The optimal situation for the child is to have both an involved mother and involved father. The child is then exposed to a wider degree of adaptive characteristics.

Children who are both well-fathered and well-mothered are likely to have positive self-concepts and a comfort about their biological sexuality. They feel good about being male or female and have a pride in their basic sex role orientation. They are comfortable with themselves and their sexuality but yet are able to be relatively flexible in their interests and responsivity to others. Security in sex role orientation gives the child more of an opportunity to develop in an actualized way. On the other hand, children who are paternally deprived are more likely to take either a defensive posture of rigid adherence to cultural sex role standards or to attempt to completely avoid expected gender-related behaviors (Biller and Meredith 1974).

Similarly, school situations which give children the opportunity to interact with competent teachers of both sexes may help facilitate the child's development. Female teachers all too frequently react negatively to assertive behavior in the classroom and seem to feel much more comfortable with girls who are generally quieter, more obedient, and conforming. Boys seem to perceive that teachers are much more positive in responding to girls and to feminine behavior and interest patterns. Unfortunately, the type of "feminine" behavior reinforced in the classroom is often of a very negative quality if one is using self-actualization as a criterion. For example, timidity, passivity, dependency, obedience, and quietness are usually rewarded. The boy or girl who is independent, assertive, questioning, and challenging is typically at a great disadvantage. Even though girls generally seem to adapt more easily to the early school environment, such an atmosphere is not conducive to their optimal development. Girls need to learn how to be independent and assertive just as much as do boys.

There is an increasing amount of data indicating that the quality of father-child interactions can have much influence on the cognitive functioning and academic achievement of both boys and girls (Biller 1974a, 1974b). Furthermore, observations have suggested that competent male teachers in pre-elementary and elementary school can have a very facilitating effect on learning and overall classroom atmosphere. Paternally deprived children seem to be especially responsive to male teachers. Recent research suggests that adult male influence can have particularly profound effects in the first few years of life, a time at which females have traditionally been considered to be the sole socializing agents.

2

Fathering, Identification, and Masculine Development: Some Theoretical Perspectives

In the first section of this chapter there is a brief summary of views of the father-son relationship emanating from the major theories of identification, including Freudian theory, learning theory, and Parsonian theory. Although there is much controversy regarding the meaning and utility of the term identification, these theories suggest some potentially important dimensions of paternal behavior.

The second section of the chapter is devoted to a multidimensional conception of identification and masculine development, an attempt to integrate notions relating to the complex interactions among various dimensions of paternal behavior and different aspects of sex role development.

Theories of Identification

Theories of identification have stimulated the major hypotheses pertaining to the child's sex role development. Identification theorists attempt to account for more than sex role development and are also concerned with conscience development, impulse control, and adult role playing behavior as well. However, in an attempt to delineate possible familial antecedents, the purpose here is to discuss only hypotheses relating to the sex role development of boys (Biller 1971a).

Freudian Theory

The Freudian view of the father's role in masculine development is described first, since other identification theory hypotheses are, at least in part, derivatives (Bronfenbrenner 1960). Freud alluded to anatomical and other biological differences between the sexes as predisposing different behavior patterns, but he also believed that both males and females had bisexual characteristics. He often depicted parent-child relationships as important determinants of sex role development (Freud 1950, 1955).

Freud postulated that the boy desires to have an exclusive relationship with his mother during the Oedipal period when he is three to five years of age. Freud believed that the boy comes to see his father as a very aggressive competitor for his mother's affection and to fear that the father will castrate him. According to Freud, the normal resolution of the Oedipus complex takes place when, in order to cope with his fear of castration, the boy identifies with his father, the aggressor, and represses his desire for his mother. The boy's subsequent strong masculine strivings and desire to be like his father were seen as a by-product of his identification with his father.

Bronfenbrenner (1960) pointed out that in Freud's later writings he described "an identification of an affectionate sort" between the boy and his father, and that some affectionate dependency on the father may increase the probability of "identification with the aggressor." In an interesting account of Freud's consideration of the father's role, Burlingham (1973) also notes that Freud occasionally alluded to affectionate father-child attachments in pre-Oedipal development. Despite this, in Freudian theory, the perception of the father as punitive and threatening, as the "source of decisive frustrations" during the Oedipal period, is seen as a major prerequisite for the boy's masculine development (Fenichel 1945).

Whiting's (1959, 1960) status-envy theory of identification is an extension of the Freudian hypothesis of identification with the aggressor. Whereas, the Freudian hypothesis stressed the boy's desire to possess his mother, Whiting emphasized that the child wants to engage in many of the activities of the envied parent. For instance, Whiting argued that the boy will have a masculine identification if he perceives his father as having access to more privileges and attractive objects and activities than does his mother (Burton and Whiting, 1961). It is assumed that the child is motivated to imitate the behavior of the primary recipient of valued resources and that his identification with that person is much strengthened by fantasy rehearsal of the envied behavior. According to this conception, a young boy will develop a masculine identification only if his father (or a father surrogate) is the primary consumer of valued resources.

Status-envy theory can be seen as an extension of the Freudian hypothesis of identification with the aggressor in that "identification with the aggressor is the outcome of a rivalrous interaction between the child and the parent who occupies an envied status" (Bandura and Walters 1963, p. 94).

Learning Theory

Mowrer (1950) attempted to reformulate Freudian theory in terms of learning theory concepts. He distinguished between defensive and developmental identification. Defensive identification is synonomous with identification with the aggressor, developmental identification with anaclitic identification. Anaclitic identification, a concept at times used in Freudian theory to explain how girls identify with their mothers and become feminine, is based on fear of loss of love.

Although Mowrer acknowledged that identification with the aggressor may be involved in masculine development, he emphasized the importance of developmental identification in the sex role development of both boys and girls. The basis for developmental identification is an affectional-emotional link with the parent motivating the child to reproduce "bits of the beloved parent" in order to avoid the feeling of loss of love when the parent withholds rewards or is absent. The identification is supposed to develop out of a nurturant parent-child relationship and the child becomes dependent on the parent to provide nurturance and affection. Again, as in Freudian theory, the boy's initial identification is viewed as a non-sex-typed one with the mother. As the father becomes more a source of reinforcement, around the age of four, the boy imitates the father and gradually becomes masculine. Similar viewpoints are expressed by other learning theorists (Sanford 1955; Sears 1957; Sears, et al. 1965; Stoke, 1950).

Sears (1957) emphasized that the child's dependency in the face of the parent's withholding love was the basis for identification. Masculine development is positively related to the degree of warmth and affection the father gives his son, or to put it another way, the amount of love and respect the boy has for his father. The more love and respect a boy has for his father, the more reinforcing his father's approval will be for him.

Parsonian Theory and Social Power Theory

A view of identification, which in certain respects combines the Freudian and learning theory hypotheses, has been advanced by some sociologists (e.g., Cottrell 1942; Parsons 1955, 1958). According to role theory the boy identifies with the person who is most able to dispense both rewards and punishments to him—the person who most often influences his behavior. Bronfenbrenner (1960) pointed out that the novel conception of role theory, as elaborated by Parsons, is that "the child identifies not with the parent as a total person, but with the reciprocal role relationship that is functioning for the child at a particular time" (p. 32).

A basic assumption of Parsonian theory is that a child's learned behavior does not have to be typical of the parent with whom he identifies, but such behavior may be the result of a reciprocal role relationship in which the child and parent participate at various times. There are reciprocal roles which differ for male and female children. Such differential reinforcements as the father provides in these relationships are responsible, according to this theory, for the establishment of sex role learning in the developing child.

Parsons considers the father to be the primary transmitter of culturally determined conceptions of masculinity and femininity. Johnson (1963) stresses the importance of fathering in her elaboration of Parsons' theory of identification. According to Johnson, the mother has a primarily expressive relationship with both boys and girls; in contrast, the father rewards his male and female children differently, encouraging instrumental behavior in his son and expressive behavior in his daughter. The identification with the "father," leads to the internalization of a reciprocal role relationship which is crucial for the sex role development of both boys and girls. For example, with his son the father plays roughly and invites aggressive and assertive responses whereas he is flirtatious and pampering with his daughter, encouraging her to be affectionate and docile.

Similar to role theorists, social learning (or social power) theorists stress that the model who is most likely to be imitated is the one who most controls valued resources (e.g. Bandura and Walters, 1963; Mussen and Distler 1959). These theorists vary somewhat in their specifics, but there is an emphasis on basic learning principles. They stress imitation of observable behavior. The degree to which the father is observed to be a decisionmaker and controller of attractive privileges within the family will increase the probability that children will imitate him.

There are many similarities among hypotheses derived from theories of identi-fication. For example, the hypotheses stress the importance of the father-son relationship and the boy imitating his father, although with different emphases: Freudian theory, the father as punitive and threatening; status-envy theory, the father as the primary consumer of resources; learning theory, the father as rewarding and affectionate; role theory, the father as the principal rewarding and punitive agent. From each of these theories, it can be predicted that if the father were absent, or if the mother were more dominant than the father (in terms of the particular theory's emphasized function), the young boy would experience difficulties in the masculine development process. The role and social power theories provide a relatively more integrative approach than do the other theories.

A Multidimensional Conception of
Identification and Masculine Development

The most influential identification theories provide very interesting hypotheses concerning the father's role in the masculine development process. However, these hypotheses generally do not take constitutional and/or sociocultural factors into account, and most of them seem to set the initial father-child relationship and learning of specific sex role behavior quite late in the child's development. Furthermore, these formulations are not detailed enough to con-sider all the factors contributing to the different aspects and patterns of sex role development (Biller 1971a; Biller and Borstelmann 1967).

Sex Role Orientation

For many children the development of sex role orientation, an important facet of self-concept, begins in the latter part of the first year of life. The period between one and three years appears especially important in such learning. For example, the boy's perception of himself as a male and thus more similar to his father than to his mother, is an impetus for the boy to imitate his father. Discrimination between initial concepts of male and female usually develops by the third year of life and with increasing age, the basis on which the child can discriminate between male and female broadens (Brown 1958; Kagan 1958b).

Parents, by such verbal cues as "just like your daddy," facilitate their son's perception of similarity to his father, and through imitation of the father, the boy increasingly sees himself as more similar to his father. Kagan (1958b) emphasized the significance of the child's perceived similarity to the parent of the same sex, both as a motive to imitate, and as a reinforcement in the sense that the more the child imitates him, the more he perceives himself as similar. Continuing imitation of the father helps strengthen the boy's conception of himself as a male.

Fathers and sons can be very similar as a result of a common genetic inheritance. Even if the father is absent or ineffectual, the boy may appear to be much like his father. For example, his activity level, degree of emotional responsiveness, and physical characteristics may closely approximate his father's and make it easy for his mother to generalize that he and his father are similar in many other ways. The boy can receive much reinforcement for approximating his absent father's behavior. The mother's evaluation of the father can have much positive or negative influence on the boy's perception of himself. Of course, in terms of certain constitutional predispositions, the child from birth can more closely resemble his other sex parent. For example, the boy's facial characteristics, complexion, and temperament may be more like his mother's than his father's. This may make it very difficult for him to perceive himself as similar to his father. If the boy is father-absent, or has an ineffectual father, problems in sex-role development are even more likely to arise.

An important factor in the development of a masculine orientation is the availability of an involved father, or another significant older male, as a discriminable male object. If the boy is to develop a positive masculine self-concept, he must receive consistent nurturance and positive feedback. Contrary to the supposition of most identification theorists, even in the first year or two of life, many children develop firm attachments to their fathers. It is not justified to assume that all boys have an initial feminine identification with their mothers which they must later unlearn or repress.

Paternal nurturance facilitates the development of a masculine orientation, but the father's (or another older male's) availability seems the key condition. The mother may be relatively more nurturant than the father, but only if a masculine father is particularly frustrating or rejecting would consistent paternal availability be a detrimental factor. In such a situation, the boy might defensively align himself with his mother against his father and see himself as unlike his father.

Kohlberg's (1966) cognitive-developmental conception of identification and sex role development is especially relevant in discussing the development of sex role orientation. Kohlberg placed much needed emphasis on cognitive influences which, for the most part, have been ignored in identification theory hypotheses. He proposed that sex role development is a facet of the general process of cognitive development and, thus, accompanies the child's growing awareness of physical and social reality. Following Kohlberg's view, children first discover that they are either boys or girls, and on this basis they form appropriate sex role preferences, which, in turn, lead to identification with their same sex parent. According to Kohlberg, parent-child relationships are relatively unimportant. Supposedly, they are only influential to the extent that they provide a warm environment encouraging the trying out of appropriate sex role behaviors or, on the other hand, a cold hostile milieu inhibiting adequate sex role learning.

There are many similarities between Kohlberg's conception of sex role development and the present formulation; the early learning of orientation, the importance of cognitive factors, the predisposing influence of orientation on later sex role development, and the influence of self-concept and competency motivation. However, the present formulation is much more inclusive. Kohlberg gave a somewhat circumscribed description of sex role development. He seemed to assume that knowledge of sex role norms is relatively isomorphic with sex role development. Even though the ability to discriminate masculine and feminine roles, symbols, and activities is an important factor in sex-role development, it does not encompass all of sex-role development. There are many individuals who have knowledge of sex-role norms but prefer to behave in an opposite sex manner. For example, a boy can be aware that he is a male and possess knowledge about sex-typed toys yet prefer to play with girls' toys.

Sex Role Preference

The development of an individual's sex role preference, his relative desire to adhere to culturally defined sex role guidelines is usually influenced by his sex role orientation. But whereas orientation is very much related to discrimination between the specific sex role models of mother and father, preference pertains to discrimination between more general, socially defined symbols and representations of sex role. Sex role orientation is involved with the individual's evaluation of himself; sex role preference is related to the individual's evaluation of certain environmental activities and opportunities. In developing a masculine sex role preference, the boy learns to value certain toys, activities, and interests. Learning experiences are based on more than family interactions. Peers and the mass media become increasingly influential.

But knowledge of social sex role distinctions is not sufficient for the development of a masculine preference. Variations in family interactions can be very important. In a situation in which there is a close parent-child relationship and parents do not value traditional sex-typed activities, their son's sex role preference will probably be relatively unmasculine. For example, if his parents do not approve of strenuous physical activities, regarding them as dangerous, the pre-school-age boy will not desire to participate in such activities, unless he learns to value them from other sources. As his peer group interactions become more influential, he may, of course, become less comfortable conforming with parental expectations.

Even though a masculine orientation generally predisposes a masculine prefer-ence, some boys have high masculine orientations but low masculine preferences. Since rather complex discrimination learning is often involved in the develop-ment of a consistent preference, a generally limiting factor may be the child's intelligence. For example, retarded children are developmentally slower forming clear-cut sex role preferences (Biller and Borstelmann 1965). A boy could also develop a high masculine orientation and a low masculine preference if his father were present for just his first few years of life, but his mother did not expect or encourage his choice of masculine activities. Another possibility is that a father may be very nurturant and involved with his son but disapprove of traditional masculine activities.

In contrast, a boy who has a low masculine orientation can develop a high masculine preference. This type of sex role development would seem likely, if the father is absent or an ineffectual model, but the mother encourages and expects the boy to participate in masculine activities. (Much of Chapter 6 is devoted to a discussion of the mother's role in the paternally deprived boy's personality development.)

Sex Role Adoption

Sex role adoption refers to the masculinity and/or femininity of the individual's publicly observable behavior. Whereas sex role orientation is related to the individual's view of himself, sex role adoption pertains to the way in which the individual is perceived by other members of his society. Correlates of sex role adoption are present even in early infancy and sex role adoption continues to evolve in adolescence and adulthood, during which time interpersonal skill devel-opment in heterosexual relationships is particularly important. However, the third through fifth years of life appear to be a significant period for sex role adoption development. The development of a masculine sex role adoption, especially in the preschool years, is often linked to imitation of the father. A young boy's masculinity is positively related to the degree to which his father is available and behaves in a masculine manner in his interaction with his family. Male siblings and peers can, of course, also be quite influential.

Paternal masculinity is much related to what White (1960) has subsumed under the heading of competency. Much of the boy's desire to imitate his father and become masculine appears to be associated with a desire to master his environment. For example, the boy's ability to solve problems and to build and repair various objects can be much increased if he has the frequent opportunity to observe and imitate his father.

Assuming that the father is relatively masculine, paternal nurturance facilitates the boy's development of a masculine sex role adoption. A nurturant father compared to a nonnurturant father, more frequently rewards his son's approach responses—and thus provides more opportunities for his son to observe and imitate his behavior. To put it another way, a nurturant father is a more available model than a nonnurturant father. The nurturant father's behavior is more often associated with affection and praise and it acquires more reward value. Thus, a boy with a nurturant father has more incentive to imitate his father than does a boy with a nonnurturant father. Moreover, a nurturant father seems more likely to reinforce his son for imitating him.

If the father is a frequent participant in setting limits for his son, other opportunities for imitation are provided. However, if the father is much more punitive and frustrating than rewarding, his behavior will not have a high incentive value and will be less reproduced. A positive relationship between paternal limit-setting and the masculinity of the boy's sex role adoption is predicted only if the father is relatively nurturant. To the extent that limit-setting is a function of the father's masculine role in the family, it would seem to be positively related to paternal decision-making.

Frequent paternal decision-making, competence, nurturance, and limit-setting can enhance the boy's overall masculine development. The father's masculinity, nurturance, and limit-setting add to his total salience for his son. The boy's perception of his father strongly influences his perception of the incentive value of the masculine role, and all aspects of his sex role development.

Individual Differences

A boy can have a masculine orientation and preference but be limited in the development of a masculine adoption by an inadequate or inappropriate physical status. For example, a boy who is very short or very thin would seem to be at a disadvantage. Height and muscle mass seem positively related to masculinity of sex role adoption. Though a particular type of physique is not sufficient to produce masculine behavior, a boy who is tall and broad or broad though short is better suited for success in most masculine activities than a boy who is tall and thin or short and thin. Parents and others seem to expect more masculine behavior from tall, broad, and/or mesomorphic boys (Biller 1968a).

The boy's physical status can influence his sex role orientation and sex role preference as well as his sex role adoption. For example, during adolescence boys with especially unmasculine physiques are apt to have insecure self-concepts. Even though they are also likely to be low in masculinity of sex role adoption, they may express very masculine sex role preferences in an effort to convince themselves and others that they are masculine (Biller and Liebman 1971). In an effort to bolster their feelings of adequacy, many adolescent boys with insecure sex role orientations engage in body-building and weightlifting (Harlow 1951).

The boy who has a sensory-motor handicap or is intellectually limited can be extremely frustrating to his father. For example, a very sportsminded father might find it very difficult to interact with a poorly coordinated son. Similarly, an intellectually striving father may be uninterested in spending time with a son who possesses little cognitive ability. There is some evidence which suggests that fathers are more likely to reject retarded sons than retarded daughters (Farber 1962; Tallman 1965).

The child's constitutional predispositions have much to do with his personality development. A boy with a mesomorphic physique, high activity level, superior intelligence, and good coordination is likely to be perceived as masculine and attain much success in most male activities. For example, many highly successful athletes have come from father-absent homes. Anecdotal evidence suggests that during childhood these men were not restricted by their mothers and found a number of older males who encouraged them in the development of their physical skills. Older males usually respond positively to a boy who possesses exceptional physical abilities. In turn, the boy who is paternally deprived is often seeking the companionship of an older male.

The influence of older males on the father-absent boy can, of course, be negative as well as positive. For example, in their search for male role models, many lower-class paternally deprived boys have formed relationships with criminals. The boy with a superior physical endowment can use his skills in antisocial activities as well as in socially approved ways. It is interesting to note that the Gluecks found that both father-absence and mesomorphic physiques were more frequent among delinquents than among nondelinquents (Glueck and Glueck 1950; 1956).

Measurement of Sex Role

If we are going to gain a better understanding of the influence of various types of fathering, more attention needs to be paid to ways in which different aspects of sex role can be measured (Biller 1971a; Biller and Borstelmann 1967). Sex role orientation is a necessary concept, but it is difficult to operationalize. Self-description techniques such as adjective check lists are relatively clear-cut procedures to assess self-perceptions of masculinity-femininity (e.g., Biller and Bahm 1971; Heilbrun 1965a). However, sex role orientation is not easily measurable in many individuals because of their defensiveness or adherence to social expectations. Thus, special indirect or projective situations (such as drawings, fantasy play, and TAT-like responses) have often been used so that the individual may express sex role inclinations which might otherwise be constrained by social and conscious self-expectations (e.g., Davids, Joelson, and McArthur 1956; May 1969).

Assessment of an individual's human figure drawings appears to be another method of evaluating his sex-role orientation. In many studies the sex of the first figure drawn has been conceived as a measure of sex role orientation (e.g., Biller 1968a). But, particularly with adolescents and adults, sex of the first figure drawn is not in itself a reliable measure of sex role orientation (Brown and Tolor 1957). In addition to the sex of the figure drawn, it seems worthwhile to take into account specific details in drawings (e.g., Swenson and Newton 1955). The Franck Drawing Completion Test (Franck and Rosen 1948), is an attempt to assess the masculinity-femininity of subjects' elaborations of incomplete line figures (e.g., angles are considered masculine, curved lines feminine). This technique has been found to have some utility with adolescents and adults (e.g., Biller and Barry 1971; Miller and Swanson 1960).

The most widely used technique for assessing children's sex role development has been Brown's (1957) IT Scale for Children (ITSC). In the usual procedure, the child is presented with a picture of an ambiguous child figure, "IT," and is asked to choose what "IT" would like in a series of pictures of various socially sex-typed items. In this way, Brown attempted to get at the child's sex role inclinations in an indirect manner. A frequent criticism leveled against this technique is that "IT" actually looks more like a boy than a girl, and many children perceive they should make choices for a boy figure rather than "projecting" their own choices onto "IT" (Brown 1962). Despite this, the IT Scale has been found to have considerable construct validity (e.g., Hetherington 1966; Mussen and Rutherford 1963).

The concept of sex role preference calls for exposure of the individual to a choice situation in which there are relatively masculine and feminine alternatives available. Rabban (1950) developed a choice procedure consisting of eight masculine toys and eight feminine toys, and methods for assessing sex role preference through picture choices have been developed along similar lines (e.g., Anastasiow 1965; Biller 1969c). The Terman and Miles Interest Inventory and the similar masculinity-femininity scales of the Minnesota Multiphasic Personality Inventory (MMPI), Strong Vocational Interest Blank, and California Psychological Inventory (Gough Femininity Scale) seem essentially techniques to measure sex role preference in adolescents and adults (e.g., Engel 1967).

Inherent in most approaches to measuring sex role preference is an assumption that masculinity and femininity are polar opposites. Supposedly, the more boys differ from girls in their sex role preferences, the more masculine they are. Rosenberg and Sutton-Smith (1959) have developed a game preference test on which preadolescent boys and girls can be assessed on both masculinity and femininity, masculine games being those almost always selected by boys and feminine items being those almost always selected by girls. The child's preferences are compared with both same sex and opposite sex norms. With this technique, masculinity and femininity scores are not merely the converse of one another, independently scored scales being available.

It is difficult to specify the complexity and range of behaviors that can be encompassed under the rubric of sex role adoption. Some investigators have used simple point scale ratings of masculinity-femininity (e.g., Koch 1956). Peer ratings have also been used (e.g., Gray 1957), and Sears, Rau, and Alpert (1965) assessed the amount of time children spent in sex-typed play areas. Freedheim (1960) had first- to fifth-grade teachers select the boys they perceived as most and least masculine in their classes, and he was able to find out what behaviors were most characteristic of high masculine and low masculine boys. Other investigators have developed similar procedures (e.g., Biller 1968a, Vroegh et al. 1967). I have also attempted to develop a rating scale procedure with which positive masculine and positive feminine behaviors can be rated separately (Biller and Leibman 1971).

It is becoming increasingly evident that sex role development is an extremely complex process. For example, as well as there being several different aspects of sex role, each aspect of sex role can have both a masculine and a feminine component. That is, an individual can have both masculine and feminine characteristics and assessment of his masculinity may not give a meaningful estimate of his femininity. Available data indicate that there are only low positive relationships among procedures attempting to measure different aspects of sex role functioning. A multidimensional approach is necessary for adequate assessment (Biller 1968a; Biller and Borstelmann 1967).

Patterns of Sex Role Development

At several points in this book, the advantages of examining the antecedents and correlates of different aspects of sex role are stressed. Miller and Swanson (1960) put forth the related idea of the importance of delineating the antecedents and correlates of patterns of sex role development, and I have elaborated upon this point of view (Biller and Borstelmann 1967; Biller 1971a).

The sex role pattern approach takes into consideration an individual's joint status on two or more aspects of sex role and can lead to a clearer understanding of personality functioning. For example, there may be a discrepancy between an individual's basic sex role orientation and his sex role preference. By dividing measures of sex role orientation and sex role preference at the median, four different groups can be identified: A group with masculine orientations and masculine preferences; a group with masculine orientations and feminine preferences; a group with feminine orientations and masculine preferences; and a group with both feminine orientations and feminine preferences.

Previous research has revealed the importance of such orientation-preference patterns in terms of several areas of personality functioning. Miller and Swanson (1960) reported that variations in defensive styles and emotional reactivity were associated with particular sex role patterns. Lipsitt and Strodtbeck (1967) presented evidence indicating that an individual's sex role pattern was related to his perception and value judgments of others. Data collected in a study with kindergarten-age boys suggested that a high level of verbal creativity is associated with particular sex role patterns (Biller, Singer, and Fullerton 1969). Barry and I studied college males and found that individuals who were consistently masculine appeared to be more similar to their fathers and to have more adequate personality adjustments than did those with other sex role patterns (Biller and Barry 1971).

The studies just mentioned assessed just two aspects of sex role. By considering three aspects of sex role and dealing only in terms of high (H) or low (L) masculinity in each aspect, eight possible patterns can be specified. The eight patterns can be symbolized as: HHH, HHL, HLH, HLL, LHH, LHL, LLH, and LLL. If an orientation, preference, adoption ordering is used, HHH indicates that an individual has a high masculine orientation, high masculine preference, and high masculine adoption: LLL that the individual is low on masculinity in all three aspects of sex role.

The relative frequency of particular patterns seems to be a function of the age range sampled. For example, the HLL pattern may be relatively frequent at two years, because many boys do not yet have the cognitive capacity to discriminate between culturally sex-typed symbols of sex role or the general physical ability to imitate their fathers extensively. On the other hand, since a masculine orientation facilitates the development of a masculine preference and adoption, the HHL pattern would probably be quite rare among preadolescents.

It is also meaningful to consider the relative stability of each aspect of sex role. All three aspects of sex role can be influenced by the child's experiences. However, a child's orientation, being formed earliest in life, and being a basic dimension of his self-concept, seems more resistant to change than the other aspects of sex-role. A child's sex-role preference and sex-role adoption seem to be more influenced by specific situational factors than does his sex-role orientation.

In most children, because of the converging accumulation of predisposing factors, a fair degree of consistency among the aspects of sex role can be expected, at least by their late elementary school years. A masculine orientation facilitates the development of a masculine preference; a masculine orientation and preference increase the probability of the development of a masculine adoption. Similar antecedent factors can operate to produce masculinity in different aspects of behavior. For instance, the presence of an appropriate model is important for the development of both orientation and adoption. Many individuals have HHH and LLL patterns because of such consistencies in the sex role development process.

A boy is most likely to develop an HHH pattern if his father is highly available, nurturant, and masculine. The LLL patterns seem probable if the father is absent or ineffectual, and the mother is very dominating and overprotective. Interaction with an extremely frustrating and rejecting father might also lead a boy to completely reject the masculine role.

Other sex role patterns occur with less frequency than the HHH and LLL patterns. A boy can develop an LHH pattern as a compensatory reaction. For example, many boys with quite unmasculine orientations, in an effort to gain peer group acceptance, behave in an exaggerated masculine manner. Their rigidity is often expressed intellectually, emotionally, and socially. The LHH pattern is particularly common among boys in neighborhoods in which there is both a high incidence of paternal deprivation and an emphasis on toughness and strength. Incongruity between sex role orientation and other aspects of sex role can lead to very high level of anxiety and/or defensiveness.

Several sets of circumstances can promote the development of an HHL pattern. If a boy is without a masculine model after age two or three, even though he has already developed a masculine orientation and preference, it may be difficult for him to develop a masculine adoption. A boy might develop an HHL pattern if his parents encourage a masculine preference and his father is very nurturant but not masculine. In such a situation, the boy could have a masculine orientation and preference but not have a masculine model to imitate. The development of an HHL pattern might also occur if the boy has a masculine orientation and preference but a very unmasculine physique, or a physical disability which hampers his masculine role performance.

A boy could develop an LHL pattern if his father were regularly absent or ineffectual and his mother expected and encouraged a masculine preference. Assuming that he lacked an available masculine model, he might not develop a masculine orientation or adoption.

The LLH, HLH, and HLL sex role patterns appear to be relatively infrequent; the LLH pattern because a masculine orientation and preference are usually precursors of a masculine adoption, and the HLH and HLL because a masculine orientation usually leads to the development of a masculine preference. A boy can develop an LLH pattern if he has a very aggressive, assertive mother who encourages him to behave in a similar fashion, but a father who has been consistently ineffectual. A mesomorphic physique and related characteristics might add to the probability of his developing an LLH pattern. Some active male homosexuals approximate the LLH pattern.

If a boy was cognitively retarded and thus handicapped in developing a high masculine preference, but had very encouraging and appropriately sex-typed parents, and was physically well-equipped, he might develop an HLH sex role pattern. A physically handicapped and intellectually retarded boy might develop a masculine orientation and an HLL pattern if his father were very involved in interacting with him. However, the frequency of such patterns would be expected to be quite rare.

Much more data are needed in order to better understand the development of sex role patterns. It must also be emphasized that discussion of just three aspects of sex role, considering only high or low masculinity on each aspect, grossly oversimplifies the sex role development process. For example, attention must be given to feminine development because individuals can have both masculine and feminine components in their orientations, preferences and adoptions. Furthermore, there are different dimensions of each aspect of sex role that can be analyzed.

3

Fathering, Attachment and Masculine Development

The focus of this chapter is on how the quality of paternal behavior may affect the child's attachment to his father and the boy's masculine development. It is emphasized that the father's influence can begin very early in the child's life and that there are many specific dimensions of paternal behavior that must be taken into account. Topics in this chapter include the father-infant attachment and the effects of such variables as paternal masculinity, paternal nurturance, paternal limit-setting, and paternal power on the young boy's sex role development. The influence of the quality of paternal behavior on other dimensions of the child's development, in addition to sex role functioning, is considered in subsequent chapters.

Attachment and Infancy

Most theorists and researchers have emphasized the importance of the mother-infant relationship and ignored the existence of the father-infant relationship. Schaffer and Emerson (1964), in their study with eighteen month old Scottish children, were among the first to present data indicating that some infants form their principal attachments with their fathers.

A study by Pedersen and Robson (1969) suggests that the quality of the father-infant relationship is important even during the child's first year of life. In an intriguing attempt to explore the impact of fathering on infants, these investigators studied correlates of infants' attachment behavior. The infants' behavior was observed at eight months and again at nine and one-half months, and mothers were interviewed regarding father participation when the infants were nine and one-half months old. Pedersen and Robson found that the degree to which the father participated in caretaking (e.g. giving bottles, changing diapers, etc.), engaged in stimulating play (e.g., excitatory and arousing activity), and was generally emotionally involved with his infant son was related to the infant's attachment to his father (i.e., intensity of infant's greeting behavior upon the father's return, directed smiles, vocalization, increased level of excitement). The authors speculated that such early father-son attachment may be an important phase of the sex role development process. It is also interesting to note the finding that the amount of paternal play with the male infant was associated with his being reported to respond better to men than to women strangers.

There were a number of clear-cut associations between reports of paternal behavior and the male infant's attachment. However, there were no significant correlations for female infants except for a negative association between degree of the father's irritability and his daughter's attachment to him.

The reason for the scarcity of father-female findings may be the strong ambivalence many fathers feel towards infant daughters. Most men express a firm desire for having a male child as their first born and due to sex segregation in childhood, many men feel particularly ill at ease with female children (Biller 1971a). A number of Pedersen and Robson's findings do suggest that many fathers are particularly uneasy in interacting with their infant daughters. For example, there were ten fathers who were reported to be constantly irritated or angry with their infants, and of these eight were fathers of girls. Fathers of females were also reported to be more apprehensive about their infants' well-being and less likely to engage in vigorous play with them.

Individual differences in paternal behavior and infant attachment should be noted, but it is also important to emphasize that approximately three-fourths of the infants appeared to be strongly attached to their fathers. Again, such data are clearly inconsistent with the traditional notion of the infant's exclusive attachment to the mother.

Pedersen and Robson deserve much credit for their fascinating study. To my knowledge, this is the first published paper systematically concerned with variables affecting the strength of the father-infant attachment. However, as with many other studies, there was no direct assessment of the father's actual behavior; maternal reports of paternal behavior were relied upon.

Rebelsky and Hanks (1971) focused on the amount of verbalization that fathers directed toward their infants. (They connected a small microphone to the infant's clothing.) There were ten middle-class families involved in the study. Recordings were made during the time the infants were two weeks to three and a half months old. Rebelsky and Hanks found evidence of extremely little paternal verbal interaction with infants. Fathers averaged less than forty seconds of verbal interactions per day with their infants. The average amount of father-infant interaction per day was little more than ten minutes and most of the fathers, particularly those with girls, spent even less time with their infants in the later part of the study. The presence of a recording device and cord may have been an inhibiting factor in the father's interactions with his infant. It should be emphasized that many fathers have much interaction with their infants which is not accompanied by verbalization.

Ban and Lewis (1971) observed the interactions of twenty one-year-old, upper-middle-class infants with their parents. The researchers placed each infant in a room with first one parent and then the other for fifteen minutes per session. Then they measured how close the child tried to stay to the parent and how much looking and vocalization was directed at the parent. The infants displayed touching and proximity-seeking about twice as often towards their mothers than towards their fathers. In contrast, the infants, especially the boys, tended to vocalize and look more towards their fathers. Girls showed a similar amount of visual attention to both parents, but boys looked at fathers significantly more than at mothers. In general, the boys tended to have more integrated patterns of attachment than did the girls. The amounts of proximal and distal behaviors were positively correlated, particularly with respect to father attachment. Boys also tended to manifest a similar level of attachment to both parents.

The Ban and Lewis research did not reveal any variables related to strength of father-infant attachment. Paternal reports of time spent with infants did not correlate with degree of attachment to the father, but the authors did not present any data concerning the quality of father-infant interactions. Fathers reported they averaged fifteen to twenty minutes of play a day with their infants. The extremes were one father reporting no interaction because the infant was asleep when he returned home while another father reported an average of two hours a day playing with his infant.

Separation Behavior

Kotelchuck (1972), described some interesting findings in regard to the association between the father-infant relationship and the infant's separation behavior. As one would expect, he found that infants displayed less separation protest from the mother when the father remained with them. He also found that infants who had fathers who had frequent interactions with them were less upset when the father left the room. It appears that an infant who is well-fathered is not greatly disturbed by his father leaving because past experience has suggested that he can depend on him to return.

I would predict a curvilinear relationship between the level of father interaction, assuming it was positive, and a child's separation protest. When there are very low levels of father-infant interaction, an infant may even be relieved when the "father-stranger" leaves the room. At low levels of father-infant interaction an infant will begin to show separation protest behavior indicating a weak but unstable and disconcerting attachment. At moderate and especially high levels of interaction a child becomes increasingly secure in his relationship and protest behavior will infrequently occur.

From my observations of the high father interaction situation, strong separation protest usually occurs when an activity is terminated at a point where an infant is frustrated. For example, the father has just begun to play peek-a-boo, toss the child in the air, had the child in his lap for only a minute, etc. When the father's leaving is not associated with a specific frustration, the child usually will not manifest a strong protest reaction (Biller 1974c).

Spelke et al. (1973) replicated some of Kotelchuck's findings and also expanded our knowledge of paternal influence on an infants' separation behavior. One-year-old, middle-class infants were systematically observed playing in an unfamiliar setting. The situation included manipulation of the presence or absence of their mother, father, and a female stranger. The general schedule called for the arrival or departure of one of the three adults at three minute intervals. In some situations two of the adults were present in various combinations (e.g., mother and father, father and female stranger) while in others one of the adults was present. The adults were instructed to minimize their interactions with the children except if the child initiated an interaction and then to interact only as much as necessary.

Fathers had earlier been interviewed to evaluate their involvement with their infants. Assessment of degree of father-child interaction was based on several variables including the time the father and infant spent together, the extent of the father's participation in child care, the father's perception of his importance as a parent and his general responsiveness to the infant.

Spelke et al. found, as did Kotelchuck, that infants did not protest as much when the mother left if the father remained with them (or if the father left and the mother remained). Also similar to Kotelchuck, Spelke et al. found that infants who had a high level of interaction with their fathers showed little upset when alone with the stranger; whereas, those infants who had a low level of interaction with their fathers showed the most crying and disruption of their play. In particular, infants with a low level of father interaction cried more than those with either medium or high father interaction.

It should be noted that these studies strongly indicate that a high degree of stranger anxiety is *not* a measure of parental attachment. In fact, the infants strongly attached to their fathers appeared much more comfortable with the stranger than those who had a minimal attachment to their fathers. (Of course, it may be that strong mother and father attachments have differential effects on the infant's reactions to strangers; e.g., a strong mother attachment may often lead to high stranger anxiety if the mother has an inhibiting effect on exploration of the environment.)

General Adaptation

In another phase of the Spelke et al. study, the infants were exposed to three different procedures designed to measure their responses to unexpected visual discrepancy. The infant sat in his mother's lap and was exposed to visual sequences which included a cube moving in a zigzag motion and two rods moving in a circular arc from left to right setting off colored lights. Infants with low father interaction responded with more irritable fretting to the visual displays than did infants with high father interaction. This suggests that well-fathered infants adapt more readily to non-social as well as social changes in their environment. These findings are consistent with my observations concerning the seemingly high-level cognitive development of well-fathered infants. Such adaptability may be one factor in facilitating the infant's ability to explore his environment and concentrate on new experiences—an important factor in his cognitive development.

My observations have strongly suggested that well-fathered infants are much more curious in exploring their environment than are infants who are paternally deprived. Well-fathered infants seem to be more secure and more trustful in branching out in their explorations. There are also indications that their motor development in terms of crawling, climbing, and manipulating objects is advanced (Biller 1974c). There appear to be a number of reasons for this phenomenon. Fathers, when they are involved, tend to be more tolerant than mothers of physical explorations by infants and to more actively encourage physical mastery. I have often observed involved fathers encouraging their infants, both vocally and gesturally, to crawl a little further or climb a little higher. Fathers are usually less concerned if the child gets hurt or dirty than are mothers. This generally allows them to tolerate temporary discomforts which the child may experience in his exploration of the environment.

It should also be added that fathers are more likely than mothers to institute a clear-cut double standard in terms of the sex of the infant. I have observed a number of fathers who have consistently encouraged their infant sons' mastery of the physical environment but who have inhibited their infant daughters with the assertion that they might be harmed. Ironically, there have been several cases where the daughters were more robust than the sons were at a similar age.

Another factor in the early facilitation of the child's exploration or his environment is that the father provides an additional attachment figure. In many cases the paternally deprived child becomes exclusively attached to the mother, often in a clinging dependent fashion. Infants who develop an attachment to their fathers as well as their mothers are likely to also have an easier time relating to other relatives and friends. A child who has frequent interactions with both parents has access to a wider variety of experiences and may be more adaptive to changes in his environment. I have repeatedly observed less separation and stranger anxiety among well-fathered infants. The infant's positive reaction to the returning father may be a prototype to his reaction to the entry of other people into his environment, especially if they are well-regarded by those he is already attached to (Biller 1974c).

Our understanding of the father-infant relationship might be more complete if we were able to carefully examine the personality functioning of the parents even before the birth of the child. The husband-wife relationship, the expectant father's attitudes towards children, and the parents' adjustment during pregnancy should be examined in terms of their possible linkage with postpartum father-child attachment. The expectant father's adjustment has often been ignored, but recent research has suggested that it may have a significant impact on later parent-child relationships (e.g. Arnstein 1972; Biller and Meredith 1974; LeMasters 1970; Liebenberg 1968; Lynn 1974).

Dimensions of Paternal Behavior

In this section, there is a discussion of how various dimensions of paternal behavior may influence the boy's masculine development. Research concerning the effects of paternal masculinity, paternal nurturance, paternal limit-setting and paternal power is reviewed.

Paternal Masculinity

There are data which indicate that the quality of the father-son relationship is a more important influence on the boy's masculine development than the amount of time the father spends at home (Biller 1971a). A crucial factor in the father present boy's masculine development is the degree to which his father exhibits masculine behavior in family interactions. The results of some studies suggest that there is not a direct relationship between the amount the boy imitates his father and the boy's masculinity (Hartup 1962; Kohlberg and Zigler 1967). Imitation of the father directly enhances the boy's masculine development only if the father displays masculine behavior in the presence of his son.

When the father consistently adopts a maternal-like role, it is likely that his son will be relatively low in masculinity. Bronfenbrenner (1958), reanalyzing data originally collected by Lansky (1956), found that adolescent boys low in masculinity of interests often came from homes in which the father played a traditionally feminine role. The fathers of these boys took over such activities as cooking and household chores and did not generally participate in family decision-making or limit-setting. Bronfenbrenner also described the findings of a study by Altucher (1957) in which adolescent boys with low masculine interests "were likely to come from families in which there was little role differentiation in household activities, and in which the mother, rather than the father, tended to dominate in the setting of limits for the child" (p. 120). What seemed to inhibit the boy's masculine development was not the father's participation in some traditionally feminine activities in the home per se (e.g., helping with the housework), but the father's surrendering of the masculine role in the family (e.g., decision-making) and/or a relative parental role reversal.

In an investigation with elementary school children, Kagan (1958a) found that over 40 percent of the boys rated low in aggression by their teachers, as compared to only about 10 percent of those rated high in aggression, perceived their mothers "as boss at home." In Freedheim's study of second- to fifth-grade children, the degree to which boys perceived their fathers as decision-makers was related to both the masculinity of the boys' projective sex role preferences and teachers' ratings of sex role adoption. In his research with third graders, Rutherford (1969) discovered a positive association between children's ability to perceive how masculine other children were and paternal dominance.

Heilbrun's (1965b) data, based on paper and pencil tests, revealed that there was a relationship between the amount of masculinity college males attributed to themselves and to their fathers. In Rychlak and Legerski's (1967) study, most adolescent boys who viewed themselves as similar to their fathers also perceived themselves and their fathers as relatively masculine.

I found a strong relationship between kindergarten-age boys' masculinity and the degree to which they perceived their fathers as making family decisions. In terms of measures of sex role orientation, sex role preference, and sex role adoption, a high level of perceived father decision-making was associated with strongly masculine behavior. Perceived father decision-making was particularly highly correlated with sex role orientation. Perceived father competence was most related to sex role orientation, although it was also significantly related to preference and adoption (Biller 1969a).

Even though there is a consistency of findings in terms of an apparent relationship between father's and son's masculinity, the studies cited above share a common methodological shortcoming. Measurement of father and son masculinity was generally not independent, both assessments usually being deduced from the son's responses. It could be argued that such evidence is not a sufficient basis on which to conclude that father's and son's masculinity is related. For example, an alternative explanation is that masculine sons will tend to see their fathers as highly masculine regardless of their father's actual masculinity. A boy may appear similar to his father, yet have learned his masculine behavior not from him but from his peer group. As Bronfenbrenner (1958) pointed out, the boy's perceived similarity to his father is not necessarily a measure of his identification with his father. Father-son similarity may be just a reflection of exposure to a common social environment.

Parental Interaction

In a methodologically superior study, Hetherington (1965) evaluated the relative dominance of parents by placing them in an actual decision-making situation. She found that masculinity of preschool-age and preadolescent boy's projective sex role behavior (ITSC) was positively related to paternal dominance. Moreover, she discovered a general tendency for similarity between father and son and son's imitation of father to be higher in father-dominant than in mother-dominant homes (Hetherington 1965; Hetherington and Brackbill 1963; Hetherington and Frankie 1967).

Using essentially the same parental interaction procedure as Hetherington

(1965), I found that father dominance in father-mother interaction was positively related to kindergarten-age boys' sex role orientations, preferences, and adoptions (Biller 1969a). Furthermore, father dominance in father-mother interaction was positively related to the boy's perception of father dominance. However, it is also important to point out that father dominance in parental interaction showed weaker relationships with sex role development than did the boy's perception of father dominance. The boy's behavior seems to be much determined by his particular perception of family interactions; and, it may be that his view of the father is the most veritable measure. The boy's perception of his father can also be influenced by his mother's behavior. In father-mother interactions some mothers encouraged their husbands to make decisions while others appeared to prevent their husbands from serving as adeqaute models by constantly competing with them for the decision-making role.

Other analyses of the data suggested the complex influences of family interactions on the boy's sex role development. Several of the boys who were low in masculinity had fathers who were dominant in terms of father-mother interaction and generally seemed masculine. However, these fathers also appeared to be controlling and restrictive of their son's behavior. For instance, this type of dominant father punished his son for disagreeing with him. Masculine development seems to be facilitated when the father is dominant (a masculine model) and allows and encourages the boy to also be dominant. Such paternal behavior appears to be particularly important in sex role adoption development. In families in which the mother and father were competing for the decision-making function, boys were often very restricted. It seems that in some families, when the mother does not allow her husband to be influential in family decisions he is more apt to attempt to dominate his son in a restrictive and controlling manner. (In Chapter 6 there is a detailed discussion of the mother's role in the sex role development process.)

Studies just discussed have dealt with assessments of the father's sex role adoption in the family. Several researchers have not found a clear-cut relationship between fathers' and sons' sex role preferences (Angrilli 1960; Payne and Mussen 1966; Mussen and Rutherford 1963; Terman and Miles 1936).

It seems that it is the father's sex role adoption in family interactions that is crucial and not the degree of masculine behavior that he exhibits outside the home. Many fathers have masculine interests and are masculine in their peer and work relationships, but are very ineffectual in their interactions with their wives and children. The stereotype of the masculine hardworking father whose primary activity at home is lying on the couch, watching television, or sleeping, is an all too accurate description of many fathers. If the boy's father is not consistently involved in family functioning, it is much harder for his son to learn to be appropriately assertive, active, independent, and competent.

Paternal Nurturance

Throughout this book there is much discussion of the concept of paternal nurturance. In a general context paternal nurturance refers to the father's affectionate, encouraging, and attentive behavior towards his child. Such behavior may or may not be manifested in the rubric of caretaking activities which appear more common in descriptions of maternal nurturance. At this point the focus is on paternal nurturance and masculine development; the influence of paternal nurturance on other dimensions of development is also discussed in several other chapters.

In a study with elementary school age children, Bronson (1959) reported findings which indicated that both the father's masculinity and the quality of the father-son relationship have to be taken into account. Assessment of the father's behavior and the father-child relationship was based on interviews with the fathers and family history data. The masculinity of toy preferences of boys who had chronically stressful relationships with their fathers was negatively associated with the father's masculinity. Boys who had fathers who were undemonstrative, frustrating, and critical seemed to reject their fathers as models. In contrast, where the father-son relationship was non-stressful (father warm, affectionate, and supportive), the masculinity of boys' toy preferences was positively correlated to fathers' masculinity. Masculine development seems to be facilitated when the father is both masculine and nurturant.

There is other evidence that a warm, affectionate father-son relationship can strengthen the boy's masculine development. In a study by Pauline Sears (1953), preschool boys who assumed the father-role in doll play activities (used the father doll with high frequency) tended to have warm, affectionate fathers. Mussen and Distler (1959) studied the structured doll play of kindergarten boys. Their results revealed that boys who scored high in masculinity of projective sex role responses (ITSC) perceived fathers as more warm and nurturant than did boys with low masculinity scores. Using the same methodology, Mussen and Rutherford (1963) reported similar findings for first-grade boys. Studying kindergarten-age boys, I found that perceived father-nurturance was related to a fantasy game measure of sex role orientation (Biller 1969a).

According to maternal interview data collected by Mussen and Distler (1960), the high masculine boys described in their earlier (1959) article had more affectionate relationships with their fathers than did the low masculine boys. Interviews with the boys' mothers also indicated a trend for the fathers of the high masculine boys to take care of their sons more often, as well as to have more responsibility for family childrearing practices.

Sears, Rau, and Alpert (1965) did not find interview measures of fathers' nurturance and warmth related to preschool boys' masculinity. But they did find that preschool boys' masculinity was negatively related to fathers' sex anxiety; and fathers' sex anxiety, in turn was negatively associated with the amount of time that fathers participated in the infant caretaking of their sons. Paternal nurturance appears to facilitate the boy's sex role development when the father is comfortable with his masculine role.

Researchers have also found that paternal nurturance is related to older boys' masculinity and similarity to their fathers. In Bronson's (1959) investigation, preadolescent boys who had fathers who were warm, affectionate, and supportive, tended to tell TAT stories which suggested a strong, masculine sex role orientation. In Payne and Mussen's (1956) study, adolescent boys who made similar responses to their fathers on the California Psychological Inventory depicted fathers as rewarding and affectionate on a story completion task, and, in addition, had high masculinity scores. (However, the assessments of paternal similarity and masculinity were both derived from responses to the California Psychological Inventory and were not methodologically independent.)

Bandura and Walters (1959) detected an association between the degree to which adolescent males viewed their fathers as warm and affectionate and saw themselves as similar to their fathers. Mussen (1961) found that adolescent boys with masculine interests (Strong Vocational Interest Blank) described fathers in their TAT stories as more rewarding and positive in father-son interaction than did boys with unmasculine interests. In a questionnaire study with college students, Distler (1964) found a significant relationship between perceived paternal nurturance and the masculinity of the subjects' self-descriptions.

Investigations with adolescent males have provided findings indicating that general personality adjustment, as well as sex role functioning, is enhanced by a positive father-son relationship. Mussen (1961) found that in addition to having more masculine interests, adolescents who regarded their fathers as warm and affectionate were emotionally more stable and mature than adolescents who reported little positive involvement with their fathers. Heilbrun's (1962) data suggested that adolescents who perceived themselves as being unlike their fathers were anxious, feminine, socially immature, and lacking in self-confidence. There is an extensive description of evidence linking the father-son relationship to various facets of personality functioning in Chapter 5.

Paternal Limit Setting

Findings suggesting a relationship between paternal limit-setting and masculine development have been presented by several researchers. Lefkowitz's (1962) data revealed that third- and fourth-grade boys who made at least some feminine toy choices had fathers who took less part in setting limits for them than did fathers of boys who made exclusively masculine toy choices. In Altucher's (1957) study, more adolescent boys who scored high in masculinity of interests, as compared to boys who scored low, said their fathers set limits for them. Moulton et al. (1966) reported similar results with male college students, but Distler (1964) did not.

In Levin and Sears (1965) study, kindergarten boys whose fathers were the principal agents of punishment manifested high levels of doll play aggression. Maternal limit-setting was found to be associated with low aggression among the elementary school boys in Kagan's (1958a) study. Results from a series of studies revealed that third-grade boys who were punished for aggression at home by both their mothers and fathers were more aggressive in school than boys punished only by their mothers (Eron et al. 1963).

The implication of such data is that boys often learn to be aggressive and masculine by modeling themselves after their fathers, the disciplinary situation being particularly relevant. Certainly the father's firmness and decisiveness in limit-setting can help the child develop a capacity for appropriately assertive and aggressive behavior. However, the quality of the father's behavior in the disciplinary situation must be examined very carefully. For example, fathers who physically abuse their children are likely to have been physically abused by their own fathers (Lynn 1974).

Other factors may be operating to produce a relationship between paternal limit-setting and boys' aggressive behavior. Boys may be aggressive as a function of the frustration engendered by severe paternal punitiveness. Furthermore, global ratings of aggression and other complex personality traits should be viewed with caution. For example, all forms of aggression are not culturally accepted as appropriate for boys; assertiveness in play and an active physical stance in interactions with peers seem appropriate, while tattling on other children and fighting with girls seem inappropriate (e.g., Biller and Borstelmann 1967; Shortell and Biller 1970).

In any case, findings concerning the influence of paternal limit-setting are inconsistent. In Mussen and Distler's (1959) study, the kindergarten boys who manifested highly masculine projective sex role responses perceived their fathers as somewhat more punitive and threatening in structured doll play situations than did boys low in masculinity. Mussen and Rutherford (1963) found a similar trend for first-grade boys. But in both studies, perceived nurturance of father was found to be much more related to high masculine preferences. In addition, Mussen and Distler (1960) ascertained nothing to indicate that the fathers of the high masculine kindergarten boys actually punished them more than did the fathers of the low masculine boys. In my study with kindergarten-age boys, perceived paternal limit-setting was slightly related to a measure of sex role orientation, but not to measures of sex role preference or sex role adoption (Biller 1969a). Sears, Rau, and Alpert (1965) did not find a consistent relationship between interview measures of paternal limit-setting and preschool boys' masculinity.

The adolescent boys with high masculine interests in Mussen's study (1961) described fathers as nonpunitive and nonrestrictive in their TAT stories. Some of the discrepancy between this study and the Mussen and Distler (1959) and Mussen and Rutherford (1963) studies may be due to age differences. For example, by adolescence, a father who earlier was perceived as threatening because of his "awesome size" may be less threatening when his son becomes similar in size and strength. During adolescence, the father is also less likely to use physical means of punishment and more likely to set limits verbally. A related point is that limit-setting is not necessarily performed in a punitive context.

Paternal nurturance facilitates masculine development to a greater degree than does paternal punitiveness, which is more consistent with the learning theory hypothesis than with the Freudian theory hypothesis. Nevertheless, it should be noted that the Freudian hypothesis stressed paternal punitiveness during the oedipal period, and data suggesting that highly masculine adolescent boys do not perceive their fathers as punitive are not necessarily inconsistent with such a viewpoint.

When the father plays a significant part in setting limits, the boy's attachment to his father and masculine development is facilitated *only* if there is an already established affectionate father-son relationship. If the father is not nurturant, and is punitive, the boy will display a low level of father imitation. Data from a study by Bandura and Walters (1959) seem particularly relevant. Adolescent boys who had highly punitive but generally nonnurturant and nonrewarding fathers, exhibited relatively low father preference and little perception of themselves as acting and thinking like their fathers.

The stress in future research should be in gathering data on paternal participation in setting limits and expectations rather than simply on the relative amount of time the father is a punishing agent. It is relevant to mention that recent research has revealed that parental firmness and consistency of setting limits are important for the child. Firmness and consistency of setting limits relate to clear-cut expectations for the child by the parent and to what Baumrind (1967) terms authoritative childrearing. In this context, it is interesting to note that Coopersmith (1967) reported that fathers of elementary school boys with high self-esteem were more active in setting limits than were fathers of boys with low self-esteem.

Paternal Power

Mussen and Distler (1959) found that boys with highly masculine projective sex role behavior (ITSC) perceived their fathers as more "powerful" than did boys low in masculinity. When perceived nurturance and perceived punitiveness scores were combined, the difference between the masculine and nonmasculine boys was particularly clearcut. Mussen and Rutherford (1963) reported similar results for first-grade boys, but the relationship was not as strong.

Similarly, Freedheim's (1960) data point to the importance of the total pattern of the father-son relationship (Freedheim and Borstelmann, 1963). Second- to fifth-grade boys' perceptions of their fathers' decision-making, nurturance, and limit-setting were assessed in a structured interview. Perceived salience of the father was defined as the median percentage of the time the boy played with the father doll in making up doll play stories. Paternal decision-making and salience were related to both masculinity of projective sex role behavior (ITSC toy selection items) and sex role adoption (teachers' ratings). The combination of paternal decision-making and salience related highest to both measures of masculinity. Neither paternal nurturance nor limit-setting alone was significantly related to the measures of masculinity. However in combination they were related to the measures of masculinity.

In a study with kindergarten-age boys which I conducted, as in other studies just described, the role theory and the social power theory hypotheses seemed to be supported more than the Freudian or learning theory hypotheses (Biller 1969a). In my study, the overall amount of perceived father influence was more important than perception of the father as dominant in a particular area. In addition, experiments concerning the imitation process in young children have added evidence which is particularly consistent with the role theory and social power theory formulations (e.g., Bandura, Ross and Ross 1963; Bandura and Walters 1963).

Parent perception and sex role research with college students has also yielded results which are in line with formulations stressing the importance of the total father-son relationship. In Winch's (1962) questionnaire study, college males who had been separated from their fathers continually from before ten years of age, perceived their mothers as both more nurturant and controlling than their fathers and also tended to see themselves as less similar to their fathers than did college males who had not been separated from their fathers. Distler (1964) found that college males who described themselves as strongly masculine on an adjective check list viewed their fathers as high in nurturance, limit-setting, and competence; in other words, as very powerful. In Moulton et al.'s (1966) study, college males with the most masculine sex role preferences (modified version of Gough's Femininity Scale) reported that their fathers were high in affection and the dominant disciplinarians in their families.

It is also interesting to note that Bronfenbrenner's (1961) findings indicated that the development of leadership, responsibility, and social maturity in adolescent males is closely associated with a father-son relationship which is not only nurturant, but includes a strong component of paternal limit-setting. A study by Reuter and I also suggests the importance of evaluating both the quality and quantity of paternal behavior (Reuter and Biller 1973). This study is discussed in more detail in Chapter 5, but it should be noted here that the combination of at least moderate paternal availability with at least moderate paternal nurturance was associated with indications of positive personal adjustment among male college students.

Socioeconomic Status

One basis for the father's power and esteem is his ability to economically provide for his family. Fathers who have low-status occupations are more apt to be viewed in a negative way than are fathers with relatively high-status occupations. If the wife has a higher occupational status than her husband, marital conflict and problems in childrearing seem more likely to occur than if the husband has a higher occupational status than his wife. Lower-socioeconomic-status fathers appear to have particular difficulty in adjusting to wives who have higher occupational status (Gover 1963; Roth and Peck 1951, Westley and Epstein 1970).

Fathers in lower-class families often make attempts to dominate their families and support a patriarchal view of the family, but they frequently have very little actual influence in the decision-making process. Even though fathers in middle-class families seem to be less concerned with having absolute authority in family interactions, they appear to exert more influence (Blood and Wolfe 1960). Lower-class fathers are more punitive and less affectionate than middle-class fathers (McKinley 1964). Researchers have also found that the father is perceived as a less powerful figure in lower-class families than in middle-class families. For example, adolescents in lower-class families, compared to those in middle-class families, are more likely to perceive their mothers as more dominant than their fathers (e.g., Bowerman and Elder 1964; Distler 1964).

In light of such findings it might be speculated that lower-class boys experience more difficulties in their relationships with their fathers, and in their sex role and personality development than do middle-class boys. However, even though middle-class fathers may be potentially powerful models for their sons, there is other evidence which suggests that they are frequently not very involved with their children (Biller 1971a; Biller and Meredith 1974).

Type of paternal deprivation is often related to social class. The relative lack of father participation, as vividly pictured by Green (1946) in his description of the uninvolved, middle-class, commuting father, interferes with the boy's masculine development. In Rabban's (1950) study, working-class boys made exclusively sex appropriate toy choices earlier than did middle-class boys (at five years as compared to six years). Rabban noted that many of the middle-class fathers in his sample were away from home a great deal, ostensibly because of occupational demands, and seemed to interact very little with their sons.

In the lower class, paternal deprivation because of desertion, or separation is more common than in the working or middle class. Hall and Keith (1964) found that lower-class boys had more masculine IT scores than did middle-class boys, but other investigators have failed to find social class differences on the IT Scale (e.g., Brown 1957; Hartup and Zook 1960). Hartup and Zook (1960) speculated that the reason for their not finding social class differences was that more than half of their lower-class group did not have fathers living at home. Unfortunately, there has been a lack of systematic consideration of variations in fathering in investigations focusing on the relationship between social class and sex role functioning.

Methodological Issues

The bulk of the research concerning parent-child relationships and personality development can be criticized because of methodological deficiencies and/or because of limited generality. In most investigations, the father's behavior is not directly assessed, and maternal or child reports of paternal behavior are used.

In many of the studies, the sources of evidence about parental behavior and the child's behavior are not independent, leading to problems of interpretation. For example, in many studies the child is asked to describe both his own and his parents' behavior. More studies in which there is an assessment of the amount of consistency among observer ratings of familial interactions and children's and parents' perceptions of parent-child relationships should be done. In addition, procedures which allow observers, parents, and children to rate each family member independently should be compared to those in which instructions call for comparative ratings of family members. One goal of such investigations would be to examine which type or types of measures are most related to specific dimensions of children's personality functioning (Biller 1971a).

Most of the studies done concerning the father-child relationship and personality development have been of a correlational nature. Often, the child's perception of his father or some report of the father's behavior is linked to a measure of the child's personality development. For instance, when significant correlations are found between the degree to which a boy perceives his father as nurturant and the boy's masculinity, it is usually assumed that paternal nurturance has been an antecedent of masculine development. But fathers may become nurturant and accepting towards their sons when their sons are masculine, and rejecting when their sons are unmasculine. Longitudinal research would be particularly helpful in determining the extent to which certain paternal behaviors precede and/or are antecedents of particular dimensions of children's behavior.

Summary

Recent findings indicate the need to modify traditional views that the infant's attachment is usually exclusively and primarily with the mother, and that the father does not become an important figure for the child until post-infancy. Research discussed in this chapter clearly indicates that individual differences in paternal behavior can greatly influence the strength of the infant's attachment to the father. A meaningful attachment to the father can facilitate the infant's social and cognitive development.

There are data which indicate that paternal masculinity, paternal nurturance, and paternal limit-setting can be important factors in the masculine development process. However, taken separately, not one of these factors is sufficient to ensure that the boy will become masculine. A boy can have a masculine father who is not very involved in his family. His father can be nurturant but not be very effective as a masculine model. The father can be very masculine and limit-setting, yet not have developed a basic affectionate relationship with his son.

A warm relationship with a father who is himself secure in his masculinity is a crucial factor in the boy's masculine development. Boys who have punitive, rejecting fathers or passive, ineffectual fathers generally have less adequate sex role functioning than do boys who have interested, nurturant fathers who play a salient and decisive role in family interactions.

Having a father does not guarantee that the boy's sex role development will go smoothly. To put it another way, all father-present boys do not become masculine. On the other hand, in Chapter 4 it is pointed out that many father-absent boys develop masculine behavior patterns. Future studies should compare father-absent boys with boys who have highly available and involved fathers, as well as with boys who have fathers who are relatively unavailable and/or ineffectual. Such studies should also include a multidimensional assessment of sex role functioning. It can be predicted that boys with highly available and salient fathers are, as a group, more securely masculine (particularly in terms of their sex role orientations) than either father-absent boys or boys who have ineffectual fathers. It can also be predicted that father-present boys with ineffectual fathers are not more masculine (and may even be less masculine) than father-absent boys. An examination of data from one of my studies supports such predictions, but more research is needed (Biller 1968a).

A shortcoming of most of the studies discussed in this chapter was that data sources were not independent. In many of the studies both the father-child relationship and the son's sex-role development were assessed from the boy's responses. In other studies, information about the father-child relationship was gathered from maternal reports. Fathers should be included in data assessment. More direct observation of father-child interaction is needed if the father's impact on the child's personality development is to be better understood.

**Father Absence, Surrogate
Models, and Masculine
Development**

The majority of the initial studies dealing with the effects of father absence were done with children whose fathers were or had been absent because of military service during World War II. Much of the current interest in the father's role has been intensified by the growing awareness of the prevalence of fatherless families and the social, economic, and psychological problems that such families often encounter. The fatherless family is a source of increasing concern in many industrialized countries (Wynn 1964). More than 10 percent of the children in the United States—a total in excess of eight million—live in fatherless families (Herzog and Sudia 1970). Fatherless families are especially common among the lower class and particularly among lower-class black families, approaching 50 percent in some areas (King 1945; Moynihan 1965).

Many researchers have speculated that the primary effects of father absence are manifested in terms of deficits and/or abnormalities in the boy's sex role development. In this chapter, research findings concern the relationship between father absence and the boy's sex role development are discussed. (Father absence and the girl's sex role development is discussed in Chapter 7.) A comparison of the sex role development of father-absent and father-present boys suggests some of the ways paternal deprivation can influence personality development.

Sex-Typed Behavior

Sears and Sears conducted a pioneering investigation of the effects of father absence on three- to five-year-old children. Each child was given an opportunity to play with a standardized set of doll play equipment and the investigators recorded his behavior. Compared to the father-present boys, the father-absent boys were less aggressive, and they also had less sex role differentiation in their doll play activity. For example, their play contained less emphasis on the maleness of the father and boy dolls (Sears 1951; Sears, Pintler, and Sears 1946).

Bach (1946) used a similar procedure to study the effects of father absence on six- to ten-year-old children. As in the Sears study, father absent boys were less aggressive in doll play than were father-present boys. Bach observed that "the father-separated children produced an idealistic and feminine fantasy picture of the father when compared to the control children who elaborated the father's aggressive tendencies" (p. 79).

In Santrock's (1970a) study of four- and five-year-old disadvantaged black children, father-absent boys exhibited less masculine and more dependent behavior in standardized doll play situations than did father-present boys, although the two groups of boys did not differ in amount of aggressive behavior. In addition, maternal interviews suggested that the father-absent boys were less aggressive as well as less masculine and more dependent in their interpersonal relations than were the father-present boys.

In a very thorough investigation, Stolz et al. (1954) gathered data concerning four- to eight-year-old children who for approximately the first two years of their lives had been separated from their fathers. Interview results revealed that the previously father-separated boys were generally perceived by their fathers as being "sissies." Careful observation of these boys supported this view. The previously father-separated boys were less assertively aggressive and independent in their peer relations than boys who had not been separated from their fathers. They were more often observed to be very submissive or to react with immature hostility. The boys who had been father absent were actually more aggressive in doll play than boys who had not been separated from their fathers. However, the fact that the fathers were present in the home at the time of this study, and that the father-child relationships were stressful, makes it difficult to speculate about what influence father absence per se had on the children's personality development.

There is additional evidence that the effects of early father absence on boys persist even after their fathers return. Carlsmith (1964) studied middle-class and upper-middle-class high school males who had experienced early father absence because of their father's military service during World War II. Father absence before the age of five was related to the patterning of College Board Aptitude Scores. Compared to the usual male pattern of math score higher than verbal score, the pattern of the father-absent subjects was more frequently the same as the female pattern—verbal score higher than math score. Moreover, "the relative superiority of verbal to math aptitudes increases steadily the longer the father is absent and the younger the child when the father left" (p. 10). Other researchers have also found that early father absence is related to a feminine patterning of aptitude test scores (e.g., Altus 1958; Nelsen and Maccoby 1966).

Leichty (1956) compared the projective test responses of male college students who were father absent from the ages of three to five to those of a matched group who had not been father absent. In terms of responses to the Blacky Pictures, fewer of the father-absent students said "Blacky" would like to pattern himself after his father, more often choosing "Mother" or "Tippy," a sibling. Such a response can be conceived of as a projective indication of underlying sex role orientation, the father-absent males being less masculine. However, it is not clear from the data Leichty presented how many of the father-absent group chose Tippy. This response might also indicate a masculine sex role orientation if Tippy was depicted by the respondent as being a male sibling. Rabin (1958) found that fewer 9- to 11-year-old Kibbutz boys than non-Kibbutz boys said Blacky would like to pattern himself after his father. This finding is consistent with the fact that the Kibbutz boys had less contact with their fathers than did the non-Kibbutz boys. Unfortunately, as in Leichty's study, it is not evident from data presentation how many of the boys chose Tippy.

Paternal occupation can be related to frequent father absence. In a very extensive investigation Tiller (1958) and Lynn and Sawrey (1959) studied Norwegian children aged eight to nine and a half whose fathers were sailors absent at least nine months a year. They compared these father-separated children with a matched group of children whose fathers had jobs which did not require them to be separated from their families. The boys' responses to projective tests, and interviews with their mothers, indicated that father separation was associated with compensatory masculinity (the boys at times behaving in an exaggerated masculine manner, at other times behaving in a highly feminine manner). The father-separated boys appeared to be much less secure in their masculinity than did the control group boys. Consistent with the findings of Bach (1946) and Sears (1951), the father-separated boys were less aggressive in doll play than the control group.

Rogers and Long's (1968) data also suggest that boys whose fathers are away for long periods of time have difficulties in their masculine development. These investigators studied children from two communities in the Out Island Bahamas. In one community, Crossing Rocks, there was a high level of paternal deprivation because men were involved in lengthy fishing trips, being away for weeks at a time for a total of at least six months a year. In the other community, Murphy Town, men were primarily wage laborers, sometimes unemployed, but generally not away from home for any lengthy period. A preference-for-shapes procedure was administered to 6 to 15-year-old children and, among the boys, a much lower percentage (25 percent vs. 61 percent) of those from the paternally deprived community made masculine responses (chose the angular shape rather than the curved shape). Interestingly, the majority (80 percent) of the adult males in the paternally deprived community who were tested made masculine responses on the preference-for-shapes procedure. Rogers and Long speculated that there was often a shift from a feminine to a masculine sex role identification as a result of informal initiation rites during the adolescent male's first year of going on fishing trips.

Several investigators have attempted to assess differences between father-absent and father-present boys in terms of their human figure drawings. Phelan (1964) assumed that boys who drew a female when asked to draw a person had failed to make a shift from an initial identification with the mother to an identification with the father. In her study, there was a higher rate of father absence among elementary-school-age boys who drew a female first as compared to those who drew a male first. An additional analysis of some of my (1968a) data with kindergarten-age children revealed that father-absent, as compared to father-present, boys were less likely to draw a male first or to clearly differentiate their male and female drawings, particularly if they became father-absent before the age of four.

Burton (1972) asked eight- to fifteen-year old Caribbean children to draw human figures. His evidence suggested that father absence during the first two years of life was associated with relatively unmasculine self-concepts for boys. Compared to father-present boys, boys who had been father absent during their first two years of life (and did not subsequently have a permanent father figure) less often drew a male first and drew males shorter. Also the father-absent boys generally drew males shorter than they drew females.

However, clear-cut relationships between father absence and figure drawings have not been consistently found with older children. A problem with many of the studies concerned with figure drawings is that there is no presentation of specific information regarding length and age of onset of father absence (e.g., Donini 1967; Lawton and Sechrest 1962).

Developmental Stages

In Chapter 3, data are reviewed that suggest that the quality of the early father-child attachment is an important factor in the child's sex role and personality development. The degree and quality of the father's involvement even in the first year of life has much influence on the child's behavior. Research by Money and his coworkers has also pointed to the first two to three years of life as being of crucial importance in the formation of an individual's sex role orientation (Money and Ehrhardt 1972). On the basis of their clinical observations of individuals with physical-sexual incongruencies, these investigators have concluded that self-conceptions relating to sex role appear particularly difficult to change after the second and third years of life. The possibility of critical periods in sex role development is suggested and early father absence appears to particularly interfere with the development of a secure masculine sex role orientation.

Father absence before the age of four or five appears to have a retarding effect on masculine development. Hetherington (1966) reported that 9- to 12-year-old father-absent boys manifested less masculine projective sex role behavior and were rated as more dependent on their peers, less aggressive, and as engaging in fewer physical contact games by male recreation directors than were father-present boys. However, there were no consistent differences on the sex role measures when the father-present boys were compared with boys who had become father absent after the age of four.

I found that father-absent, five-year-old boys had less masculine sex role orientations (fantasy game measure) and sex role preferences (game choice) than did father-present boys (Biller 1969b). Moreover, the boys who became father absent before the age of four had significantly less masculine sex role orientations than those who became father-absent in their fifth year. In an investigation Bahm and I conducted with junior high school boys, those who became father-absent before the age of five scored less masculine on an adjective check list measure of masculinity of self-concept than did those who were father present (Biller and Bahm 1971). Research by Burton (1972) with Caribbean children also indicates the disruptive effect of early father absence on masculinity of self-concept.

Almost one half (17 out of 38) of the extremely feminine boys in Green's (1974) investigation experienced at least three consecutive months of father absence prior to the age of four. The separations were temporary in only three of the cases and most, if not all of the other 21 feminine boys who were not father-absent appeared to suffer from some other form of paternal deprivation during their first few years of life. However, Green's research reveals that many other factors in addition to early paternal deprivation are involved in the development of extremely feminine behavior patterns among boys. (There is further discussion of Green's research in Chapter 6.)

From their cross-cultural perspective, Burton and Whiting (1961) discussed the possible differential impact of father absence at different stages of the sex role development process. Burton and Whiting pointed out that many societies have a "discontinuous identification process." The father is virtually excluded from contact with his young children. Supposedly, a discontinuity in identification is produced when the boy is pushed into masculine behavior sometime in preadolescence or adolescence, particularly through his experiences during initiation rites. In contrast to earlier female domination, the boy is suddenly under the direct control of adult males, and feminine behavior is negatively reinforced. It is assumed that the boy has to learn to repress his earlier feminine identification. Whiting, Kluckhohn, and Anthony (1958) discovered that societies with exclusive mother-son sleeping arrangements and long postpartum sex taboos were likely to have elaborate male initiation rites; Burton and Whiting hypothesized "that the initiation rites serve psychologically to brainwash the primary feminine identity and establish firmly the secondary male identity" (p. 90).

In support of their "sex-role identification conflict hypothesis," Burton and Whiting (1961) reported some rather dramatic cross-cultural evidence. In societies in which rules of residence were matrilocal and in which the infant sleeps and interacts almost exclusively with females during the first few years of his life, a custom called the couvade was likely to occur. This custom stipulates that the husband retire to his bed upon the birth of his offspring and act as though he had just gone through childbirth. This custom can be interpreted as symbolic of an underlying feminine identification.

The effects of early father absence are not restricted to sex role functioning and many other personality characteristics can be influenced. A study of lower-class fifth-grade boys by Santrock (1970b) suggested that boys who became father absent before the age of two were more handicapped in terms of several dimensions of personality development than were boys who became father absent at a later age. For example, boys who became father absent before age two were found to be less trusting, less industrious, and to have more feelings of inferiority than boys who became father absent between the ages of three to five. The impact of early paternal deprivation is also supported by Carlsmith's (1964) findings concerning cognitive functioning. Other evidence is consistent with the supposition that early father absence is associated with a heightened susceptibility to a variety of psychological problems (Biller 1971a, 1972a). Studies relating to the effects of the timing of father absence on various dimensions of personality development are reviewed in later chapters.

Different Aspects of Sex Role Development

As the findings relating to developmental stages have suggested, different aspects of sex role may not be affected in the same way by father absence. It is common for young father-absent children to intensely seek the attention of older males (McCandless 1967). Because of deprivation effects, father-absent children often have a strong motivation to imitate and please potential father figures (Freud and Burlingham 1944). Father-absent boys may strive to act masculine in some facets of their behavior while continuing to behave in an unmasculine or feminine manner in others. For example, a paternally deprived boy may be exposed only to females who encourage passivity and dependency in the first four or five years of his life, while later there is much peer and societal pressure for him to behave in a masculine manner. Demands for masculine behavior may not become apparent to the boy until he reaches school age or even adolescence, but in any case under such conditions his sex role preference and/or sex role adoption may differ from his basic sex role orientation.

The results of many studies can be construed as indicating that the effect of father absence varies in terms of which aspects of sex role are considered. D'Andrade (1962) investigated the impact of several kinds of family patterns on the sex role development of 5- to 14-year-old children. One of his procedures can be considered to be a measure of sex role preference. (The child was asked whether he preferred to pretend to be the father, mother, brother, or sister, if he were playing a game.) In terms of this procedure, boys whose fathers had been continually absent made just about as many masculine choices as boys whose fathers had been continually present. D'Andrade also used a projective drawing completion test (Franck Test) to assess the boys' sex role development. The number of subjects at different age levels was very small, but assessment of the completed drawings suggested that some of the boys who were without fathers during their first few years of life had unmasculine and/or feminine sex role orientations even though they appeared quite masculine in their sex role preferences.

Barclay and Cusumano (1967) did not find any differences between father-present and father-absent adolescent males on a measure of sex role preference (Gough Femininity Scale). However, the father-absent males, as compared to the father-present males, were more field-dependent in terms of Witkin's rod and frame test. Barclay and Cusumano conceptualized the field-dependence-field independence dimension as reflecting underlying sex role orientation. Louden (1973) used a different measure of field-dependence-field independence but reported similar results.

In a study I did with lower-class, six-year-old children, father-absent boys were significantly less masculine than father-present boys on a measure of projective sex role behavior (ITSC). Such a procedure can be assumed to assess sex role orientation. However, the two groups were not consistently different in terms of their direct sex role preferences (the toys and games they said they liked) or teachers' ratings of sex role adoption (Biller 1968b). Results from one of my studies with five-year-old boys also suggested that sex role orientation is more affected by father absence than are sex role preference or sex role adoption (Biller 1969b). Even though the father-absent boys had significantly less masculine game preferences than the father-present boys, differences between the groups were most clear-cut in terms of responses to the sex role orientation procedure.

Social Background

If it can be assumed that attending college is more typical of middle-class adolescents than of lower-class adolescents, an investigation by Altus (1958) involving college students suggests that father-absent, middle-class boys remain relatively low in masculinity of sex role preference throughout adolescence. Father-absent and father-present male freshmen at the University of California were compared. Father absence was due to divorce, but no data on the age of onset of father absence were reported. The father-absent group scored significantly higher than the father-present group on the masculinity-femininity scale of the MMPI, indicating less masculinity of interests and attitudes.

In contrast, an examination of data from several other studies suggests the hypothesis that, particularly by adolescence, there is relatively little difference among lower-class father-present and father-absent boys with respect to many facets of sex role awareness, preference, and adoption (Aldous 1969; Barclay and Cusumano 1967; Greenstein 1966; Miller 1961; Mitchell and Wilson 1967; McCord, McCord, and Thurber 1962; Tiller 1961).

Greenstein (1966) studied adolescent boys referred to a juvenile court affiliated diagnostic center. Father-absent and father-present males were not found to be significantly different in terms of their response to a masculinity-femininity inventory and other sex role measures. Subjects were considered to be father absent if, at least three years prior to age twelve, no adult male was living in their home. However, at the time of the study, 10 of the 25 father-absent boys were residing in homes in which an adult male was present.

Miller (1961), with a seemingly more representative subject population, compared father-absent, lower-class, junior high school boys, predominantly black and Puerto Rican, with a matched group of father-present boys. There were no clear-cut differences, on either a masculinity-femininity interest inventory or in teachers' ratings of aggression and dependency. A boy was considered to be father-absent if no male lived in his home for at least two years prior to the study.

Such a short-term criterion of father absence does not indicate in how many cases the father (or a father surrogate) was available in the preschool years, and if so, for how long. For example, paternal availability during the preschool years for the adolescent father-absent boys could account for their relatively masculine sex role development.

McCord, McCord, and Thurber (1962) analyzed social workers' observations of predominantly lower-class 10- to 15-year-old boys. These investigators did not find any differences in the sex-appropriate behavior of boys separated from their fathers before the age of six and father-present boys. However, many boys separated from their fathers between the ages of six and twelve exhibited a feminine-aggressive pattern of behavior. A feminine-aggressive pattern of behavior can be a consequence of sex role conflict and insecurity. Tiller (1958) described a somewhat similar pattern of behavior for Norwegian father-separated boys.

The masculinity of many father-absent boys may be a reflection of conflict-generated overcompensation. Father-absent boys, particularly those in the lower class, seem to have an abundance of highly masculine peers whom they can emulate. Some observers have speculated that among lower-class adolescent boys, those who are father absent often exceed those who are father present in certain dimensions of masculine behavior (e.g., Burton and Whiting 1961; Miller 1958). Terman and Miles (1936), although not describing their father-absent subjects in sufficient detail, did note that this group scored significantly above the median for males in terms of masculinity of interests. Santrock and Wohlford (1970), in their study of lower-class, fifth-grade boys, found that teachers rated father-absent boys as more aggressive and masculine than they did father-present boys. By late childhood lower-class, father-absent boys appear to score at least as high as their father-present counterparts on certain measures of sex role preference and sex role adoption.

Surrogate Models

All children experience father absence to some degree. Usually it is while the father is away at work. The father may be separated from his children for prolonged periods or permanently because of economic factors, occupation, war, desertion, divorce, hospitalization, or death. An almost infinite variety of patterns of father absence can be specified. Many factors need to be considered in describing a particular father-absent situation: type (constant, intermittent, etc.), length, cause, the child's sex and age, quality of mother-child interactions, sibling constellation, sociocultural background, and the availability of surrogate models.

The absent father can still have an ongoing psychological impact on his child. The child may have memories of past interactions and/or develop a perception of his father from what others tell him. In this way the absent father can function as a model for the child. One of Freud's and Burlingham's (1944) case studies provides a poignant illustration. Tony, a two-year-old, only lived with his family up until the age of eighteen months, and he saw his father very little. His actual relationship with his father was very limited, but Tony perceived himself as having an extremely close relationship with his father. He talked about his father doing everything with him and he attempted to emulate every detail about his father's behavior that he could remember.

Paternal absence or paternal inadequacy does not rule out the possible presence of other male models. A brother, uncle, grandfather, or male boarder may provide the boy with much competent adult male contact. An important role can be played by male neighbors and teachers. Chapter 8 contains a detailed discussion of the possible effects of male teachers on boys. Male teachers seem to have a particularly great potential for influencing father-absent boys.

The child may even learn some masculine behaviors by patterning himself after a movie or television star, an athlete, or a fictional hero. Freud and Burlingham (1944) described how a fatherless, two-year-old boy developed a fantasy role model. Bob's mother had told him about a nine-year-old boy whom he referred to as "Big Bobby" and thereafter Bob actively used Big Bobby as a masculine model, attempting physical feats that he thought Big Bobby could perform. Bob perceived Big Bobby as physically superior to everyone else.

Some investigators have found that masculinity is related to the general amount of contact boys have with adult males. Nash (1965) studied a group of Scottish orphans who went to live in cottages run by married couples, the husbands thus offering them a masculine model. Even though less masculine (in terms of a variety of sex role measures) than boys who were raised in a typical family setting, they were more masculine than a group of orphans brought up entirely by women. Similarly, Steimel (1960) reported that adolescent boys who were high (compared to those who were low) in masculinity of interests on both the MMPI and Strong Vocational Interest Blank, recalled more childhood experiences with older males. In terms of maternal interview data, Santrock (1970) found that father-absent boys with a father substitute were significantly less dependent than father-absent boys with no father substitute.

There are additional data that suggest that stepfathers can have a facilitating effect on the father-absent child's development, particularly if the stepfather-child relationship begins before the age of four or five. Research relating to cognitive functioning has indicated that previously father-absent children who gain a stepfather in early childhood are not usually handicapped in their cognitive functioning; whereas, children who remain without a father substitute are likely to suffer in at least some facets of their cognitive functioning, often in areas that are considered to be masculine related skills (Lessing, Zagorin and Nelson 1970; Santrock 1972).

However, there has been a general lack of systematic consideration of the role of the stepfather in the child's personality development. Some investigators have found evidence suggesting that the presence of a stepfather can negatively affect the child's psychological functioning (e.g., Benson 1968; Langner and Michael 1963). On the other hand, Anderson (1968) presented evidence that the early presence of a stepfather can lessen the chance of the father-absent boy becoming delinquent. It is, of course, the quality of the stepfather-child relationship and not the presence of a stepfather per se which affects the child's personality development. The child's age at the time the mother remarries seems to be a critical variable. For example, the young child who feels paternally deprived may find it much easier to accept a stepfather than the adolescent who may have established a strong sense of independence. Similarly, the stepfather may react more favorably to the young affectionate child than to the older child who refuses to accept his authority. The quality of the mother-child relationship and the mother's attitude toward the stepfather are also very important factors (Biller and Meredith 1974).

Sibling Factors

Older brothers as well as fathers can provide the child with a masculine model. There has been a considerable amount of research linking the sex of siblings with the child's sex role development. In a classic study of five- and six-year-olds, Koch (1956) found that a boy with an older sister was more likely to be rated a sissy by teachers than a boy with an older brother. Similarly, a girl with an older brother was more likely to be rated a tomboy than a girl with an older sister. Brim (1958) reanalyzed Koch's extensive data and found more clear-cut evidence concerning sex of sibling effects. For example, in terms of teacher ratings, boys with older brothers were much more likely to exhibit positive masculine (instrumental) behaviors and much less likely to exhibit positive feminine behaviors than are boys with older sisters. Girls with older brothers were more likely to exhibit positive masculine behaviors than were girls with older sisters.

In two-child families where the children are relatively close in age, boys with brothers have stronger masculine sex role preferences than boys with sisters. Rosenberg and Sutton-Smith (1964) studied elementary school children's play and game preferences. In two-child families, boys with brothers had more masculine sex role preferences than boys with sisters. Girls with sisters had more feminine sex role preferences than girls with brothers. In a study with college students using the MMPI masculinity-femininity scale, similar findings were reported for males but not for females (Sutton-Smith and Rosenberg 1970).

However, it is interesting to note that in three-child families, elementary school boys with two sisters had more masculine sex role preferences than did boys with two brothers. Males in female environments often compensate by manifesting strong masculine sex role preferences. Similarly, it has been found that fathers who have two daughters and no sons tend to have very masculine sex role preferences (Rosenberg and Sutton-Smith 1968). Sex role insecurity is often manifested in the form of rigid sex role preferences. Again, it should be emphasized that sex role preferences are relatively changeable dimensions of sex role functioning and are not particularly indicative of underlying sex role acceptance or personality adjustment.

The results of family structure studies have been very interesting. Nevertheless, greater understanding of the potential effects of ordinal position and sibling status calls for a systematic consideration of interactions among the quality of parent-child relations and the various dimensions of family structure. For example, paternal deprivation may have a much different effect on a five-year-old boy who is an only child than on a five-year-old boy who has two older brothers who themselves were not paternally deprived in early childhood. Obviously, many other variables have to be considered including the frequency and quality of interactions among siblings. A problem with many of the sibling studies is that they consider only the presence or absence of a particular type of sibling. This is somewhat analogous to studies which take into account only whether a child is father present or father absent.

Interestingly, in two-child, father-absent families, there is some evidence that boys with brothers suffer less of a deficit in academic aptitude than do boys with sisters (Sutton-Smith, Rosenberg and Landy 1968). In Santrock's (1970a) study father-absent boys with only older male siblings scored more masculine (on a maternal interview measure of sex role behavior) than father-absent boys with only older female siblings. In an extension of Santrock's investigation Wohlford et al. (1971) found that father-absent children with older brothers were less dependent than those without older brothers in terms of both doll play and maternal interview measures. However, the presence or absence of older female siblings was not related to the sex role measures and did not affect the older brother's influence. It is also interesting to note that the five-year-olds in the Sears' research appeared to be less influenced by father absence than did the three or four year olds (Sears 1951); an examination of the Sears' data indicates that the five-year-old boys had more siblings than did the younger children. Unfortunately, no details are given in terms of the sex and age of siblings, but it is possible that the older children had more male siblings thereby lessening the effects of father absence (Biller and Borstelmann 1967).

Although the presence of male siblings may lessen the effects of father absence, data from one of my investigations was consistent with the conclusion that the presence of a father is generally a much more important factor in masculine development than is the presence of an older brother (Biller 1968a). It is also relevant to note that the sibling constellation in a family may influence aspects of sex-typing in parents as well as in children. For example, there is evidence that fathers' attitudes concerning what constitutes appropriate sex role behavior are influenced by the sex of their children (Lansky 1967; Rosenberg and Sutton-Smith 1968).

Peer Group

Peers are very important models for masculine behavior. The masculine role models provided by the peer group can be particularly influential for the paternally deprived boy. In a social class or subculture in which instrumental aggression and physical prowess are very important as a means of achieving peer acceptance, many father-absent boys are likely to emulate their masculine peers. Peer models seem especially important in lower-class neighborhoods. Miller (1958) emphasized the centrality of such traits as toughness and independence in the value system of lower-class adolescents. Lower-class boys honor aggressiveness more than do middle-class boys, and one of the types of boys they most admire is the aggressive, belligerent youngster who earns their respect because of his toughness and strength (Pope 1953).

The focus on masculine behavior in the adolescent gang provides the father-absent, lower-class boy with many substitute masculine models. Miller (1958) emphasized that:

For boys reared in female-based households the corner group provides the first real opportunity to learn essential aspects of the male role in the context of peers facing similar problems of sex-role identification (p. 14).

During the elementary school years, and in some cases even earlier, peer group pressure for masculine behavior begins to have an effect on most paternally deprived boys. There are some family situations in which emotional and instrumental dependency on the mother is so strong that peer influences do not have an effect or are delayed until adolescence. Because of certain physical handicaps such as lack of strength or coordination, it may be relatively impossible for a boy to successfully interact with a masculine striving peer group.

On the other hand, the boy who is physically well-equipped may find it relatively easy to gain acceptance from his peers. Many paternally deprived boys behave in a generally effective and masculine manner. For example, an additional case-study analysis of some of the five-year-old boys in my (1968a,

1969b) studies has indicated that father-absent boys who are relatively meso-morphic are less likely to be retarded in their sex role development than are father-absent boys with unmasculine physiques. A boy's physique has an important stimulus value in terms of the expectations and reinforcements it elicits from others and it may, along with correlated constitutional factors, predispose him toward success or failure in particular types of activities. The influence of the child's anatomical, temperamental, and cognitive predispositions on parental and peer behavior must be taken into account (e.g., Bell 1968).

Summary

Comparisons of father-absent and father-present boys suggested that availability of the father is an important factor in the masculine development of young boys. There is evidence that the young father-absent boy is more dependent, less aggressive, and less competent in peer relationships than his father-present counterpart. He is likely to have an unmasculine self-concept. However, analysis of previous investigations revealed methodological difficulties and indicated that a number of factors must be taken into account if the impact of father absence on masculine behavior is to be fully understood.

The first few years of life appear to be particularly important in masculine development, and father absence during this period seems to have an especially retarding effect. If the boy becomes father absent after the age of five, his sex role development appears to be much less affected than if he becomes father absent early in life, particularly if the absence began during his first two years. Different aspects of sex role development are not influenced to the same extent by father absence. Sex role orientation, that aspect of sex role relating to self-concept, seems to be most hampered by father absence in the first few years of life. Sex role preference and at least some facets of sex role adoption appear to be less influenced by father absence.

Father-absent boys learn many masculine behaviors. Even in the father's absence, other males such as neighbors, teachers and siblings can play a very important role in the boy's masculine development. For example, lower-class, father-absent boys usually learn many masculine behaviors from their peers and generally behave in a masculine manner, although there is evidence that they are likely to have unmasculine sex role orientations and to behave in an overly rigid fashion.

In addition to the obvious theoretical and practical relevance of studying the effects of father absence, a possible methodological justification is that father absence is a naturalistic manipulation. It can be argued that father absence must be an antecedent rather than a consequence of certain behaviors in children. However, a general problem with studies comparing father-absent and father-present children is that investigators have usually treated both father-absent children and father-present children as if they represented homogeneous groups. There has been a lack of concern for the meaning of father absence and father presence. For example, there have been few attempts to ensure that a group of consistently father-absent boys is compared with a group of boys who have a high level and quality of father availability.

Most researchers have treated father absence in an overly simplistic fashion. In many studies, there has been no specification of such variables as type, length, and age of onset of father absence. Potentially important variables such as the child's sex, IQ, constitutional characteristics, birth order, relationship with his mother, and sociocultural background, as well as availability of father surrogates, are often not taken into account, either in subject matching or in data analysis. When careful matching procedures are followed, more clear-cut findings seem to emerge (e.g., Biller 1969b, 1971a; Hetherington 1966).

Investigators have made inferences about the effects of father absence and variations in paternal behavior on sex role development and the identification process, but measurement of hypothesized dependent variables has often been indirect or included only a very narrow range of behaviors. Data concerning a limited measure of masculinity have frequently been used to make inferences concerning overall patterns of identification and sex role development; multi-dimensional assessment procedures are needed if we are to gain a clearer understanding of the influence of father absence of the child's sex role development.

Fathering and Personal and Social Adjustment

This chapter covers a diverse array of material indicating the importance of the father-child relationship in the boy's personal, emotional, and social adjustment. Topics include the influence of insufficient fathering on self-concept, anxiety, impulsiveness, moral development, self-control, and delinquent behavior. There is a consideration of the ways in which the father-child relationship may affect the boy's interactions with others. Both peer relationships and sexual relationships are examined and there is a discussion of data linking paternal deprivation to difficulties in heterosexual adjustment and the development of homosexuality.

The final section of this chapter is concerned with the influence of paternal deprivation in the etiology of psychopathology. Studies revealing an association between inadequate fathering and various forms of psychopathology are summarized. There is an emphasis on how the father-mother relationship and family interaction patterns are related to psychopathology, since many forms of psychopathology appear to be directly related to inadequate interpersonal relationships among family members.

Self-esteem and Personal Adjustment

Several researchers have presented data indicating an association between self-esteem and various facets of paternal behavior. The father's interest and consistent participation seems to strongly contribute to the development of the child's self-confidence and self-esteem. In Coopersmith's (1967) study of elementary school boys, paternal involvement in limit-setting was associated with high self-esteem. In contrast, boys with low self-esteem were much more likely to be punished exclusively by their mothers. Coopersmith also noted that boys who were able to confide in their fathers were likely to have high self-esteem. Sears (1970) found a relationship between mother-reported paternal warmth and a questionnaire measure of sixth grade boys' self-esteem.

Mussen et al. (1963) found that adolescent boys with unaffectionate relationships with their fathers were particularly likely to feel rejected and unhappy. Medinnus (1965a) reported that college students' self-esteem was positively related to paternal love and negatively related to paternal rejection and neglect. Rosenberg's (1965) results suggested that the early father-child relationship is especially important for the child's self-esteem. Among adolescents, those who were father absent had lower self-esteem than those who were father present, particularly when father absence had begun in early childhood.

Slater (1962) examined the relationship between college men's personality characteristics and their perceptions of their parents. Students who scored high on questionnaire measures of ego strength and social competence were likely to perceive their fathers as affectionate and emotionally supportive. In contrast, students who responded in a manner suggesting low ego strength, impulsiveness, and social introversion were likely to see their fathers as being inhibiting in their demands and discipline. Paternal involvement was positively associated with the son's responsivity toward others. Baggett (1967) found that college students who had experienced continual father absence since before the age of eight were less well-adjusted on personality measures than those who had been father present.

Reuter and I studied the relationship between various combinations of perceived paternal nurturance-availability and college males' personality adjustment (Reuter and Biller 1973). A family background questionnaire was designed to assess perceptions of father-child relationships and the amount of time the father spent at home when the subjects were children. The personal adjustment scale of Gough and Heilbrun's Adjective Check List, and the socialization scale of the California Psychological Inventory, were employed as measures of personality adjustment. High paternal nurturance, combined with at least moderate paternal availability, and high paternal availability combined with at least moderate paternal nurturance, were related to high scores on the personality adjustment measures. A male who has adequate opportunities to observe a nurturant father can imitate his behavior and develop positive personality characteristics. The father who is both relatively nurturant and relatively available may have a more adequate personality adjustment than other types of fathers.

In contrast, high paternal nurturance combined with low paternal availability and high paternal availability combined with low paternal nurturance were associated with relatively poor scores on the personality adjustment measures. The boy with a highly nurturant but seldom-home father may feel quite frustrated that his father is not home more often and/or may find it difficult to imitate such an elusive figure. Males who reported that their fathers had been home much of the time but gave them little attention seemed to be especially handicapped in their psychological functioning. The unnurturant father is an inadequate model and his consistent presence appears to be a detriment to the boy's personality functioning. To put it another way, the boy with an unnurturant father may be better off if his father is not very available. This is consistent with evidence that suggests that father-absent boys often have better personality adjustments than boys with passive ineffectual fathers (Biller 1971a, 1972a).

Adjustment and Perceived Similarity
to the Father

The results of many investigations have suggested that low perceived similarity to the father is related to maladjustment among males. Cava and Rausch (1952) had adolescent boys fill out a vocational interest test for themselves and then as they thought their fathers would. Boys having low perceived similarity to the father generally scored high in castration anxiety as measured by projective test responses. Sopchak (1952) had college students fill out the MMPI for themselves and as they perceived their parents would. Men who perceived themselves as dissimilar to their fathers were more likely to be anxious and maladjusted in terms of their MMPI responses. Lazowick (1955) found that the more the son perceived himself to be similar to his father on a personality inventory, the lower his score was likely to be on an anxiety scale. In Helper's (1955) study, there was a positive relationship between perceived similarity to the father and peer acceptance.

Gray (1959) studied fifth through eighth graders and reported a positive association between boys' perceived similarity to fathers and peer ratings of adjustment. Lockwood and Guerney's (1962) study revealed that fathers as well as their adolescent sons were likely to perceive strong father-son similarity when the son scored high on an adjustment inventory. In David's (1968) study there was an association between low perceived similarity to the father and low ego strength among both college males and females. Manis (1958) appears to have been the only investigator who did not report a relationship between perceived similarity to the father and adjustment among males.

Anxiety

Inadequate fathering is often associated with a high level of anxiety in children. The paternally deprived child's insecurity in his interpersonal relationships can contribute to feelings of anxiety and low self-esteem. In addition, the paternally deprived child may experience much anxiety because of an overly intense relationship with his mother (see Chapter 6). The father-absent child, in particular, is likely to encounter economic insecurity and, depending on the reason for paternal absence, may be concerned with his father's well-being. Feelings of being different from other children may also increase his anxiety and perception of being inadequate. A principal role of the father is to help the family deal with environmental problems, and the paternally deprived child may encounter more than his share of many seemingly unsolvable crises. Children with adequate and available fathers are exposed to a model who can realistically and creatively deal with some of the problems that a mother may not have the experience or time to solve (Biller 1971a).

Stolz et al. (1954) reported that four- to eight-year-old children, father-absent the first few years of life while their fathers were away in military service, were more anxious than children whose fathers had been consistently present. Previously father-separated children were observed to be more anxious with peers and adults, in story completion sessions when the situation involved the father, and in terms of maternal reports of seriousness and number of fears. It is important to note that the fathers were not absent at the time of the study and were having stressful relationships with their children. In a study of nursery school children, Koch (1961) found that father-absent children (eight boys and three girls) exhibited more anxiety on a projective test than did a matched group from intact families. The father-absent children more often selected unhappy faces for the central child depicted in various situations.

McCord, McCord, and Thurber (1962) analyzed social workers' observations of 10- to 15-year-old, lower-class boys. They concluded that father-absent boys manifested more anxiety about sex than a matched group of father-present boys, although the difference concerning amount of general fearfulness was insignificant. In a retrospective study, Stephens (1961) asked social workers about their experiences with father-absent boys. Father-absent boys were described as being more effeminate and anxious about sex than were father-present boys. Leichty (1960) did not find any evidence that father absence during early childhood was associated with castration anxiety in college males, although some of her findings did suggest that father absence was related to anxiety concerning mother-father sexual interaction.

A high level of anxiety is often an outcome of inadequate sex role development. Some investigators have found that males low in masculinity and/or those with inappropriate sex role preferences are highly anxious (e.g., Mussen 1961; Rosenberg and Sutton-Smith, 1964). Similarly, there is evidence which suggests that poor father-child relationships are related to both a high level of anxiety and poor sex role adjustment (Beier and Ratzeburg 1953; Lazowick 1955). For example, Lazowick (1955) found that the less the son perceived himself as similar to his father, the higher his score was likely to be on an anxiety scale. However, other research has revealed that highly masculine behavior is sometimes associated with intense anxiety (e.g., Gray 1957; Webb 1963).

It could, of course, be argued that there are many different types and/or definitions of anxiety and this may help to explain these seemingly contradictory findings. A *secure* sex role development is accompanied by a relatively low degree of anxiety in most situations. However, many boys who exhibit high masculine preferences and high masculine adoptions are actually quite insecure in their sex role development. Sex role anxiety may lead many paternally deprived boys to overcompensate and become hypermasculine in their behavior. Lack of a firmly masculine sex role orientation can be reflected in overly rigid sex role preference and sex role adoption behavior. There may be a curvilinear relationship between anxiety and certain facets of masculine behavior, particularly in adolescence. For example, both boys very low and boys very high in masculinity of sex role preference may be relatively anxious.

Chronic anxiety and poor adjustment seem uncommon among boys who have solid identifications with their fathers (Lynn 1969; Schoeppe, Haggard, and Havighurst 1953). Males who perceive themselves as being similar to their fathers, particularly when their fathers are masculine, are likely to be relatively free of serious psychological difficulties (Cava and Rausch 1952; Heilbrun 1962; Heilbrun and Fromme 1965; Sopchak 1952).

Vocational Adjustment

A number of investigators have speculated that the type of work in which a father engages can influence the personality development of his children (e.g., Bronfenbrenner 1958; Miller and Swanson 1958). For example, Miller and Swanson suggested that fathers who are entrepreneurs, those who take risks and individual responsibility in their business ventures, encourage the development of self-control, self-reliance, and assertive mastery of the environment. According to Miller and Swanson, fathers who are engaged in bureaucratic occupations take few risks and encourage more conformity behavior in their children. There is some evidence that fathers with entrepreneurial occupations are more likely to be dominant family decisionmakers than are fathers with bureaucratic occupations (Gold and Slater 1958). However, as Benson (1968) pointed out, many studies do not support conceptualizations which predict a direct relationship between fathers' occupations and the personality development of children.

Nevertheless, even in our highly mobile society the boy's career choice is often very much influenced by his father's occupation (Mussen, Conger and Kagan 1974). Fathers still appear to be the most influential models in the male's vocational adjustment (Bell 1969). Jenson and Kirchner (1955) point out that when the son goes into an occupation in a different field from his father, it is usually of a higher status. When fathers have careers in such fields as medicine and law or the physical or social sciences, sons are especially likely to choose the same profession (Werts 1968). Of course, even when high status occupations are considered, the majority of sons do not choose the same career as their fathers.

The quality of the father-child relationship is a much more important factor than the father's specific occupation. Crites (1962) had college men fill out a vocational interest inventory and a questionnaire relating to their perceptions of their parents. Men who perceived themselves as more similar to their fathers generally had masculine vocational interests whereas those who perceived themselves as being more similar to their mothers generally had more vocational interests in fields emphasizing verbal and linguistic skills. Interestingly, men who perceived themselves as being about equally similar to both parents expressed interests relating to the expression of both masculine and feminine characteristics. For example, they preferred occupations which involved both helping people and doing research.

Green and Parker's (1965) findings suggested that the quality of parent-child relationships of young children is likely to influence the types of jobs they say they would prefer to have when they become adults. For example, boys were likely to choose person-oriented vocations if they perceived either their mothers or fathers positively, whereas girls were likely to make a non-person-oriented choice if they viewed either parent as negative, especially the father. However, research with adolescents and adults has not been consistent with the supposition that quality of parent-child relations is a major determinant of choosing a person-oriented or a non-person-oriented occupation (e.g., Brunkan 1965; Byers, Forrest and Zaccaria 1968; Switzer et al. 1962).

Certainly, the father in his work role can provide an important model for his son, but the amount of opportunity the son has to interact and observe his father is the critical variable. Fathers in many different occupations often have very little to do with their children. If the quality of the father-child relationship were taken into account, more clear-cut findings pertaining to relationships among paternal occupation and personality development might be forthcoming.

Males who have experienced inadequate fathering are likely to have vocational adjustment problems. Studying Peace Corps volunteers, Suedfield (1967) discovered that those who were father absent during childhood were much more likely not to complete their scheduled overseas tours than were those who had not been father absent. Premature terminations were associated with problems of adjustment and conduct, and included some psychiatrically based decisions. Bell (1969) found that adolescent males whose fathers were strong and positive role models, personally as well as occupationally, achieved higher levels of vocational adjustment than did those whose fathers were absent or were weak or negative role models. The vocational adjustments of those whose fathers were negative role models was somewhat better than those whose fathers were absent or were weak role models; the father who is a negative role model may at least provide the boy with a clearcut frame of reference to react against. There is other research which suggests that there is a relationship between father absence in childhood and poor occupational adjustment and unemployment in adulthood (Gay and Tonge 1967; Hall and Tonge 1963).

Frequent opportunities for observing a competent adult male in a variety of problem-solving situations are important in the development of the child's maturity and responsibility. Bronfenbrenner (1961) found that the amount of time adolescent boys spent with their fathers was positively related to the degree of leadership and responsibility that the boys displayed in school. On the basis of their findings, Mussen et al. (1963) concluded that instrumental achievement striving was more frequent among adolescent boys with adequate (affectionate) father-son relationships than among those with inadequate father-son relationships. Findings from some studies suggest that males who have been father absent during childhood generally have lower achievement motivation and experience less career success than do males who have been father present (McClelland 1961; Terman and Oden 1947, Veroff et al. 1960).

McClelland et al.'s (1953) findings indicate that achievement motivation may be stifled by fathers who are over-involved or under-involved with them and also by fathers who occupationally are extremely successful or clear-cut failures. Moderately nurturant and moderately successful fathers may have sons with the highest motivation to achieve. It is important to emphasize, however, that motivation to achieve is not necessarily linked with achievement and that many individuals are frustrated by overly strong needs to prove themselves, which in turn may interfere with their personal and social development. The male who feels he must prove his masculinity via occupational success and cannot find time for nonvocational and family pursuits is a rather common phenomenon (Biller and Meredith 1974).

The involved father can do much to help his child to function independently and competently, and to motivate him to achieve success. Rosen and D'Andrade (1959) observed that fathers of adolescent boys with high achievement strivings encouraged their sons' self-reliance and independence. The father's role in fostering independence and achievement often revolves around being the boy's model and allowing him to make his own decisions. The quality of father-mother interactions are very important. The father who is dominated by his wife is not an effective model for his son. Many boys from maternally dominated families are dependent and unsuccessful in their academic performance (e.g., Devereux, Bronfenbrenner, and Suci 1962; Elder 1962; Smelser 1963).

The father who is decisive and competent and also allows his child to be independent facilitates his child's ability to cope with his environment. Paternal self-confidence, encouragement, and involvement can be important factors in the development of the boy's assertiveness, problem-solving skills and ability to think flexibly. However, paternal interference in the son's activities can hamper the boy's functioning (Busse 1969; Rosen and D'Andrade 1959). A domineering father, as well as a domineering mother, can undermine the boy's competency by not allowing him sufficient opportunity to solve his own problems. Paternal domination and rigid subordination of the mother and child by the father stifles the boy's independence and achievement strivings (Strodtbeck 1958). The child needs to develop a feeling that he is capable of being similar to a highly competent father and that as he grows older he can successfully imitate and learn his father's skills. (In Chapter 8 there is a more thorough discussion of the father's influence on achievement and academic functioning).

Fathers who encourage autonomy and independence also seem to aid in the development of their children's concern for constructive social change. Some data suggest that students who are striving to change society are likely to have politically liberal fathers who were involved, warm, and permissive in child rearing (Flacks 1967). There is evidence indicating that both male and female college students who are supporters of the Women's Liberation Movement frequently come from homes where flexible fathers encourage their autonomy and independence (Lynn 1974). On the other hand, Lane (1959) presented evidence linking men's authoritarianism and political passivity with inadequate relations with their fathers.

Longitudinal Studies

Block (1971) presented complex longitudinal findings which underscored the impact of father's behavior, and the father-mother relationship, on the child's later personality development. The subjects were drawn from the Berkeley Longitudinal Study. There are many facets to this fascinating study, but here I am focusing on attempts to relate ratings made on the early family atmosphere of the individuals when they were children with their personalities in adolescence and adulthood. (Findings concerning the female groups are discussed in Chapter 7.) A Q-sort methodology was used on a vast array of data collected at three age periods; junior high school, high school, and adulthood (when the subjects were in their 30s). A factor analytic approach was used to differentiate personality types and these types were analyzed with respect to a number of criteria including family background data.

The findings seem most striking in emphasizing the importance of a positive home environment with two competent involved parents. Overall, the findings reinforce the notion of the facilitating effect of the father being a positive masculine figure and the mother a positive feminine figure.

Males who were classified as ego resilient (well-adjusted and emotionally and interpersonally successful) had fathers who were described as outgoing, bright, and productive. Their mothers were highly intelligent, warm, and psychologically healthy. Both parents took their child-rearing responsibilities very seriously.

Another male group achieved a positive but belated adjustment in adulthood even though they had many psychological difficulties during their adolescent years. They became hardworking and conscientious individuals. In general, their parents were described as warm, responsible, and unambitious. This group appeared to be well-adjusted but not to as high a degree as those who were described as ego resilient. It is interesting to note that the ego resilient group was higher in intellectual ability (IQ, 128) than was the belated adjustment group (IQ, 106). Both of these groups could be described as developing their intellectual potentialities in adulthood.

In contrast to these groups of well-adjusted males, there were three groups who did not achieve adequate psychological adjustments. One group was labeled "vulnerable overcontrollers." They had passive, withdrawn, and timid fathers and rigid, neurotic, and sexually conflicted mothers. This group seemed to model the neurotic traits expressed in both parents (just as the two well-adjusted groups seemed to mirror the competence of both their parents). Another group, "anomic extraverts," were frequently noted to have fathers who were undemonstrative, uninvolved, and domineering. Their mothers were apathetic and seemed uninterested in either their husbands or children. This group seemed to react against their ignoring parents during adolescence, but by adulthood they appeared to have developed an affective blandness and detachment similar to their parents.

The third group of poorly adjusted males, "unsettled undercontrollers," also had inadequate and neglecting parents. Their fathers were highly selfish, uninterested, and remote from them (and often physically absent from the home). The mothers were described as unstable and there was frequent parental disagreement. It is relevant to note that this group was extremely bright (IQ, 128) but that their inadequate home background seemed to interfere with the development of their potential.

Block, von der Lippe, and Block (1973) reported data which also indicate the complexity of the associations between parental behavior and the child's later personality functioning. They studied a sample of adult males and a sample of adult females from the Berkeley Longitudinal Studies. The sex role and socialization status of the subjects was determined by their scores on the Femininity and Socialization Scales of the California Psychological Inventory. The males and females were separately grouped according to their sex role and socialization patterns. (Data concerning the female groups are discussed in Chapter 7.)

Comparisons of the personality characteristics of different groups were done with respect to Q-sort analyses of extensive interview data. The various groups were also compared in terms of observational and interview ratings of the subjects' family background based on data collected during their childhood, and there were also contemporaneous interviewer judgments based on the subjects' retrospective reports of their home environments.

The high masculine, high socialized males were perceived as being self-confident, competent, optimistic, and buoyant in affect. Analyses of their family background suggested that their parents had a compatible relationship and that the father was the most important person in their personality development. The fathers of such men granted their sons autonomy and were highly available as models as well as accepting of their sons.

The low masculine, high socialized males were seen as over-controlled conventional, conscientious, and productive. They were viewed as markedly unaggressive yet seemed to be quite responsible and successful. Their fathers were depicted as very positive models in terms of success, ambition, adjustment, and interpersonal relations. The researchers stress that the father's capacity for delay of gratification and long-term commitment seems most evident in this group. This group also appeared to have particularly admirable mothers and been exposed to highly compatible father-mother interactions.

The high masculine, low socialized males were perceived as hypermasculine in a compensatory manner. They presented a constellation of traits including egotism and lack of impulse control. Family background data clearly indicated that these men had weak, neurotic, and somewhat rejecting fathers. The mother-father relationship was described as very poor and the mothers seemed resentful and dissatisfied with their husbands. In general, the fathers seemed to be very poor models.

The low masculine, low socialized males communicated an attitude of submissiveness, self-doubt, vulnerability, and defensive blame of others. Their fathers appeared to have been relatively uninvolved with their families and yet at the same time conflict-producing. The mothers also appeared very inadequate and were described as neurotic, lacking in energy, and rejecting of the maternal role. There was also some evidence indicating that both parents, particularly the fathers, had difficulties in maintaining marriage relationships.

Impulsive and Antisocial Behavior

Mischel conducted a series of studies concerning the antecedents and correlates of impulse control in Caribbean children (e.g., Mischel 1961c). In an earlier phase of his research, Mischel (1958) discovered that 7- to 9-year-old, black, West Indian children chose immediate gratification significantly more frequently than did white West Indian children. The differences between the black and white children appeared to be related to the greater incidence of father absence among the black children. Studying 8- and 9-year-olds, Mischel (1961b) found that father-absent children showed a stronger preference for immediate gratification than did father-present children. Father-absent children, for instance, more often chose a small candy bar for immediate consumption rather than waiting a week for a large candy bar.

Mischel (1958) speculated that father absence interferes with the young child's development of trust of other people. It is also possible that many young father-absent children trust adult females but not adult males; in Mischel's research an adult male offered the choice between immediate and delayed gratification. The young, father-absent child may learn to be secure in the presence of his mother and generalize this trust to other females, but a basis for trusting adult males may be lacking.

When Mischel (1961b) studied 11- to 14-year-olds, he did not find an association between father absence and preference for immediate gratification. Perhaps, as Mischel suggested, as the father-absent child grows older, his wider experience helps him to develop a trust of others beyond those in his immediate family. With added experience most father-absent children may learn to trust males. In addition, according to Mischel, many of the older, father-absent children may have been without their fathers for a relatively brief period. The older, paternally deprived children may have been father present during the age period most crucial to the development of trust. In Mischel's·studies the criterion of father absence was simply whether or not the father was living at home and there was no measure of duration of father absence. In research with fifth-grade boys, Santrock (1970b) found that father absence beginning in the first two years of life was more disruptive to the development of trust than father absence during the ages of three to five.

Santrock and Wohlford (1970) studied delay of gratification among fifth-grade boys. They found that boys who were father absent because of divorce, as compared to those who were father absent because of death, had more difficulty in delaying gratification. Boys who were father absent because of divorce more often chose an immediately available small candy bar than waiting till the next day for a much larger one. Boys who became father-separated before the age of two or between the ages of six to nine were more likely to choose the immediate reward than those who were separated from their fathers between the ages of three to five.

Moral Development and Impulse Control

Paternal dominance in discipline, when combined with a high level of paternal affection, is strongly associated with male children's sensitivity to their moral transgressions (Moulton et al. 1966). The father who is able to firmly set limits and can also be affectionate and responsive to his child's needs seems to be a particularly good model for interpersonal sensitivity and moral development. Holstein (1972) found that adolescents who were morally mature were likely to have fathers who were warm and nurturant and high in their own level of moral development.

Hoffman (1971a) reported data concerning the conscience development of seventh-grade children. Father-absent boys consistently scored lower than father-present boys on a variety of moral indexes. They scored lower on measures of internal moral judgment, guilt following transgressions, acceptance of blame, moral values, and rule-conformity. In addition, they were rated as higher in aggression by their teachers, which may also reflect difficulties in self-control. Although the influence was less clear-cut, weak father identification among father-present boys was also related to less adequate conscience development. Father identification was determined by responses to questions involving the person the boy felt most similar to, most admired, and most wanted to resemble when he grew up. Boys with strong father identification scored higher on the measures of internal moral judgment, moral values, and conformity to rules than did boys with low father identification (Hoffman 1971a,b).

Whiting (1959) hypothesized that paternal deprivation is negatively related to the strength of the child's conscience development. Doing a cross-cultural analysis, he assumed that self-blame for illness is an indication of strong conscience development. In societies in which fathers have little contact with their young children, there is more of a tendency to blame others and/or supernatural beings for one's illness. Blaming one's self for illness was strongest in nuclear households and least in polygynous mother-child households. Such evidence is also consistent with the view that paternal deprivation can inhibit the development of trust in others.

The quality of the father-child relationship seems to have particular influence on whether the child takes responsibility for his own actions or acts as if his behavior is controlled by external forces. Children who have a warm relationship with a competent father who can constructively set limits for them are much more likely to develop a realistic internal locus of control. There is beginning to be more attention paid to the familial antecedents of variations in locus of control among children (e.g., Davis and Phares 1969; MacDonald 1970; Nowicki and Segal 1974).

A number of clinicians, including Aichorn (1935) and Lederer (1964), have speculated about inadequacies in the self-control and conscience development of the father-absent boy. In his experience as a psychotherapist, Meerloo (1956) found that a lack of accurate time perception, which is often associated with difficulties in self-control, is common among father-absent individuals. In a study of elementary school children in a Cuban section of Miami, Wohlford and Leiberman (1970) reported that father-absent children had less well-developed future time perspectives than did father-present children. Tolor, Brannigan, and Murphy (1970) investigated the relationship between perceived psychological distance from the father and future perspective among college students. Students who perceived themselves as distant from their fathers were less able to extend themselves into a future perspective than were students who felt close to their fathers.

Meerloo (1956) assumed that the father represents social order and that his adherence to time schedules gives the child an important lesson in social functioning. The paternally deprived boy may find it very difficult to follow the rules of society. Antisocial acts are often impulsive as well as aggressive, and there is evidence that inability to delay gratification is associated with inaccurate time perception, lack of social responsibility, low achievement motivation, and juvenile delinquency (e.g., Mischel 1961a, 1961c).

The father-absent boy often lacks a model from whom to learn to delay gratification and to control his aggressive and destructive impulses. A boy who has experienced paternal deprivation may have particular difficulty in respecting and communicating with adult males in positions of authority. Douvan and Adelson (1966) observed much rebelliousness against adult authority figures and particularly a rejection of men among adolescent, father-absent boys. (It is interesting to contrast such a reaction to the continual seeking of male adults among many young father-absent children—perhaps there has been a disillusionment process.)

The boy whose father has set limits for him—in a nurturant and realistic manner—is better able to set limits for himself. There is also some evidence that perceived similarity to father is related to positive relationships with authority figures (Bieri and Lobeck 1959). Investigators have found that boys who receive appropriate and consistent discipline from their fathers are less likely to commit delinquent acts even if they are gang members (Glueck and Glueck 1950; Stanfield 1966).

Delinquency

Juvenile delinquency can have many different etiologies, but paternal deprivation is a frequent contributing factor. Many researchers have noted that father-absence is more common among delinquent boys than among nondelinquent boys. Studying adolescents, Glueck and Glueck (1950) reported that more than two-fifths of the delinquent boys were father absent as compared with less than one-fourth of a matched nondelinquent group. McCord, McCord, and Thurber (1962) found that the lower-class, father-absent boys in their study committed more felonies than did the father-present group, although the rates of gang delinquency were not different. Gregory (1965a) listed a large number of investigations linking father absence with delinquent behavior and also detected a strong association between these variables in his study of high school students. Other researchers relying on self-report measures have also detected that individuals from fatherless families are more likely to engage in delinquent behavior (e.g., Slocum and Stone, 1963).

Early father absence has a particularly strong association with delinquency among males. Siegman (1966) analyzed medical students' responses to an anonymous questionnaire concerning their childhood experiences. He compared the responses of students who had been without a father for at least one year during their first few years of life with those of students who had been continuously father present. The father-absent group admitted to a greater degree of antisocial behavior during childhood. Anderson (1968) found that a history of early father absence was much more frequent among boys committed to a training school. He also discovered that father-absent, nondelinquents had a much higher rate of father substitution (stepfather, father surrogate, etc.) between the ages of four to seven than did father-absent delinquents. Kelly and Baer (1969) studied the recidivism rate among male delinquents. Compared to a 12 percent rate among father-present males, they found a 39 percent recidivism rate among males who had become father absent before the age of six. However, boys who became father absent after the age of six had only a 10 percent recidivism rate.

Miller (1958) argued that most lower-class boys suffer from paternal deprivation and that their antisocial behavior is often an attempt to prove that they are masculine. Bacon, Child, and Barry (1963), in a cross-cultural study, found that father availability was negatively related to the amount of theft and personal crime. Degree of father availability was defined in terms of family structure. Societies with a predominantly monogamous nuclear family structure tended to be rated low in the amount of theft and personal crime, whereas societies with a polygamous mother-child family structure tended to be rated high in both theft and personal crime. Following Miller's hypothesis, Bacon, Child, and Barry suggested that such antisocial behavior was a reaction against a female-based household and an attempted assertion of masculinity. A large number of psychiatric referrals with the complaint of aggressive acting-out are made by mothers of preadolescent and adolescent, father-absent boys, and clinical data suggest that sex role conflicts are frequent in such boys (e.g., MacDonald 1938; Wylie and Delgado 1959).

Herzog and Sudia (1970) carefully analyzed the methodological defects of studies linking father absence and delinquency. They pointed out that socioeconomic and sociocultural factors are often not taken into account in comparisons of father-absent and father-present children. Furthermore, Herzog and Sudia emphasized that law enforcement officials and other community agents may react differently when a father-absent child, rather than a father-present child, behaves in an antisocial manner, especially when the child comes from an economically disadvantaged family. For example, they may expect the father-absent child to commit increasingly serious offenses and he may be dealt with more severely. Such treatment may negatively influence the father-absent child's self-concept and strengthen the probability that he will become involved in more antisocial acts.

The difficulty that boys from father-absent homes often have in relating to male authority figures can also contribute to the reactions of law enforcement officials. The father-absent boy's "lack of respect" can lead to negative interactions with male authority figures. In fact, some data suggest that father-absent boys are more prone to commit offenses against authority than against property (Herzog and Sudia 1970; Nye 1958).

Herzog and Sudia (1970) also cited much evidence indicating that lack of general family cohesiveness and supervision, rather than father absence per se, is the most significant factor associated with juvenile delinquency. Many familial and nonfamilial factors have to be considered, and in only some cases is father absence directly linked to delinquent behavior. For example, boys in father-absent families who have a positive relationship with highly competent mothers seem to be less likely to become delinquent than boys in father-present families who have inadequate fathers.

Father-present juvenile delinquents appear to have very poor relationships with their fathers. Bach and Bremer (1947) reported that pre-adolescent delinquent boys produced significantly fewer father fantasies on projective tests than did a nondelinquent control group. The delinquents portrayed fathers as lacking in affection and empathy. Similarly, Andry (1962) found that delinquents characterized their fathers as glum, uncommunicative, and as employing unreasonable punishment and little praise. Father-son communication was particularly poor.

Andry's findings are consistent with those of Bandura and Walters (1959), who reported that the relationship between delinquent sons and fathers is marked by rejection, hostility, and antagonism. McCord, McCord, and Howard (1963) found that a deviant, aggressive father in the context of general parental neglect and punitiveness was strongly related to juvenile delinquency. Medinnus (1965b) obtained data suggesting a very high frequency of negative father-child relationships among delinquent boys. The delinquent adolescent boys in Medinnus's study perceived their fathers as much more rejecting and neglecting than their mothers.

Shaefer's (1965) data also revealed the particularly negative way delinquent boys often perceive their fathers. Compared to nondelinquent boys, delinquent boys viewed their fathers as laxer in discipline, more neglecting, and generally less involved. Surprisingly, the delinquents described their mothers as more positive and loving than did the nondelinquents. It is also interesting to note that Gregory (1965a) found a higher rate of delinquency among boys living with their mothers following father loss than among boys living with fathers following mother loss. Such data suggests that paternal deprivation is more of a factor in the development of delinquency than is maternal deprivation.

There is considerable evidence that father-present delinquents are likely to have inadequate fathers who themselves have difficulties in impulse control. Jenkins (1968) found that the fathers of delinquent children seen at a child guidance clinic were frequently described as rigid, controlling, and prone to alcoholism. McCord, McCord, and Howard (1963) reported that criminal behavior in adulthood was often found among men whose fathers had been criminals, alcoholics, and/or extremely abusive to their families. Several other researchers have presented data suggesting a link between paternal inadequacy and delinquent behavior (Bennett 1959; Gardiner 1959; Glueck and Glueck 1950).

Boys who commit delinquent acts by themselves appear to have poorer relationships with their fathers than do boys who commit delinquent acts with other gang members (Brigham, Ricketts, and Johnson 1967). On the other hand, boys who have positive relationships with their fathers are likely to engage in constructive and prosocial gang behavior (Crane 1955; Thrasher 1927). Such findings indicate that the quality of fathering a boy receives is of much influence in his peer relationships.

Interpersonal Relationships

As was discussed in Chapter 3, the father-infant relationship can have much impact on the child's subsequent relationships with others. For example, data was presented which indicated that infants who had little contact with their fathers were more likely to experience greater separation anxiety from their mothers and more negative reactions to strangers. The way the father interacts with the child presents a particularly potent modeling situation which the child is apt to generalize to his relationship with others.

Paternal deprivation can severely interfere with the development of successful peer relationships. Stolz et al.'s (1954) observations, as well as mothers' and fathers' reports indicated that four- to eight-year-old children who had been father absent for the first few years of life had poorer peer relationships than children who had not been father absent. The Norwegian, father-separated boys in Tiller's (1958) investigation were judged to have less adequate peer relationships than nonfather-separated boys. Other investigators have reported that continuously father-absent boys are less popular and have less satisfying peer relationships than do father-present boys (e.g., Leiderman 1953; Miller 1961; Mitchell and Wilson 1967).

Paternally deprived boys are often handicapped in their peer relationships because they lack a secure masculine orientation. Sex-appropriate behavior is very important in the formation of friendships among elementary school children. For instance, Tuddenham (1951, 1952) found that the most popular boys in the first grade were those who were considered by their peers to be good sports, good at games, daring, not bashful, and "real boys." Gray (1957, 1959) reported similar results for fifth- to eighth-grade boys. In addition, boys who were rated high in popularity perceived themselves as more similar to their fathers than did boys who were rated low in popularity (Gray 1959).

A positive father-son relationship gives the boy a basis for successful peer interactions. Rutherford and Mussen (1968) reported evidence indicating that nursery school boys who perceive their fathers as warm and nurturant are likley to be generous with other children. Fourth-grade boys in Leiderman's (1953, 1959) study who had high acceptance among their peers had warmer relationships with their fathers than did those with low peer acceptance. Cox's (1962) data also suggest a consistency between boys' relationships with their fathers and with their peers. Payne and Mussen (1956) found that adolescent boys who were similar to their fathers in terms of responses to the California Psychological Inventory were rated as more friendly by their teachers than were boys who had responses markedly different from their fathers.

Mussen et al.'s (1963) study also revealed that positive father-son relationships were associated with successful peer interactions and self-confidence among adolescent males. Studying high school boys, Helper (1955) found that boys who perceived themselves as similar to their fathers were likely to be highly accepted by their peers. Lois Hoffman's (1961) results indicated that boys from mother-dominant homes had much more difficulty in their peer relationships than did boys from father-dominant homes. Maternal dominance was associated with impulsiveness and an inability to influence peers. On the other hand, self-confidence, assertiveness, and overall competence in peer group interaction were related to a warm father-son relationship.

For boys, the presence of a masculine father, a positive father-son relationship, generally sex-appropriate behavior, and popularity with peers are strongly related. The absence of a warm, affectionate relationship with an adult male, during which mutual enjoyment of sex-typed interests and activities takes place, can seriously interfere with the boy's social development. The case of the maternally overprotected boy is relatively easy to understand. His mother strongly discourages his participation in masculine peer group activities, and his interests are very different from his male contemporaries. The unmasculine boy seems particularly likely to search for platonic relationships with girls or to associate with unmasculine boys.

The case of the paternally deprived boy who is well-motivated to be masculine seems more complex. During preadolescence and adolescence many father-absent boys feel that they have to continually prove themselves because they lack a secure masculine self-concept. However, lack of self-confidence and a high level of anxiety are not viewed as appropriate for males and can lead to further interpersonal difficulties.

A paternally deprived boy might have poor peer relationships despite rigid denial of anxiety and seeming bravado. The boy who continually challenges and berates others in his effort to prove his masculinity can become very unpopular, although he may be feared and respected by his peers. Father-absent boys can, of course, form close relationships with other children. In fact, masculine-striving, father-absent boys are likley to form relationships with older boys. Such relationships often facilitate their personality development, but because of dependency on peer acceptance, paternally deprived boys may passively conform to the wishes of an older peer group. This is an expression of their desire to have the masculine role model they lack at home. A related factor in their seeking relationships with older males may be the threat to their insecure masculine images of not performing as well in athletic and physical competition as boys their own age.

Family-functioning

There needs to be a consideration of how certain interpersonal variables in the father-mother relationship influence a boy's interactions with others. There have been numerous studies which have suggested that father and mother agreement about their child, and childrearing issues, is associated with positive social and emotional adjustment among children. Farber (1962) found 11- to 16-year-old boys' initiative and responsibility was related to the degree of their fathers' and mothers' consensus on domestic values. Medinnus (1963a) reported that strong disagreement between fathers' and mothers' childrearing and educational values was associated with poor overall school and peer adjustment among first graders.

Wyer's (1965a) findings indicated a link between degree of parental discrepancy in childrearing attitudes and preschool children's social uncertainty. Wyer (1965b) also detected a relationship between degree of mother and father similarity in perception of their children and the children's self-acceptance and academic achievement in college. Van der Veen (1965) found a positive association between parental agreement about family interactions and the social and emotional functioning of children at school.

Satisfaction of mothers with their husbands' childrearing approach was ascertained by Coopersmith (1967) to be related to high self-esteem among elementary school boys. Friedman (1969) described data indicating high mother-father agreement on basic family issues among seven- to thirteen-year-old children who emerged as leaders during a summer camp. However, in such studies it is very difficult to evaluate how much of the relationship between parental agreement and the child's adjustment is due to the child's influence on the parents. Some children from birth seem to be extremely adaptive to parental expectations, but other children, often because of temperamental or intellectual incompatibilities with their parents, can cause great tension and disagreement in a marital relationship.

A frequently researched factor in family functioning is the amount of father or mother dominance in decision-making. However, dominance is not an all or none phenomena; sometimes one parent will have authority in mundane day-to-day decisions, but in actuality the other parent has the final say on major decisions. Also there are many different areas in which a parent may be dominant, but usually the same parent is not dominant in all dimensions of family life. In general, evidence does suggest that there is a relative equality of sharing in most marriages, and that in nonegalitarian marriages fathers are more likely to dominate than are mothers (Blood and Wolfe 1960; Lynn, 1974). In the present discussion the focus is not on the issue of whether the father or mother is generally the most dominant parent, but rather how differences in degree of father dominance are related to variations in children's interpersonal adjustment.

Relying on college students' reports, Distler (1965) found a positive relationship among paternal dominance and power, parents' compatibility, and the child's satisfaction with his parents. Hurvitz (1965) and Ryder and Goodrich (1966) also presented evidence suggesting that wives in husband-dominated homes are more satisfied with their family life than are wives or husbands in wife-dominated homes. In earlier parts of this book, I have already discussed many studies which indicate a relationship between maternal dominance and difficulties in the boy's sex role and social adjustment.

There is considerable evidence linking very low paternal dominance with academic underachievement as well as interpersonal difficulties. Grunebaum et al. (1962) reported clinical data which suggested that underachieving elementary school boys were likely to come from homes in which the mother dominated and the father felt very inadequate. Elder (1962a) found that male adolescents who perceived their mothers as dominant in family decision-making were low in both academic motivation and achievement. Smelser (1963) presented findings indicating that maternal dominance was associated with sons not being as successful as their fathers. Cervantes (1965) reported that high school dropouts are likely to come from homes in which the father lacks influence.

On the other hand, Bowerman and Elder (1964) found that superior academic achievement was associated with fathers being perceived as dominant in family decision-making and democratic in parent-child relations. However, it is important to emphasize that overly dominating fathers often undermine their children's development of intellectual and interpersonal competence. Strodtbeck (1958) found that fathers who severely dominated their wives and sons were likely to have sons who felt little control over their environment and had low academic motivation.

There is some evidence that overdominating fathers are especially likely to have shy and fearful children (Alkire 1969; Becker and Krug 1969). Trapp and Kausler's (1958) findings are consistent with the supposition that overdominance by either parent can be socially inhibiting for a child. They found that children who had moderately dominant parents were most likely to positively interact with an adult, whereas high or low parental dominance was associated with avoidance of adult contact.

Straus (1962) studied the relationship between male adolescents' emotional and academic adjustment and their perceptions in terms of which parent bossed the other in various situations. He found that boys who perceived neither parent as bossing the other were most satisfied with their parents, less anxious, and had more perspective on the future than boys who perceived mother or father dominance, or those who saw their parents as trying to boss each other. Boys who perceived their parents as trying to boss one another were relatively high in anxiety and rejection of their parents and had the least perspective on the future. Perceived mother dominance was most associated with anxiety and rejection of parents.

Westley and Epstein (1970) conducted a research project which supports the view that the father-mother relationship is a crucial factor in the psychological development of their children. They intensively studied a total of 59 English Protestant families with a child who at the onset of the study was a first-year McGill University student. About two-thirds of the students were males. Their families were all intact and generally of middle or above-socioeconomic status. The researchers used intensive psychiatric interviews, sociological interviews and questionnaires, extensive psychological testing and lengthy home visits with individuals in those cooperating families that had either a very emotionally healthy or emotionally disturbed child attending McGill. Level of psychological adjustment was determined by the combined judgments of a psychiatrist who had interviewed each student and a psychologist who had administered the Rorschach and TAT to each student. A third group of moderately adjusted students and their families was also studied but not in as great detail. There was a relatively large number of methodological problems with this study including frequent lack of independent judgments and very incomplete reporting of specific data. However, the in depth study of the families and the provocative interdisciplinary approach warrant at least some heuristic discussion of the findings and conclusions.

Westley and Epstein found that the emotional health of the children, and the father-mother relationship, was associated with the father having a higher initial social status than the mother, a balanced relatively sex-typed parental division of labor, and a father-led pattern of authority (father and mother discussion but with the father making the majority of decisions). The child's emotional health appeared to be closely related to the quality of the emotional relationship between the parents. This usually meant the parents were emotionally healthy individuals but Westley and Epstein pointed out there were exceptions and emphasized that the quality of the father-mother relationship was more important than the psychological status of the individual parents. However, the father appeared to play a particularly important role as a family problem solver and the mother seemed crucial in permitting her children to function autonomously.

Westley and Epstein presented some provocative data relating to the associations between different types of parent authority and the personality functioning of children. The father-led families seemed the most successful. In such families discussions were arrived at through discussion, but the father more often had the final say, making the decisions between 55 and 65 percent of the time. The children from these families appeared to be good leaders, particularly stable and assertive. In equalitarian families where there was an approximately equal sharing of parental decision-making, the children seemed to be quiet, friendly and industrious. Compared to the father-led children, they seemed to be followers rather than leaders. In contrast to children from the father-led or equalitarian families, children from either father dominant or mother dominant homes seemed to have poorer psychological adjustments. Children from father dominant homes seemed timid, withdrawn, submissive and to have low self-confidence. However, they also appeared to be self-disciplined and industrious. Children from mother-dominant homes appeared to be consistently maladjusted; they were timid, withdrawn, lacked self-discipline and manifested severe psychopathologic symptoms. Westley and Epstein claimed that few of the children in the mother-dominant group were emotionally healthy.

Lack of paternal involvement and an excessive level of maternal influence in the family is particularly common in the development of psychopathology among males. There is a growing literature indicating that father-present males having uninvolved fathers, compared to those with involved fathers, are much more likely to develop severe behavior disturbances (e.g., Alkire 1969; Anderson 1969; Biller and Davids 1973; Farina 1960; Johnson and Meadow 1966; Kayton and Biller 1972; Piety 1967; Warren and Cameron 1950).

Sexual and Marriage Relationships

A positive father-child relationship can greatly facilitate the boy's security in interacting with females. (Research focusing on the father-daughter relationship and female sexual development is discussed in Chapter 7.) The boy who has developed a positive masculine self-image has much more confidence in hetero-sexual interactions. There is longitudinal data which suggests that the male who develops a strong sense of masculinity in childhood is likely to be successful in his heterosexual relationships in adulthood (Kagan and Moss 1962).

There is considerable evidence indicating that the male's adjustment to marriage is related to his relationship with his father and his parents' marital relationship (Barry 1970; Cross and Aron 1971). Difficulty in forming lasting heterosexual relationships often appears to be linked to paternal deprivation. Andrews and Cristensen's (1951) data suggested that college students whose parents had been divorced were likely to have frequent but unstable courtship relationships.

Winch (1949, 1950) found that father- absence among college males was negatively related to degree of courtship behavior (defined as closeness to marriage). He also reported that a high level of emotional attachment to the mother was negatively related to the degree of courtship behavior. In their interview study Hilgard, Neuman, and Fisk (1960) detected that many men whose fathers died when they were children continued to be very dependent on their mothers, if their mothers did not remarry. For example, only one of the ten men whose mothers did not remarry seemed to manifest a fair degree of independence in his marital relationship.

Jacobson and Ryder (1969) did an exploratory interview study with young marrieds who suffered the death of a parent prior to marriage. Death of the husband's father prior to the age of twelve was associated with a high rate of marriage difficulty. Husbands, father absent early in life, were described as immature and as lacking interpersonal competence. Participation in feminine-type domestic activities and low sexual activity were commonly reported for this group. In general, their marriages were relatively devoid of closeness and intimacy. In contrast, when the husbands had lost their fathers after the age of twelve, they were more likely to be involved in positive marriage relationships.

Other researchers have reported evidence indicating that individuals who have experienced father absence because of a broken home situation in childhood are more likely to have their own marriages end in divorce or separation (Landis 1965, Rohrer and Edmonson 1960). In many of these situations there is probably a strong modeling effect; children see parents attempting to solve their marital conflicts by ending a marriage and are more likely to behave in a similar fashion themselves. Research by Pettigrew (1964) with lower-class blacks is consistent with the supposition that father-absent males frequently have difficulty in their heterosexual relationships. Compared to father-present males, father-absent males were "more likely to be single or divorced—another manifestation of their disturbed sexual identification" (p. 420). Pettigrew also cited evidence suggesting that black males are less securely masculine in certain facets of their behavior than are white males.

Because of frequent paternal deprivation, and maternal disparagement of maleness, lower-class black males often suffer in terms of their sex role orientations, even though they may be quite masculine in other facets of their behavior. In two studies, both father availability and sociocultural background were significantly related to what could be considered measures of sex role orientation (Barclay and Cusumano 1967; Biller 1968b). Studying lower-class black and white lower-class boys, I did not find any clear-cut differences in sex role preference or sex role adoption. However, in terms of a projective sex role orientation responses (ITSC), black father-absent boys were the least masculine; there was no significant difference between white father-absent and black father-present boys; and white father-present boys were the most masculine (Biller 1968b).

A great deal of the heterosexual difficulty that many paternally deprived, lower-class males experience is associated with their compulsive rejection of anything that they perceive as related to femininity. Proving that they are not homosexual and/or effeminate is a major preoccupation of many lower-class males. They frequently engage in a Don Juan pattern of behavior, making one conquest after another, and a stable emotional relationship with a female may not be formed even during marriage. The fear of again being dominated by a female, as they were as children, contributes to their need to continually exhibit their masculinity by new conquests. The perception of childrearing as an exclusively feminine endeavor also interferes with their interaction with children and helps perpetuate the depressing cycle of paternal deprivation in lower-class families. Although such a pattern of behavior seems particularly prevalent among lower-class black males, it is by no means exclusive to this group.

Sexual Inadequacy

In their monumental work, Masters and Johnson (1970) describe the complex and varied etiology of sexual inadequacy. Parental factors are but one set of variables which may be antecedents to sexual problems. Nevertheless, paternal deprivation does appear with some frequency in the backgrounds of the sexually inadequate individuals Masters and Johnson have treated.

When discussing primary male impotence, Masters and Johnson note three specific instances of overt mother-son sexual encounters (genital stimulation by the mother) and add that in all these cases the father was either absent or minimally available. In six other cases there had been an overt pattern of homosexuality during adolescence; three of these males had totally dominant mothers and extremely uninvolved fathers.

Masters and Johnson mention the existence of a great number of cases in the clinical literature in which maternal dominance was a major factor in secondary impotence. In addition, as of 1970, they reported thirteen of their own cases with such a pattern. The passive, ineffectual father consistently emerges from such histories. The mother looms large as all-knowing and all-doing. The mother was often in full control of the boy's social contacts even when he reached adolescence.

Masters and Johnson also report five cases of secondary impotence associated with paternal over-control. Such fathers seemed to demand that all their wishes be met but had no sensitivity for the needs of their wives or children. Often the father was still dominating his son in adulthood, sometimes in a business relationship. Anxiety about trying to match his father's image or expectations was a major difficulty for the son. Masters and Johnson stress that unopposed maternal or paternal domination, irrespective of its etiology, can undermine the boy's sense of masculine competency. Of course, inadequate parenting does not necessarily lead to sexual inadequacy. Many men from such backgrounds are quite successful in their sexual relationships.

Homosexuality

As a group, homosexuals tend to have more psychological problems than do heterosexuals, but many of their conflicts are exacerbated by social rejection. It is important to emphasize that homosexuality is not necessarily associated with psychopathology. There are wide individual differences in adjustment and general competency among homosexuals as there are among heterosexuals. There is much recent research which indicates that there are many homosexuals who are very effective and competent in their interpersonal relationships and careers. On a variety of criteria such individuals rank high in personal, emotional, and social adjustment (e.g., Freedman 1971; Hooker 1969).

Although no systematic studies have been made concerning the rates of homosexuality among father-absent males, some investigators have suggested that father-absent males are more prone than father-present males to become homosexual. Both West (1959) and O'Connor (1964) reported that homosexual males more often than neurotic males had histories of long periods of father-absence during childhood. The paternally deprived boy's search for a father figure can often be involved in the development of homosexual relationships.

West (1967) presents an excellent review of data pertaining to the antecedents of male homosexuality: males who as children are father absent or have ineffectual fathers, together with being involved in an intense, close-binding relationship with their mothers, seem particularly prone to develop a homosexual pattern of behavior. A close-binding, sexualized, mother-son relationship seems more common in father-absent homes than in father-present homes and may, along with related factors, lessen the probability of the boy entering into meaningful heterosexual relationships. A significant proportion of homosexuals during childhood were discouraged by their mothers from participating in masculine activities and were often reinforced for feminine behavior (e.g., Bieber et al. 1962; Gundlach 1969).

There is much evidence that male homosexuals do not develop strong attachments to their fathers. Chang and Block (1960) compared a group of relatively well-adjusted male homosexuals with a heterosexual control group. They found that the homosexuals responded with stronger identifications with their mothers and weaker identifications with their fathers. A study by Nash and Hayes (1965) suggests that male homosexuals who take a passive feminine role in their sexual relationships have a particularly weak identification with their fathers and strong identifications with their mothers.

Both Bieber et al. (1962) and Evans (1969) found that more fathers of homosexuals than fathers of heterosexuals were described as detached and hostile. Mothers of homosexuals were depicted as close-binding with their sons and relatively uninvolved with their husbands. Bené (1965) reported that more male homosexuals than heterosexuals perceived their fathers as weak and were hostile towards them. Similarly, studies by Apperson and McAdoo (1968) and Saghir and Robbins (1973) suggested a pattern of very negative father-child relations during the childhoods of male homosexuals.

A particularly extensive study of the family backgrounds of homosexuals was conducted by Thompson et al. (1973). College-age, well-educated homosexuals were recruited through their friends, and their family backgrounds and childhood activities were compared with those of a control group. Homosexual men described very little interaction with their fathers and a relative lack of acceptance by their fathers during their childhoods. The homosexuals generally viewed their fathers as weak, hostile, and rejecting. In general, Thompson et al. found the classic male homosexual pattern of paternal deprivation coupled with an over-intense, mother-child relationship and early expression of avoidance of masculine activities.

Heterosexuals as well as homosexuals who avoided masculine activities in childhood reported more distance from both their fathers and men in general. It may be that the major difference between these homosexuals and heterosexuals was their adolescent sexual experience. For example, opportunities for positive heterosexual relationships may have been more readily available for some of the boys. It should also be noted that more homosexuals than heterosexuals described themselves as frail or clumsy during childhood; again there may be mediating constitutional factors in the development of some cases of homosexuality. The data fit well with a hypothesis suggesting that early paternal deprivation makes the individual more vulnerable to certain influences in later development. The particular form of adjustment the paternally deprived individual makes is determined by a complex interaction of factors (Biller 1972a).

Psychopathology

Much data relating paternal deprivation and childhood maladjustment have already been reviewed. In this section, the investigations generally focus on clinically diagnosed individuals. In most of the studies discussed previously, the individuals were grouped according to their test responses, behavior in specific situations, and/or in terms of ratings made by others; they were not individuals who were clinically diagnosed as having some form of psychopathology or being treated at a clinic or hospital. It is important to emphasize that individuals who are clinically labeled are not necessarily more psychologically impaired than individuals who have not been clinically diagnosed. Much of the time, the major difference is that so-called mentally disturbed individuals have simply come into contact with a mental health facility.

The Becker and Peterson research group has conducted extensive studies designed to ascertain the association between parental behavior and specific types of clinically diagnosed psychological disturbance among six- to twelve-year-old children (Becker et al. 1959, 1962; Peterson et al. 1959). Children who had conduct problems (problems in impulse control and/or aggressiveness) frequently had fathers who were poor enforcers of discipline, especially of rules established by the mother. Children who had personality problems (shy, oversensitive, low self-concept) frequently had fathers who were insensitive and dictatorial. Rosenthal et al. (1962) also found that inadequate fathering was associated with a number of psychological problems in children, particularly those of an antisocial nature. However, as with the Becker and Peterson studies, no specific analyses in terms of how the sex of the child might be related to parental behavior were reported.

Block (1969) also attempted to distinguish between the parental characteristics of children in different diagnostic groupings. Although, the findings from Block's study were not specifically consistent with the Becker and Peterson studies, a picture of paternal inadequacy as a major factor in childhood psychopathology again emerged. Liverant (1969) found that fathers of disturbed children responded in a much more negative fashion on the MMPI than did fathers of nondisturbed children. The responses of the fathers of disturbed children indicated that they were impulsive, anxious, depressed, and concerned with bodily complaints.

Father Absence

Research indicating a higher than average frequency of interpersonal difficulties among paternally deprived individuals has already been reviewed. Thus, it is not surprising that many studies have suggested that father-absent children often act very immature and frequently have a high rate of severe behavior problems associated with school adjustment (e.g., Garbower 1959; Gregory 1965a; Hardy 1937; Holman 1953; Layman 1960; Palmer 1960; Risen 1939; Rouman 1956; Rowntree 1955; Russell 1957; Seplin 1952; Tuckman and Regan 1966; Wylie and Delgado 1969).

An examination of the files of child guidance centers also reveals that both father absence and inadequate sex role development are much more common among disturbed children than among children in the general population. However, methodological limitations make for problems in interpreting the findings of many of the studies linking father absence with emotional disturbance in children. In particular, analyses in terms of sex of child and control groups of nonproblem children are often not included.

Garbower (1969) studying children from Navy families, found that those who were seen for psychiatric problems had more frequent and lengthy periods of father absence than did a non-disturbed comparison group. The fathers of the disturbed children also seemed less sensitive to the effects of their being away from their families. Although Pedersen (1966) found a similar amount of father absence among 11- to 15-year-old boys, irrespective of whether they were referred for psychiatric help, he did find the degree of pathology among disturbed children highly associated with the amount of father absence they had experienced.

Trunnell (1968) studied children seen at an outpatient clinic and found that severity of psychopathology varied with the length of father absence and the age of onset of the father's absence. The longer the absence and the younger the child at the onset of his absence, the more serious the psychopathology. Oltman and Friedman (1967) found particularly high rates of childhood father absence among adults who had chronically disturbed personalities and inadequate moral development. In addition, they found above-average rates of father absence among neurotics and drug addicts. Rosenberg (1969) also reported extremely high rates of frequent childhood father absence among young alcoholics and drug addicts. Maternal dominance combined with father absence or inadequacy is common in the histories of drug addicts (Chein et al. 1964; Wood and Duffy 1966).

There is a high rate of father loss among patients hospitalized for attempting to commit suicide (e.g., Gay and Tonge 1967; Robins, Schmidt, and O'Neal 1957). Other evidence indicates that individuals who have been father absent are more likely to exhibit, to a pathological degree, feelings of loss and depressed behavior (e.g., Beck, Sehti, and Tuthill 1963; Haworth 1964; Hill and Price 1967; Keeler 1954; Travis 1933).

Brown (1961) and Beck, Sehti, and Tuthill (1963) found that paternal absence before the age of four was highly associated with depression, but other studies have suggested that loss of father between the ages of 10-14 may also be particularly predisposing to depression (Dennehy 1966; Hill and Price 1967). Loss of father due to death may be more strongly related to chronically depressed behavior than is loss of father due to other factors. Research concerning father absence and depressed behavior, although of heuristic value, has not been carefully controlled. For instance, many of the subjects suffering from paternal loss have frequently also had a history of institutionalization.

Brill and Liston (1966) reported that loss of father due to death in childhood was not unusually high among mental patients. However, the frequency of loss of father due to divorce or separation in childhood was much higher for individuals suffering from neurosis, psychosis, or personality disorders than for a number of different comparison groups. Consistent with Brill and Liston's data, father absence due to divorce, separation, or desertion has also been found to be more highly associated with delinquency (Goode 1961), maladjustment (Baggett 1967), low self-esteem and sexual acting out (Hetherington 1972) and cognitive deficits (Santrock 1972). Other researchers who have reported that rates of childhood father absence are higher among adult patients classified as neurotic or schizophrenic than among the general population, have not done systematic analyses in terms of reason for father absence (e.g., Da Silva 1963; Ingham 1949; Madow and Hardy 1947; Norton 1952; Oltman, McGarry, and Friedman 1952; Wahl 1954, 1956).

Gregory (1958, 1965b) critically evaluated many of the relevant studies and emphasized some of the methodological pitfalls in comparisons involving the relative incidence of mental illness among father-present and father-absent individuals. Lack of consideration of the possible effects of socioeconomic status is a major shortcoming of most of the studies. Cobliner (1963) reported some provocative findings which suggested that father absence is more likely to be related to serious psychological disturbance in lower-class, as compared to middle-class, individuals. Middle-class families, particularly with respect to the mother-child relationship, may have more psychological as well as economic resources with which to cope with paternal deprivation (Biller 1971a).

Family Interaction Patterns

Some of the most intriguing, as well as methodologically sound studies have provided observations of family functioning in standardized problem-solving situations. Mishler and Waxler (1968) and Schuham (1970) found that high paternal involvement and decision-making are uncommon in families in which there is a severely disturbed son. In families with nondisturbed sons, the father was most often the ascendant figure, and mutually acceptable decisions were much more common (Schuham 1970).

In his observational study, Alkire (1969) found that fathers usually dominated in families with normal adolescents while mothers dominated in families with disturbed adolescents. Other research concerning interactions among disturbed families has indicated several sub-types of inappropriate fathering (McPherson 1970). Paternal hostility toward the child and mother and lack of open communication among family members were very common. Leighton, Stollak and Ferguson (1971) compared the interactions of families which had disturbed young children with families which had nondisturbed children. In general, fathers in normal families were in a dominant position and their role was accepted by family members. In contrast, clinic families were usually dominated by mothers even though the rest of the family was opposed and uncomfortable with this arrangement. Maternal dominance has been found to be associated with a varied array of psychopathological problems, especially among males (e.g., Alkire 1969; Chein et al. 1964; Gassner and Murray 1969; Goldberg 1958; Kohn and Clausen 1956; Lidz et al. 1957; Schuham 1970).

However, it must again be emphasized that many investigators have found evidence which indicates that overly dominant fathers can have just as negative an effect on their child's development as can overly dominant mothers. Researchers have reported much data relating arbitrary paternal power assertion and overcontrol to poor adjustment and psychopathology among children (Bodin 1969; Ferreira et al. 1966; Hoffman 1960; Hutchinson 1969; Murrell and Stachowiak 1967; Rubenstein and Levitt 1957; Strodtbeck 1958; Trapp and Kausler 1958).

The degree of husband-wife dominance may not be a particularly good indication of degree of paternal deprivation, except where there is extreme maternal dominance. Extreme paternal dominance is indicative of inadequate fathering and squelches the child's development of independence and competence as much as does extreme maternal dominance.

Adequate personality development is facilitated in families in which the father clearly represents a positive masculine role and the mother a positive feminine role. Kayton and I (1971) studied matched groups of nondisturbed neurotic, paranoid schizophrenic, and nonparanoid schizophrenic adult males. We found that the nondisturbed subjects perceived their parents as exhibiting sex-appropriate behaviors to a greater extent than did the disturbed subjects. A smaller proportion of individuals in the disturbed groups viewed their fathers as possessing masculine-instrumental traits, and particularly among the schizophrenic groups, their mothers as having feminine-expressive characteristics. Severely disturbed behavior is often associated with difficulties and/or abnormalities in sex role development (e.g., Biller 1973b; Biller and Poey 1969; Cheek 1964; Gardner 1967; Kayton and Biller 1972; McClelland and Watt 1968; Zeichner 1955, 1956).

Types of Paternal Deprivation

There are some data which suggest that boys from father-absent homes are, in many cases, less retarded in their personality development than are boys from intact maternally dominated homes (Biller 1968a, Reuter and Biller 1973). In Nye's (1957) study, children from broken homes were found to have better family adjustments and to have lower rates of antisocial behavior and psychosomatic illness than were children from unhappy unbroken homes. Other research has also suggested that a child may function more adequately in a father-absent home than in one in which there is an inappropriate husband wife relationship (e.g., Benson 1968; Landis 1962).

Father-absent children may be more influenced by factors outside the home than are children from intact but unhappy and/or maternally dominated homes. Some children may be particularly affected by attention from an adult male because of their intense feelings of paternal deprivation. Children with inadequate fathers often become resigned to their situation. For example, the father-present, but maternally dominated child is likely to develop a view of men as ineffectual, especially if his father is continually being controlled by his mother. On the other hand, the father-absent child may develop a much more flexible view of adult male behavior.

Research that is described in this chapter and in other chapters indicates that inadequate fathering and/or father-absence predisposes children toward certain developmental deficits. However, there are many paternally deprived children who are generally well adjusted. Such children should be more carefully studied, in order to determine why they differ from less well-adjusted, paternally deprived children. Investigators should include consideration of both type of child maladjustment and type of family inadequacy.

On the other hand, extremely severe psychopathology such as autism or childhood schizophrenia does not develop simply as a function of disturbed parent-child relationships. The child's genetic and/or constitutional predispositions play an important part in determining the severity of his psychopathology as well as the quality of parent-child interactions. Most children are handicapped if they have experienced paternal deprivation or inadequacy and they are likely to have much difficulty in their emotional and interpersonal development. But in the great majority of cases, insufficient or inappropriate fathering (and/or mothering) per se does not account for children who are unable to develop basic communication skills and to form interpersonal attachments. For example, the child's neurological malfunctioning or extreme temperamentally related hypersensitivity or hyposensitivity can make it very difficult for the parent to respond in a positive manner. In some cases, constitutionally atypical children contribute to the development of psychopathology in their parents.

Summary

The father is an important model for his child. The father's positive involvement facilitates the development of the boy's cognitive functioning, self-concept, his ability to control his impulses and to function independently and responsibly, and his overall interpersonal competence.

Much of the father's influence is related to his impact on the boy's sex role development. Certain skills are relatively sex-typed and mastery of the environment and problem solving are often learned in the context of traditionally masculine activities. When the boy has a warm relationship with a masculine and competent father, he is well on his way to learning how to master his social and physical environment. His ability to understand the world outside of his home, to plan for the future, and to cope with crises can all be facilitated by his experiences with his father.

Much of what the boy learns about the masculine role comes from peer group interactions. The boy who receives positive fathering is particularly well-suited to both learn and effectively influence his peer group. He is motivated to interact with other males, but he is also independent enough to resist passive conformity. He is more likely to be a leader and is better able to communicate with his peers. He is more comfortable with his masculinity and has little need to prove himself by means of overcompensatory behavior.

Having observed his father's relationship with his mother, he has learned basic skills in interacting with females. He can communicate adequately with females. He does not feel intimidated by women, yet he does not have to constantly dominate them. He can accept their femininity because he is secure in his masculinity. He can succeed in marriage as well as in his occupation. Because he has experienced positive fathering, he is also more able to be a successful father.

On the other hand, the paternally deprived boy is likely to have developmental difficulties. This is especially true if he comes from a generally disadvantaged background. Father absence and/or father inadequacy can be highly debilitating for the lower-class boy, particularly if it beings in early childhood. The paternally deprived boy is likely to be insecure in his peer relationships as well as in his relationships with authority figures. Not having a consistently interested adult male with whom to interact, he may experience problems in learning to control his impulses. He may become tied to his mother, or may become equally as dependent on his peer group. He may be less able to act independently and competently. Lack of masculine behavior and/or a compensatory overstriving are more frequent among inadequately fathered boys than they are among adequately fathered boys.

Paternal deprivation has often been found to be associated with high anxiety and a proneness to the development of severe psychopathology. Inadequate fathering is a frequent concomitant of children's and adults' psychological problems. Early father absence, particularly when it is in the context of divorce, separation or desertion, seems to be a very frequent factor in the etiology of psychopathology. However, much more research is needed to determine why some paternally deprived children become emotionally disturbed and others do not. Sociocultural variables, constitutional factors and the quality of the mother-child relationship can be very significant in determining the impact of variations in fathering on the developing child. In the next chapter the mother-child relationship is considered in much more detail.

6

Paternal Deprivation and The Mother-Child Relationship

There are many factors which can affect the way in which the child is influenced by his relationship with his father or by father absence. The quality of mothering a child receives is crucial and can become even more important when the child is paternally deprived. In this chapter there is emphasis on the way in which variations in mothering may be related to individual differences in the paternally deprived boy's behavior. The major topics considered include the influence of the mother's evaluation of the father, matrifocal families, maternal overprotection, the mother's sex role development, maternal employment, and dimensions of effective mothering.

Mother's Evaluation of the Father

Maternal attitudes relating to the father can be an important factor in the sex role and personality development of boys in intact homes. Pauline Sears (1953) noted that mothers of kindergarten boys who took the feminine role in doll play tended to be critical of their husbands. In a clinical study of academically underachieving boys, Grunebaum et al. (1962) observed that a contributing factor to boys' difficulties was mothers' perceptions that their husbands were inadequate and incompetent. In contrast, Farber (1962) found that a salient aspect of well-functioning marriages was the mother's support of the child's positive feelings toward the father. The mother helped support the father as an identification model for the boy and also helped to smooth over tensions in the father-daughter relationship by clearly communicating her love and respect for the father.

Helper (1955) compared high school boys' self-descriptions with the boys' perceptions of their fathers. He found that son-father similarity was significantly related to the mother's approval of the father as a model for the child. Bronfenbrenner (1958) pointed out that similarity of father and son " . . . does not necessarily mean that the child wanted to be like his father, that his motivation was *personally directed*." He goes on to summarize Helper's findings as follows:

A boy is more likely to aspire to and take on characteristics that are typically masculine in our culture when his mother regards such characteristics as desirable; the fact that these characteristics are also possessed and approved by the father may be merely a reflection of the cultural norm and quite incidental to the child's learning process (p. 119).

Maternal attitudes are of critical significance when a boy is father absent. In his study of children separated from their fathers during wartime, Bach (1946) described "curiously ambivalent aggressive-affectionate father fantasies in some cases where maternal father-typing tended to be depreciative" (p. 76). Wylie and Delgado (1959) analyzed the family backgrounds of aggressive fatherless boys referred to a child guidance clinic. With few exceptions the mothers depicted their ex-husbands and sons in highly negative terms, emphasizing the dangerously aggressive quality of their behavior. Kopf (1970) found that poor school adjustment among father-absent boys was associated with their mothers' negative attitude toward their absent husbands. Clinical cases dramatically illustrate how the mother's consistently derogatory comments about the absent father can contribute to the development of a poor self-concept and maladaptive behavior in the son (Diamond 1957; Neubauer 1960). As might be expected, maternal attitudes concerning the absent father influence the child's reaction if the father returns home (Baxter, Horton, and Wiley 1964; Stolz et al. 1954).

The mother's evaluation of the absent father is often much related to the reason for his being absent. Feelings of resentment and loneliness can be associated with many different reasons for husband absence, but it is usually easier for a mother to talk positively about a husband who has died than one who has divorced or deserted her (Benson 1968; Hetherington 1972). Discussing the absent father with her children may be very frustrating for the mother, and when the father is absent because of divorce or desertion, such discussion may be even more painful. It is very difficult to maintain a positive image of the father in the face of the conflict and competition concerning children that often takes place before, during, and after a divorce. Sociocultural factors can also influence the family's reaction to father absence. For example, divorce seems to be less acceptable and more disruptive for Catholic and Jewish families than for Protestant families (Rosenberg 1965).

Loss of father due to death may lead to more acute behavioral reactions in children than loss of father due to other factors, but father-absence may have general effects on personality development irrespective of reason for father-absence (Biller 1971b). If the reason for father-absence has an impact on the child's personality development, much of the effect is mediated through the mother-child relationship. Researchers should also examine why, after husband absence, certain women remain unmarried or without consistent male companionship. Long-term father or father-surrogate absence, as well as onset of father absence is, in some cases, much a function of the mother's attitudes toward men.

The father-child relationship prior to father absence and the child's age at the onset of the absence are also very important factors in determining the extent of the influence of maternal attitudes toward the absent father. For example, the father-absent boy who has had a positive relationship with his father up until ten years of age is less likely to be influenced by negative maternal views concerning the father than the boy who was paternally deprived even before his father's absence. Unfortunately, there have not been systematic investigations of how the reason for father absence at different developmental periods influences the mother-child relationship.

Matrifocal Families

Negative evaluation of the father often occurs in matrifocal families. (The female-centered family is sometimes referred to as "matriarchal" but the term "matrifocal" seems a more accurate label.) This type of family is very common in lower socioeconomic neighborhoods, and appears to be particularly prevalent among lower-class blacks (Pettigrew 1964). There are many black families of lower socioeconomic status in which the father is a respected and integral member, but there seem to be even more in which he is absent or a relatively peripheral member (Frazier 1939). This phenomena was cogently described by Dai (1953):

One interesting feature of the broken home situation among Negroes is the dominance of the mother or mother substitutes, such as grandmothers, aunts, and sisters. This phenomenon may also be found in homes that are not broken, but in homes where the fathers are no longer important; they are, therefore, about as good as absent. Another related feature of the situation is the preference for girls shown by many Negro mothers and grandmothers (p. 558).

Dai's (1953) contention that girls are often preferred to boys by lower-class black women is consistent with Rohrer and Edmonson's (1960) findings. As part of their extensive research project, black women were interviewed concerning their adoption preferences. These women generally expressed preferences to adopt girls rather than boys. This clear-cut preference for girls by black females seems in marked contrast to the findings of a survey study at a large midwestern university by Dinitz, Dynes, and Clarke (1954) which revealed that a majority of females would prefer to have a male child as their first child, or if they could have only one child. The white middle class puts more value on the male role than on the female role (Brown 1958; Lynn 1959). However, this high valuation of maleness and masculinity is not supported by "matriarchal" black women. According to Rohrer and Edmonson (1960):

The matriarchs make no bones about their preference for little girls, and while they often manifest real affection for their boy children, they are clearly convinced that all little boys must inexorably and deplorably become men with all the pathologies of that sex (p. 161).

Sociocultural factors lessen the probability of long-term marriage relationships among lower-class blacks (Pettigrew 1964). The instability of marriage relationships among lower-class blacks may be related to the fact that individuals with certain personality patterns are predisposed to become divorced and/or to seek out very tangential marriage relationships (Grønseth 1957; Loeb 1966). Because of their inability to tolerate close relationships with men, some women marry men who, due to their personality functioning and/or occupational commitments, cannot get very much involved in family life. The wife's negative attitudes concerning men can be a central factor in the husband's decision to desert her and his children.

However, the mother who has a positive attitude concerning masculinity can facilitate her father-absent child's personality development. For instance, by praising the absent father's general competence in dealing with his environment and his strength and physical prowess, she may be able to help her son learn to value his own maleness. On the other hand, maternal depreciation of the father's masculinity can lead the young boy to avoid acting masculine at least until the time he comes into contact with his male peer culture.

Maternal attitudes concerning masculinity and men form a significant part of the mother-son relationship, and a mother is apt to view her husband and her son in a similar manner. Nevertheless, maternal reactions are not independent from individual differences in children. The degree to which a mother perceives her son as similar to his father is often related to the boy's behavioral and physical characteristics. For example, if the boy very much resembles his father, facially and physically, it is more likely that the mother will expect her son's behavior to approximate his father's than if there was little father-son resemblance.

Maternal Overprotection

Maternal overprotection is a frequent concomitant of paternal deprivation. In families in which maternal overprotection exists, the father generally plays a very submissive and ineffectual role (Levy 1943). When fathers are actively involved with their families, they are usually very critical of having their children overprotected and they also serve as models for independent behavior. If the father is absent, the probability of a pattern of maternal overprotection is often increased. The child's age at the onset of father absence is an important variable. The boy who becomes father absent during infancy or during his preschool years is more likely to be overprotected by his mother, but if father absence begins when the boy is older, he may be expected to take over many of the responsibilities his father had previously assumed.

Stendler (1952) described two critical periods in the development of overdependency: (1) at around age nine months, when the child first begins to test out if his mother will meet his dependency needs; and (2) from two to three years of age, when the child must give up his perceived control of his mother and learn to act independently in culturally approved ways. Paternal deprivation during these periods can make the child particularly prone to overdependency. Studying first-grade children, Stendler (1954) found that many children who were seen as overdependent by their teachers came from families with high rates of father absence. Among the 20 overdependent children, 13 lacked the consistent presence of the father in the home during the first three years of life, compared to only 6 of 20 in the control group. Moreover, the 6 relatively father-absent children in the control group had generally been without their fathers for a much shorter time than the overdependent children. The actively involved father discourages the mother's overprotecting tendencies and encourages independent activity, especially in the boy. Unfortunately, Stendler did not give separate data analyses for boys and girls.

Retrospective maternal reports compiled by Stolz et al. (1954) suggested that mothers whose husbands were away in military service tended to restrict their infants' locomotor activities to a greater extent than did mothers whose husbands were present. However, these findings might also be more meaningful if the researchers had presented separate analysis in terms of sex of child. Similar results were reported by Tiller (1958) in his study with mothers of eight- and nine-year-old Norwegian children. Compared to the control group mothers, mothers whose husbands were seldom home (sailor officers) were more overprotective, as judged by maternal interview data and by the children's responses to a structured doll-play test.

The Stolz et al. (1954) and Tiller (1958) investigations suggested that paternally deprived and maternally overprotected boys are particularly likely to suffer in terms of their masculine development. In her study of kindergarten boys, Pauline Sears (1953) reported that many boys who took the feminine role in doll play had mothers who restricted their sons' mobility outside the home. In a study of five-year-old children, I found that mothers of father-absent boys were less encouraging of independent and aggressive behavior than were mothers of father-present boys. Many of the informal responses of the husband-absent mothers indicated that they were particularly fearful of their children being physically injured (Biller 1969b).

Physical Status

The child's behavior and overall physical status can, of course, be a factor influencing maternal reactions. If a child is particularly frail, such maternal concern may be very realistic. Children who have had frequent or chronic illnesses are likely to have very close relationships with their mothers. In some cases constant maternal attention is necessary. Fathers usually find it very difficult to interact with a chronically sick child; and relatively exclusive mother-child relationships often develop. Unfortunately, the intense mother-child relationship, which was originally related to the child's illness, frequently persists even after the child is well. For example, the mother may still perceive that her child needs to be protected from vigorous activities with other children. Such a situation can be very inhibiting to peer relationships and adequate sex-role development.

The mother whose child has been very sick in infancy may be prone to overreact to the child's later illnesses. She is apt to become overrestrictive and overprotective. The child, in turn, may receive much attention for reporting his complaints and physical discomforts. Males who have psychosomatic disorders have often had extremely close relationships with their mothers, poor relationships with their fathers, and inadequate sex-role development (Lipton et al. 1966). For example, maternal dominance has been found to be associated with duodenal ulcers and a large number of other forms of psychosomatically-related organ dysfunctions (Goldberg 1958). There are also data which suggest that father-absent children are more likely than are father-present children to develop psychosomatic symptoms (Rosenberg 1965).

Of course, it is difficult to determine whether the familial situation was an etiological factor or merely an outcome of an originally circumscribed illness. There are physiologically based individual differences with respect to predispositions towards certain types of psychosomatic disorders (e.g., Lipton et al. 1966). Whether family etiology is primary or secondary, maternal overprotection and paternal deprivation often lead to the development of maladaptive behavior patterns. Such familial factors can also play a significant role in the etiology of alcoholism and drug addiction (Chein et al. 1964; Rosenberg 1969).

Sociocultural Milieu

In assessing variables that influence the behavior of the husband-absent mother, economic and social difficulties cannot be overlooked (e.g., Glasser and Navarre 1965; Hartley 1960). Kriesberg (1967) poignantly described the plight of the mother whose husband is absent:

His absence is likely to mean that his former wife is poor, lives in poor neighborhoods, and lacks social, emotional, and physical assistance in childrearing. Furthermore, how husbandless mothers accommodate themselves to these circumstances can have important consequences for their children (p. 288).

The degree to which the husbandless mother has social and economic resources available to her can influence the child's interpersonal and educational opportunities. When we take such factors into consideration, the lower-class child seems even more disadvantaged by fatherlessness than does the middle-class child.

Paternal absence or inadequacy adds to the generally debilitating effects already experienced by the economically disadvantaged segment of our society.

Paternal absence or inadequacy is often associated with a lack of material resources. Economic deprivation can make it much more difficult for the father-absent child to avail himself of experiences which might positively affect his development. Consistent economic deprivation makes it easy to develop a defeatist attitude about one's potential impact on the environment. As Herzog and Sudia (1970) cogently pointed out, many researchers uncritically assume that a child's personality difficulties are due simply to father absence without also considering the impact of economic deprivation.

The mother's attitudes are related to her social and economic opportunities and are readily transmitted to the child. Maternal views concerning the worth of education are linked to sociocultural background. As a function of differing maternal values and reinforcement patterns, middle-class father-absent children are less handicapped in intellectual pursuits than are lower-class father-absent children. Middle-class father-absent boys appear to receive more maternal encouragement for school achievement than do lower-class father-absent boys (Biller 1974a, 1974b). The interacting effect of social class and maternal behavior on the cognitive functioning of paternally deprived children is discussed in much more detail in Chapter 8.

Sociocultural background is also associated with the frequency of maternal overprotection. McCord, McCord, and Thurber (1962) found no evidence of maternal overprotection or overdependency among lower-class father-absent boys. Consistent with McCord, McCord, and Thurber's findings are the case studies of lower-class father-absent males presented by Kardiner and Ovesey (1951) and Rohrer and Edmonson (1960). A lower-class mother may have less opportunity to overprotect a father-absent child than does a middle-class mother, because she is more often engaged in a full-time job (Heckscher 1967). In addition, there is less of a social stigma attached to father absence by lower-class families, especially among lower-class black families (King, 1945). A mother without a husband who has young children is a more common phenomenon in the lower class. In contrast, the middle-class mother appears to be more predisposed to feel guilty if her child, particularly her son, is being deprived of a father. The middle-class mother seems more likely to overprotect and overindulge her child.

On the other hand, maternal rejection and neglect are quite common among husbandless, lower-class mothers (e.g., Heckscher 1967; McCord, McCord, and Thurber 1962). Compared to middle-class mothers, lower-class mothers without husbands seem more concerned with their own needs and their day-to-day existence and often withdraw from their children. Lower-class mothers are particularly likely to reject their male children (Beller 1967; Dai 1953).

Either overprotection or rejection can reduce the probability of the boy's feeling a sense of worth in terms of his maleness. Maternal indifference or rejection makes a boy more vulnerable to be indiscriminately influenced by the gang milieu than does maternal overprotection. The maternally overprotected, paternally deprived boy may be quite timid and passive in peer interactions, whereas the maternally rejected father-absent boy is more likely to actively seek peer acceptance.

The frequent depreciation of maleness by their mothers contributes to the meaningfulness of the gang milieu for lower-class boys. A boy who is neglected or rejected can have his needs for attention, recognition, and affection satisfied by becoming a member of a gang. Masculine behaviors, particularly clear-cut acts of physical prowess and aggression, are highly valued by the gang, and behaviors perceived as feminine are anxiously avoided. The boy's physical status can be a major factor in determining whether he can achieve peer acceptance. The boy who is big and muscular will have a much greater chance of impressing his peers than the boy who is small and frail. If he has the ability to perform in an aggressive and competitive manner, participation in a gang milieu may help bolster the paternally deprived boy's self-image. However, the gang milieu promotes very rigid interpersonal and cognitive functioning.

Sex-role Conflicts

Low paternal availability often leads to an increase in the intensity of the emotional relationship between mother and child, especially during infancy and early childhood. A strong and relatively exclusive attachment to his mother can severely hamper a boy's peer interactions and sex role development. Miller (1961) discovered a negative relationship between degree of maternal attachment and masculinity of interests among lower-class adolescent boys. Winch's (1950) questionnaire data suggest that college males' courtship behavior is inversely related to their attachment to their mothers.

Anthropologists have described intense mother-child relationships which often develop in preliterate societies during postpartum taboos concerning sexual intercourse. Such taboos may last two to three years, during which time the family is relatively father absent. In a cross-cultural investigation, Stephens (1962) presented evidence indicating that long postpartum taboos tend to make mothers closer to their children and less husband-centered. In societies with long postpartum taboos, mothers tend to be overprotective as well as more indulgent of dependency than are mothers in societies in which postpartum taboos are of short duration. Cross-cultural data suggest that sex-role conflicts are frequent in societies in which young children have a relatively exclusive relationship with their mothers (e.g., Burton and Whiting 1961; Stephens 1962). Sociocultural variations, especially those reflected in terms of prevalent patterns of mothering, may account for marked differences between father-absent and father-present children in some societies but not in others (e.g., Ancona, Cesa-Bianchi, and Bocquet 1964).

On the basis of his experience with middle-class American families, Levy

(1943) found that excessive physical contact was a frequent concomitant of maternal overprotection. Among 19 cases of maternal overprotection involving boys, 6 of the boys slept with their mothers long past infancy, 3 during adolescence. In almost one-half of Wylie and Delgado's (1959) cases involving father-absent, preadolescent and adolescent boys, mother and son slept together in the same bed or bedroom. Sons often serve as husband-surrogates for husbandless mothers. In his review of psychoanalytic case studies, Neubauer (1960) emphasized how difficult sex role development is for the young father-absent boy who has a highly sexualized relationship with his mother. Such an intense relationship affords the boy little opportunity to interact with masculine role models. In addition, the boy's inability to cope with his sexual feelings toward his mother may lead to a defensive feminine identification (Freud 1947).

An intense relationship with the mother, and little opportunity to observe appropriate male-female interactions, is more common when the boy is pater nally deprived. As discussed in Chapter 5, a close-binding mother-son relationship, in the context of paternal deprivation, is a frequent factor contributing to difficulties in heterosexual relationships and in the etiology of male homosexuality.

In addition to lacking a male role model during the preschool years, the father-absent boy is likely to be confronted by a mother who does not encourage masculine behavior. As father-absent boys come into contact with boys from intact homes, especially as they begin school, they may be ignored or rejected because of their lack of masculine behavior. Many father-absent boys who are strongly motivated to adopt masculine behavior will do so if they have sufficient opportunity to interact with their peers. Their mothers may react negatively to such behavior and thus create conflict, and some degree of sex role confusion. The boy will learn to modify his behavior according to whether he is interacting with his mother or his peers, but the development of a secure sex role orientation may be very difficult.

If a boy is extremely emotionally and instrumentally dependent upon his mother, he may not become involved in the masculine subculture. A boy with a strong but a less intense mother-son relationship can learn to act feminine in the presence of his mother and masculine with his peers. However, keeping behavior consistent with an internal standard of masculinity-femininity can be very difficult and anxiety-producing for the father-absent boy.

The boy's sex role conflicts are often manifested by difficulties in interacting with females. Ruth Hartley (1959) interviewed eight- to eleven-year-old boys from intact homes and delineated the following types of sex role development: (1) overly intense masculine striving combined with rigidity concerning male and female activities and hostility toward women; (2) overly-intense masculine striving combined with rigidity concerning male and female activities, but no hostility towards women; (3) inclinations and attempts to withdraw from the masculine role and related activities; and (4) a positively integrated and balanced sex role. Behaviors related to types (1), (2), and (3) are more frequently displayed by paternally deprived boys than by adequately fathered boys. However, in order to make meaningful predictions, peer group interactions, the quality of the mother-child relationship, and various family structure variables need to be carefully considered.

For example, birth order and age and sex of siblings can interact with maternal behavior to influence the father-absent child's personality development. If a father-absent boy is an only child or the only boy in an all female family, the probability of maternal overprotection is increased. On the other hand, if the boy has frequent opportunity to interact with older male siblings, peers, and adults, who encourage the development of his autonomy and assertiveness, the chance of a close-binding mother-son relationship is lessened.

Transsexual Behavior

Stoller (1968) described the case histories of several boys who felt that they were really females. These boys represented an extreme in terms of the pervasiveness of their femininity. Stoller referred to them as being transsexual. These boys had extremely close physical relationships with their mothers. Mutual mother-child body contact during infancy was especially intense and there was much evidence that the mothers reinforced many forms of feminine behavior. In none of these cases was the father masculine or involved with his child. Stoller's book is replete with references to case studies suggesting that disturbed sex role development in males is associated with an overly intense, relatively exclusive mother-son relationship.

Green (1974) reported a high rate of early paternal deprivation among extremely feminine boys who wished they were girls and preferred to dress as females. These boys had exceedingly strong identifications with their mothers and were very feminine in their sex role orientations, preferences, and adoptions, generally manifesting a transsexual behavior pattern. Of the 38 boys that Green intensively studied, 13 became father-absent prior to age four. Among the other boys, who were father-present, father-son relationships seemed to have been very limited or distant.

In contrast, the mothers were excessively attached to their sons and many had difficulty in perceiving that there was anything deviant in their boys' behavior. Although many of the fathers were quite upset that their sons continued to behave in a feminine manner when they reached four or five years of age, they had been generally tolerant, and were probably at least indirectly reinforcing, of feminine behavior during the infancy and toddler period. Such data suggest that these fathers were very different from most men who are very uncomfortable when their young children, especially their sons, deviate from culturally-expected sex role behavior (Biller 1971a).

Green's work is particularly valuable because he traces the complex interaction of various factors in the development of extremely feminine boys. He discusses how, in some cases, sibling and peer group reactions as well as parental behavior can strongly reinforce inappropriate sex role behavior. Perhaps most important, his research suggests ways in which the child's characteristics may influence parental behavior. For example, in at least several of his cases, paternal deprivation was increased because of the young boy's disinclination to participate in masculine activities and seeming inability to relate to his father.

It is important to emphasize that constitutional predispositions, as well as direct parental influence, are often involved in the child developing a transsexual behavior pattern. Boys who become transsexual are frequently rather "pretty," delicate, non-mesomorphic, and resemble their mothers in outward appearance more than their fathers. This is not to say that biological factors caused the children to become transsexual but that constitutional predispositions may increase the likelihood that certain children will develop "feminine" behavior patterns. Parents' expectations are very much influenced by their children's appearance and behavior. There are some cases where biological factors such as genetic anomolies have a relatively more direct impact on the development of transsexualism or other forms of atypical sex role development (Green 1974; Hampson 1965; Money and Ehrhardt 1972).

The Mother's Sex Role Development

A boy whose mother is uncomfortable with her femininity is likely to have difficulties in his sex role development. An important facet of the sex role development process is learning how to interact with the other sex; and the boy whose mother is ambivalent about her sexuality is at a disadvantage in trying to generalize his experiences to his relationships with other females. Case study data indicate that mothers with severe sex role conflicts discourage their sons' masculine development (e.g., Bieber et al. 1962; Fenichel 1945; Green 1974; Levy 1943; Neubauer 1960; Stoller 1968).

Levy (1943) claimed that many of the maternally overprotecting mothers he studied had severe problems in sex-role identification. He speculated that their insecurity in being feminine was a factor in their inappropriate mothering techniques. Anxiety concerning their children's sexuality is common among mothers with sex role conflicts. Sears, Rau, and Alpert (1965) found evidence indicating that maternal sex anxiety was negatively associated with preschool-age boys' masculinity.

The boy's masculine development can be facilitated if his mother is secure in her femininity. Payne and Mussen (1956) found a negative correlation between mothers' and son's scores on the Gough Femininity Scale; feminine-scoring mothers tended to have masculine-scoring sons. Steimel (1962) reported a tendency for boys with low masculine interests to perceive their mothers as having masculine interests. However, data from other studies do not suggest that there is a clear-cut relationship between the sex typing of mothers' and sons' interests (Angrilli 1960; Mussen and Rutherford 1963; Terman and Miles 1936).

In terms of available evidence, the degree of femininity of the mother's interests does not appear to be critical, but the general role she assumes in her family does seem important. For example, a mother can express feminine interests and yet basically not feel very secure about being a woman and a mother. On the other hand, she can be involved in traditionally masculine-type activities and yet still interact with her children in a feminine-expressive manner. In fact, there is some evidence that highly competent and self-confident mothers are relatively flexible in their sex role preferences (Coopersmith 1967). The key factor seems to be the mother's realistic and positive acceptance of her motherhood.

Maternal Employment

Many effective mothers are employed and have demanding extrafamilial responsibilities. Nye (1959) reported a tendency among father-absent children for those whose mothers were employed, to be better adjusted than those whose mothers were not employed. Kriesberg (1967, 1970) also presented evidence indicating that maternal employment among father-absent lower-class families can be a positive factor in the child's adjustment. Among low income families, father-absent children whose mothers were employed achieved higher school grades than those whose mothers did not work. However, there was no relationship between maternal employment and school grades for children from intact families. Kriesberg's findings are very provocative but unfortunately his comparison groups were not carefully matched and there was no analysis concerning sex of child.

In a post-hoc analysis of data from her study of lower-class adolescents, Barbara Miller (1960) found that maternal employment was negatively related to masculinity of interests among father-present boys, but positively related to masculinity of interests among father-absent boys. She speculated that in the lower-class father-absent family the mother who works may present her son with a model of competence and independence, whereas maternal employment in the lower-class father-present family may imply that the father is inadequate and an economic failure. Consistent with Miller's supposition, some studies have indicated that lower-class father-present boys perceive their fathers less positively when their mothers work full time than when their mothers do not work (Douvan 1963; Etaugh 1974; Hoffman 1974; McCord, McCord, and Thurber 1962; Propper, 1972).

The mother's having a more prestigious and well-paying job than the father can be an additionally disruptive factor in the boy's sex role development, particularly if he is from a lower class background. In such a sitaution, it is likely that the family will be maternally dominated and the father will play a passive, ineffectual role. There does not appear to be any systematic research concerning how such factors might influence the child's personality functioning, but frequent marital conflicts are reported in families in which the wife has a more prestigious job than the husband (Gover 1963; Roth and Peck 1951). Such findings are interesting, but unfortunately there is a paucity of research dealing with the possible differential effects of various types of maternal employment on father-absent and father-present children as a function of social class level.

The middle-class father generally seems less threatened by his wife's employment than does the lower-class father, and is more likely to facilitate her working. King, McIntyre, and Axelson (1968) found that children's acceptance of maternal employment was increased as a function of how much their fathers participated in household tasks. The father's attitude toward the mother's working and his willingness to share domestic responsibilities can be a major factor in the way maternal employment affects the child. For example, in some cases maternal employment actually helps the father become more involved with his children while in others the child may suffer the joint effects of paternal as well as maternal deprivation (Biller and Meredith 1974).

Middle-class mothers are more likely to feel good about their jobs which, if they are full time, are usually more prestigious and well-paying than those of lower-class mothers. When a mother feels positively about her job she is more apt to have effective interactions with her family than if she considers it unfulfilling or demeaning (Hoffman 1974). For example, Coopersmith (1967) presented some data suggesting that regular maternal employment is related to high self-esteem in children when mothers feel positively about their work. If a mother feels positively about her work, there is also much less chance of her becoming overly focused on her children. Maternal employment may be especially beneficial in allowing both mother and children to successfully accept the child's growing needs for independence and autonomy (Biller and Meredith 1974).

Maternal employment also lessens the child's stereotyped perception of male and female roles. Hartley and Klein (1959) investigated the relationship between maternal employment and the sex role perceptions of elementary school children. Children who had working mothers made fewer sex-linked distinctions on a sorting task involving various occupations than did children who had nonworking mothers. Studying college students, Vogel et al. (1970) found that those with working mothers had less polarized views of sex differences than did those with nonworking mothers. However, the groups did not differ in terms of the masculinity-femininity of their self-perceptions.

Maternal employment per se does not seem to have a clear-cut effect on the child's personality development (Etaugh 1974; Hoffman 1974). What seems to be important is how the mother feels about being a woman and how secure she is in her basic femininity. The quality of mothering and fathering a child receives is of much more significance than whether or not his mother is employed. The next section includes evidence and speculation relating to the facilitating effects that particular types of mothering can have on the child's personality development.

Effective Mothering

The mother-son relationship can stimulate or hinder adequate personality development. When the boy is paternally deprived, his relationship with his mother is particularly influential. McCord, McCord, and Thurber (1962) analyzed social workers' observations of 10- to 15-year-old, lower-class boys. The presence of a rejecting and/or disturbed mother was related to various behavior problems (sexual anxiety, regressive behavior, and criminal acts) in father-absent boys; but father-absent boys who had seemingly well-adjusted mothers were much less likely to have such problems.

Pedersen (1966) compared a group of emotionally disturbed boys with a group of nondisturbed boys. The boys were all from military families and ranged in age from 11 to 15. Relatively long periods of father absence were common for both the emotionally disturbed and nondisturbed children. However, it was only in the disturbed group that degree of father absence was related to level of emotional disturbance (measured by the Rogers Test of Personality Adjustment). Pedersen also found that the mothers of the emotionally disturbed children were themselves more disturbed (in terms of MMPI responses) than were the mothers of the nondisturbed children. An implication of these findings is that psychologically healthy mothers may be able to counteract some of the effects of paternal deprivation.

Using a retrospective interview technique, Hilgard, Neuman, and Fisk (1960) studied adults whose fathers had died when they were children. These investigators concluded that the mother's ego strength was an important determinant of her child's adjustment as an adult. Mothers who could utilize their own and outside resources, and assume some of the dual functions of mother and father with little conflict, appeared to be able to constructively deal with the problems of raising a fatherless family. Such women were described as relatively feminine while their husbands were alive but as secure enough in their basic sex role identifications to perform some of the traditional functions of the father after he had died. It is important to emphasize that the mother's ego strength rather than her warmth or tenderness seemed to be the essential variable in her child's adjustment. If a child is paternally deprived, excessive maternal warmth and affection may be particularly detrimental to his personality development. A close-binding, overprotective relationship can severely hamper his opportunities for interpersonal growth.

When a mother is generally competent in interpersonal and environmental interaction, she may be an important model for her child. However, a child's personality development seems to be facilitated only if the parent allows him sufficient freedom and responsibility to imitate effective parental behaviors (Biller 1969a, 1971a). For example, the young boy from a typical matrifocal family is often not encouraged to display assertive behavior. Mothers in such families often interfere with their son's attempts at mastery, and reward submissive responses. These women seem to be insecure in terms of their underlying femininity and have difficulty in their interactions with males.

Maternal Encouragement

Colley (1959) suggested that "even in a father's absence, an appropriately identified mother will respond to the boy 'as if' he were a male and will expect him to treat her as a male would treat a female" (p. 173). In intact homes, fathers seem to vary their own behavior more as a function of sex of child than do mothers. Fathers are reported to be more concerned with sex-typing and to more often base their expectations and reinforcements on the basis of sex of child (e.g., Goodenough 1957; Tasch 1955). In the paternally deprived home, the degree to which the mother can take over the sex-role differentiation function may be of critical importance in the boy's personality development (Biller 1971a).

A mother can facilitate her father-absent son's sex role development by having a positive attitude toward the absent father and males in general, and by consistently encouraging competence in her son. In intact homes, parental reactions to aggressive and assertive behavior do influence the boy's personality development. For example, in Sears, Rau, and Alpert's (1965) investigation with nursery school children, parents who permitted and accepted aggressive and assertive behavior in their preschool-age sons had highly masculine sons. In contrast, boys low in masculinity were found to have parents who were anxious, nonpermissive, and severely punishing of aggression. In the context of warm parent-child relationships, restrictive and autocratic parents tend to have passive, conforming, and dependent children (e.g., Baldwin, Kalhorn, and Breese 1949; Becker 1964).

Maternal encouragement of masculine behavior seems particularly important for the father-absent boy. In a study of kindergarten boys, I assessed maternal encouragement of masculine behavior with a multiple choice questionnaire (Biller 1969b). The measure of maternal encouragement of masculine behavior was significantly related to the father-absent boys' masculinity, as assessed by a game preference measure and a multidimensional rating scale filled out by teachers. Father-absent boys whose mothers accepted and reinforced assertive, aggressive, and independent behavior were more masculine than father-absent boys whose mothers discouraged such behavior. The degree of maternal encouragement for masculine behavior was not significantly related to the father-present boys' masculine development.

The father-son relationship appears to be more critical than the mother-son relationship when the father is present, and it can be predicted that maternal encouragement and expectations concerning sex role behavior are less important when the father is present than when he is absent. For instance, a warm relationship with a masculine and salient father can outweigh the effects of a mildly overprotective mother. However, maternal behavior is an especially significant variable in facilitating, or inhibiting, masculine development in the young, father-absent boy. The mother can, by reinforcing specific responses and expecting masculine behavior, increase the father-absent boy's perception of the incentive value of the masculine role. Such maternal behavior can, in turn, promote a positive view of males as salient and powerful, and thus motivate the boy to imitate their behavior.

Father absence generally has more of a retarding impact on the boy's sex role orientation than it does on his sex role preference or his sex role adoption (see Chapter 4). Sex role preference and sex role adoption seem more easily influenced by maternal behavior. However, if a father-absent boy develops a masculine preferdnce and adoption on the basis of both consistent maternal and peer group reinforcement, he is likely to view himself and his masculinity positively, and to develop a masculine sex role orientation at least by his middle school years.

Father absence before the age of five has more effect on the boy's masculine development than does father absence after the age of five, and the mother-child relationship is particularly crucial when a boy becomes father absent early in life. Bahm and I found that degree of perceived maternal encouragement for masculine behavior was highly related to the masculinity of junior high school boys who had been father absent since before the age of five. (Perceived maternal encouragement for aggressive behavior was assessed by the subjects' responses to a Q-sort procedure and their masculinity by their self-descriptions on an adjective checklist.) Among the boys who became father absent before the age of five, those who perceived their mothers as encouraging assertive and aggressive behavior had much more masculine self-concepts than did those who perceived their mothers as discouraging such behavior (Biller and Bahm 1971).

Future research should lead to a much clearer delineation of the kinds of maternal behaviors, and the dimensions of the mother-child relationship, that are relevant to the father-absent boy's personality development. In Chapter 7 some research concerning the effects of father absence on the girl's personality development is reviewed, and it is important for investigators studying the impact of father absence to systematically examine the possible differential effects of the mother-child relationship as a function of the sex of a child. Data from such studies can be useful for programs designed to maximize the interpersonal and intellectual potential of father-absent children, and to help mothers in father-absent families to become more effective parents.

Summary

The mother's evaluation of the father can be an important determinant in the boy's personality development. If the mother is constantly critical of the father, it can interfere with the boy's viewing himself positively. When a boy is father absent, the mother's view of the father may have particularly strong consequences. Mothers who feel abandoned or deserted by their husbands often develop a negative attitude toward males. Mothers in matrifocal homes are likely to devalue their sons and the masculine role.

In matrifocal families and in families in which there is maternal overprotection, there is generally paternal deprivation. If the father is present, he plays a submissive and ineffectual role. When fathers are absent or uninvolved, the probability of maternal domination and/or maternal overprotection is much increased. Mothers who excessively restrict their sons and consistently reward dependent behavior are likely to interfere with their sons' psychological development. Maternal overprotection inhibits the development of independent and responsible behavior. Paternal deprivation also is often associated with a highly intense close-binding mother-child relationship. The boy's excessive emotional dependency on his mother can hamper his peer relationships and his heterosexual development.

Lower-class boys seem less likely to be maternally overprotected than do middle-class boys. However, the incidence of matrifocal homes is greater among the lower class. In addition, the lower-class paternally deprived boy more often seems to rebel against his unmasculine family environment and to engage in overcompensatory gang behavior. The lower-class boy is more often maternally neglected or rejected than the middle-class boy. He seems to be more influenced by his peers and often develops a very negative attitude toward any endeavors that he perceives as feminine.

Although the probability of an inappropriate mother-son relationship is increased when the father is absent, it is clear that the mother can positively influence her paternally deprived son's personality development. Mothers who are psychologically healthy and competent can be models for effective behavior. The mother's security in her femininity is very important. If she feels comfortable in interacting with males and in accepting and encouraging a male's masculine responses, she can do much to aid in her son's masculine development.

When the father is absent or ineffectual, the mother-child relationship assumes even more importance. In the father-present home, a warm relationship with a masculine father can outweigh the effects of an overprotecting mother, but in the father-absent home an overprotective mother can greatly interfere with her son's personality development. On the other hand, if a boy has a passive and ineffectual father who is frequently available to imitate, the mother might find it difficult to foster her son's masculine development. The mother of the father-absent boy may have more of an opportunity to encourage the boy's masculine development than the mother of the boy who has an available but inadequate father. The former does not have to counteract the influence of an inadequate model.

The effects of the mother-child relationship cannot be fully understood if they are considered in isolation from the father-child relationship, and the child's constitutional characteristics, sociocultural background, and peer relationships. For example, if the child is father-absent, the length and age of onset of father absence should be taken into account; when boys become father absent early in life, the mother-child relationship is especially influential.

More research is needed in which there is direct observation of family interactions. Data are presented in this book which indicate that the husband-wife relationship is very important in influencing the father's interaction with his children. The mother's view of the father and her own sex role development are factors which can affect the father's involvement in his family. In turn, the father's behavior has much impact on the mother's ability to relate to her children. The complexity of family functioning calls for systematic observations of the ways in which various family members interact and communicate with one another.

7

The Father-Daughter Relationship

Compared to the emphasis on the father-son relationship, there has been relatively little attention given to the impact of the father-daughter relationship. In this chapter, much data are presented which indicate that variations in fathering have important effects on the female's psychological functioning. There is a focus on the influence of paternal deprivation on the girl's emotional development and social and sexual relationships.

Theoretical Perspectives

Unfortunately, much of the theorizing about the father-daughter relationship is marred by negative conceptions of feminine behavior. Freud's theory of identification for girls centers around the Oedipus complex. When the girl discovers she lacks a penis after being exposed to her brother or male peer, she supposedly blames her mother. She then seeks out her father in an attempted retaliation against her mother. Freud speculated that the daughter never fully resolved the Oedipus conflict and therefore maintained a certain type of love relationship with her father, even in adulthood. Because of her wish to replace her mother, the girl is supposed to become fearful that she will suffer maternal rejection. In an attempt to ward off this fear of loss of love, the girl identifies with her mother. But again, according to Freud, the fear of loss of love is not as strong as the fear of castration and the girl does not identify completely enough with her mother to fully resolve the Oedipus complex (Freud 1924, 1933, 1950).

Deutsch (1944) described the traditional psychoanalytic viewpoint in her discussion of Freud's conception of the process of feminine development. According to Deutsch (1944), the father plays an important function in leading the girl to adopt an erotic-passive mode of interacting with males. He showers her with love and tenderness when she acts passive, helpless, and/or femininely seductive, but discourages her masculine and/or aggressive strivings.

The importance of successfully resolving the feminine oedipal complex was stressed in a somewhat more positive way by Leonard (1966), who suggested the need for a girl to "establish a desexualized object relationship to her father" in order for her to be able "later to accept the feminine role without guilt or anxiety and to give love to a young man in her peer group" (p. 332). Adequate fathering is assumed to be an essential requirement for the success of this phase of psychosexual development. Without paternal participation the girl may idealize her father and later, as an adolescent, seek a love object similar to this ideal or maintain a pre-Oedipal narcissistic attitude, such that in adolescence she may be "unable to give love but rather seeks narcissistic gratification in being loved (Leonard 1966, p. 332)." Leonard suggested that a father who ignores or rejects his daughter may contribute to her remaining at a phallic, masculine identified, phase of development because in this way the daughter hopes to receive the love of both parents—the mother's love because the daughter is like the father whom the mother loves and the father's love because the daughter has become the boy he once was or the son he wished for.

Some psychoanalytic theorists have emphasized that sex role development begins before the oedipal period and have pointed to the emergence of the girl's feminine behavior patterns by the time she is two or three (Horney 1933; Stoller 1968). In fact, Kleeman (1971a,b) and Green (1974) stressed that the dynamics of the father-daughter relationship can stimulate or disrupt the girl's feminine development even during her first year of life.

Such learning theorists as Mowrer (1950) and Sears (1957) focused on the importance of parental nurturance in the rewarding of the child's sex-appropriate behaviors. They hypothesized that the child becomes strongly dependent on the parents for supplying nurturance and learns to perform those behaviors which the parents reward. Learning theorists do not generally attach special significance to the father-daughter relationship. However, to the extent that the father has the ability to reward particular behaviors, it can be argued that he has a significant influence on his daughter's personality development. Paternal reinforcement of the girl's attempts to emulate her mother's behavior and the father's general approval of the mother's behavior, seem particularly important.

Parsons (1955, 1958) emphasized the role of the father in feminine development. He viewed the mother as very influential in the child's general personality development, but not as significant as the father in a child's sex role functioning. He emphasized that the mother does not vary her role as a function of the sex of the child as much as does the father. The father is supposed to be the principal transmitter of culturally based conceptions of masculinity and femininity. Johnson (1963) stressed that the mother has a primarily expressive relationship with both boys and girls whereas the father rewards his male and female children differently, encouraging instrumental behavior in his son and expressive behavior in his daughter. For example, the father's flirtatious and pampering behavior is expected to elicit affection and docility in his daughter.

Feminine Development

As can be seen from some of the theoretical perspectives just described there has been a marked tendency to define femininity in negative terms and/or as the opposite of masculinity; for instance, stressing passivity and dependency (Bardwick 1971; Bieliauskas 1965; Salzman 1967). Using a group of college students as judges, Rosenkrantz et al. (1968) assessed cultural stereotypes of masculinity and femininity. An inspection of the 41 items on which there was 75 percent or better agreement yielded a relatively negative definition of femininity. Although some items reflected positive feminine qualities, many items related to passivity, dependency, narcissism, and irresponsibility. Femininity, as traditionally defined, appears to involve passivity, dependency, an internal focus on a world of emotion and fantasy rather than an inclination towards thought and action. Traditional femininity is often found to be negatively associated with adjustment among females (Bardwick 1971; Biller 1971a).

Value judgments are made, to some extent, in definitions of appropriate sex role behavior. Obviously, one has to base any definition of sex roles in relation to a particular sociocultural milieu. Since a focus of the present discussion is on ways in which the father can facilitate his daughter's personality development, it is relevant to analyze elements of femininity which are related to psychological adjustment. As emphasized in Chapter 1, it is meaningful to define feminine behavior in positive terms. For example, femininity in social interaction is related to skill in interpersonal communication, expressiveness of warmth, and sensitivity to the needs of others.

Parsons (1955) has differentiated masculinity and femininity on the basis of the predominance of instrumental needs, interests, and functions in the former and of *expressive* needs, interests, and functions in the latter. Men are seen as assuming more technical, executive, and judicial roles; women more supportive, integrative, and tension-managing roles. In a study emanating from the Parsonian framework, Heilbrun (1965b) obtained ratings from four clinical psychologists as to the instrumental or expressive nature of the adjectives included in Gough and Heilbrun's Adjective Check List. Femininity, as reflected in the expressive adjectives, consists of warmth, sensitivity to the needs of others, the ability to communicate positive feelings, and general social competence.

The girl's perception of herself, and of the value of traditional feminine behavior, can be much influenced by family structure. For example, in two-child families, girls with sisters tend to be more feminine in their interests than girls with brothers (e.g., Brim 1958). The family's sociocultural background also can be very influential. Girls in upper-middle-class homes appear to be much less satisfied with the traditional feminine role than do lower-middle-class girls (e.g., Hartley 1964). The domestic role is often devalued in homes in which there is emphasis on professional accomplishment and the opportunity for the mother to turn over certain household responsibilities to a person of lower status. However, it is important to point out that femininity, according to the present definition, is based upon a positive feeling about being a female—and a particular patterning of interpersonal behavior. Whether or not a woman enjoys housework, or chooses a career, should not be used as the ultimate criterion in assessing her femininity.

Women who possess both positive feminine and positive masculine characteristics and secure sex role orientations are most able to actualize their potential. Women who have pride in their femininity and are independent and assertive *as well as* nurturant and sensitive are likely to achieve interpersonal and creative fulfillment (Biller 1972b; Biller and Meredith 1974).

Paternal Differentiation

A girl's feminine development is much influenced by how her father differentiates his "masculine" role from her "feminine" role and what type of behavior he considers appropriate for his daughter. Studying first grade children, Mussen and Rutherford (1963) found that fathers of highly feminine girls encouraged their daughters more in sex-typed activities than did fathers of unfeminine girls. These investigators suggested that masculine fathers who actively encourage and appreciate femininity in girls are particularly able to facilitate their daughter's sex role development. Similarly, in their study with nursery school children, Sears, Rau, and Alpert (1965) reported a significant correlation between girls' femininity and their fathers' expectations of their participation in feminine activities.

In an examination of the familial antecedents of sex role behavior, Heilbrun (1965b) concluded that fathers are more proficient than mothers in differentiating between their male and female children. Heilbrun emphasized that "fathers are more capable of responding expressively than mothers are of acting instrumentally . . . that fathers systematically vary their sex role as they relate to male and female offspring" (p. 796). Heilbrun found that daughters who perceive themselves as feminine, as well as sons who perceive themselves as masculine, are likely to view their fathers as masculine.

Goodenough's (1957) results support the view that fathers influence their children's sex role development more than do mothers. Goodenough focused upon the influence of the parents in determining the social interests of nursery school children. She found that " . . . the father has a greater interest in sex differences than the mother and hence exerts stronger influence in general sex-typing" (p. 321); for example, there was much more paternal encouragement for girls to develop skills in social interaction. Strong paternal emphasis on sex role differentiation was also found in a study by Aberle and Naegele (1952). Differences in parent-child interactions are a function of the sex of the child as well as the sex of the parent (e.g., Bronfenbrenner 1961; Emmerich 1962; Papenek 1969; Rosenberg and Sutton-Smith 1968; Rothbart and Maccoby 1966).

Tasch (1952, 1955) interviewed fathers of boys and girls in order to learn about their conceptions of the paternal role. She found much evidence of paternal differentiation in terms of sex of child. Her results indicated that fathers viewed their daughters as more delicate and sensitive than their sons. Fathers were found to use physical punishment more frequently with their sons than with their daughters. Fathers tended to define household tasks in terms of their sex-appropriateness. For example, they expected girls to iron and wash clothes and babysit for siblings, while boys were expected to be responsible for taking out the garbage and help their fathers in activities involving mechanical and physical competence. Unfortunately, fathers often have rigid sex role stereotypes and in their zeal to "feminize" females they actively discourage the development of intellectual and physical competence in their daughters (Biller and Meredith 1974).

Nevertheless, the child is not merely a passive recipient of familial and sociocultural influences. As has been stressed in earlier sections of this book, the child's constitutional predispositions can play a very important part in influencing parent-child and environmental interactions. For example, the young girl who is temperamentally responsive to social interaction and is very attractive may make it especially easy for her father to encourage her positive feminine development. Similarly, if the girl facially and physically resembles a highly feminine mother, the father is likely to treat her as a female. On the other hand, the girl who is physically large and unattractive may be perceived as unfeminine by her father. The father may reject his daughter if she does not fit his conception of the physical characteristics of femininity. If the father does not have a son and his daughter is particularly vigorous and well-coordinated, he is likely to treat her as if she were a boy.

Personal and Social Adjustment

When the father is not involved in the family, his daughter is likely to have problems in her sex role and personality development. Hoffman (1961a) found that girls from mother-dominant homes had difficulty relating to males and were disliked by boys. However, Hetherington (1965) did not find a clear-cut relationship between parental dominance and girls' sex role preferences, although girls with dominant fathers were much more likely to imitate them and to be similar to them than girls with dominant mothers. Other studies are also consistent with the supposition that paternal dominance is a less influential factor for girls than it is for boys (Biller 1969c; Hetherington and Frankie 1967).

My results suggested that the girl's feminine development is facilitated if the mother is seen as a generally salient controller of resources (Biller 1969c). Kindergarten-age girls perceived their fathers as more competent and more decision-making, their mothers as more limit-setting, and both parents as similar in nurturance. I found a subgroup of girls whose femininity scores were low and who perceived their mothers as relatively high in decision-making and limit-setting, but quite low in nurturance and competence. In most cases, at least a moderate level of paternal involvement in decision-making seemed important in the girl's feminine development.

Zung and I reported data which suggest that very strong maternal control and dominance hampers girls' as well as the boys' personality development (Biller and Zung 1972). We found that high maternal control and intrusiveness was associated with sex role conflict and anxiety among elementary school girls. For girls the *optimal level* of paternal dominance may be moderate, allowing the mother to also be viewed as a "salient controller of resources" yet in a general context of paternal involvement. It is important that the girl perceive her father as competent and as appreciating her behavior, even if she does not perceive him as the dominant parent.

Results of an investigation by Fish and myself (1973) suggest that the father plays a particularly important role in the girl's personality adjustment. College females' perceptions of their relationships with their fathers during childhood were assessed by means of an extensive family background questionnaire. Subjects who perceived their fathers as having been very nurturant, and positively interested in them, scored high on the Adjective Check List personal adjustment scale. In contrast, subjects who perceived their fathers as having been rejecting scored very low on the personal adjustment measure. Findings from other investigations have also pointed to the influence of positive paternal involvement in the girl's interpersonal adjustment (e.g., Baumrind and Black 1967; Torgoff and Dreyer 1961).

Block's (1971) analysis of data collected from the Berkeley Longitudinal Study highlights the importance of both the father-daughter and father-mother relationships in the quality of the female's personality functioning. (There is a fuller description of the methodology of this study in Chapter 5.) The most well-adjusted females were from homes with two positively involved parents. Their mothers were described as affectionate, personable, and resourceful and their fathers as warm, competent, and firm. A second group of relatively well-adjusted females came from homes with extremely bright, capable, and ambitious mothers but rather passive but warm fathers.

Four other groups of females were poorly adjusted. The "hyperfeminine repressives" had fathers who were inadequate, conforming, and sexually ambivalent. Their mothers seemed very mediocre and placid. (This group appeared to model after both parents and be generally inadequate.) In contrast, another poorly adjusted group, "dominating narcissists," seemed more similar to fathers who were dominant, self-centered, and outgoing. Their mothers were despairing and neurotic and their fathers presented relatively more positive models. Women who fit the "vulnerable overcontroller" category, similar to their male counterparts, had extremely inadequate parents. Both their mothers and fathers were described as very dissatisfied and neurotic. The last group of women discussed were the "lonely independents." These women had some very positive qualities, including assertiveness and a drive for achievement, which they seemed to learn from fathers, who were vital, opinionated, and arrogantly self-assured. However, their mothers presented very poor models, being meek and easily overwhelmed. Perhaps the problems of the women in this group (like the other poorly adjusted groups) stemmed from having little opportunity to view a positive father-mother relationship.

Block, von der Lippe, and Block's (1973) study also helps to convey some of the complexity of the associations between parental behavior and later personaltiy functioning. As mentioned when their results concerning male personality development were discussed in Chapter 5, these investigators studied groups of subjects who differed in terms of their femininity and socialization scores on the California Psychological Inventory.

Highly feminine, highly socialized women were described as fitting comfortably into the culturally-expected role for females. They were described as conservative, conventional, dependable, and docile. However, there was not a completely tranquil picture, since interviewers frequently perceived vulnerability, indecision, and personal dissatisfaction among this group. They appeared to come from a family-centered environment and have particularly close, warm, and sharing relationships with their mothers. Their mothers seemed to also typify a positive adjustment to the stereotypic feminine role. Interestingly, no distinctive picture of the father seemed to emerge for this group. (I would speculate that a relatively passive father who reinforced stereotyped feminine behavior could easily contribute to such overly conforming behavior.)

The high feminine, low socialized females in many ways seemed to resemble the high masculine, low socialized males. They seemed quite narcissistic and hedonistic. Similar to their mothers they seemed to have unstable marital relationships. These women appeared to have very inadequate and rejecting mothers. Their relationships with their fathers seemed stronger but appeared to have been overly seductive and may have prematurely stimulated these females into early sexual experiences. (The investigators noted that this group was particularly attractive. I would emphasize that their appearance may have had a strong impact on their parents. For example, a very attractive daughter may exacerbate an insecure mother's anxiety about herself and increase the probability of seductive behavior on the part of the father.)

The low feminine, high socialized women conveyed a relaxed, poised, and outgoing appearance and generally seemed to be the most well-adjusted group. They were viewed as conservative and not at all introspective. Their family backgrounds seemed stable, affectionate, and comfortable. Their fathers were described as warm and accepting and their mothers appeared to be oriented toward rationality, achievement, and intellectual attainment.

The low feminine, low socialized women appeared to be assertive, critical, and rebellious. (As with the high feminine, low socialized group, they seemed to be unhappy with life but communicated their displeasure in a much different manner.) They were aggressively insistent upon their autonomy and independence and communicated decisiveness and competence. These women came from very conflicted and inadequate backgrounds. Their mothers appeared to be neurotic, vulnerable, unhappy, and generally interpersonally incompetent. Their fathers were hard driving and status oriented. The fathers were uninvolved with their families and tended to reject their daughters.

Marital and Sexual Adjustment

Many women choose to pursue a full-time career rather than marriage because of very realistic factors, such as self-fulfillment and economic need. However, the choice of a career is sometimes motivated by a fearful avoidance of marriage. Unmarried career women often have much underlying sex role conflict (Levin 1966). In Rushing's (1964) study with adolescents, girls who reported satisfactory relationships with their fathers were less likely to give priority to a career than were those who had unsatisfactory relationships with their fathers. When a girl is continually frustrated in her interactions with her father, she may develop a negative attitude toward close relationships with men and marriage. White (1959) compared the self-concepts and familial backgrounds of women whose interests focused on marriage and childrearing with those whose interests revolved around a career. More of the women who were interested in marriage appeared to have close relationships with both parents and to be comfortable in their self-concepts. More of the women interested in careers came from homes in which the father had died or in which there was inadequate parent-child communication.

Of course, one problem with such studies is that they do not include a group of women who were interested in both careers and in marriage and childrearing. Women who can comfortably pursue their occupational interests and develop their intellectual competence as well as being successful wives and mothers are more likely to have come from homes in which they had both positively involved fathers and mothers. Data reviewed in Chapter 8 indicate the importance a positive father-daughter relationship can have in the female's achieving a high level of intellectual competence and career success.

Lozoff's (1974) findings strongly suggest that father-daughter relationships are very crucial in the development of college-educated, primarily upper middle-class women who are able to be successful in both their heterosexual relationships and in their creative, professional endeavors. Such women had brilliant fathers who were personally secure, vital and achievement-oriented. The fathers treated their children with much respect. They valued their daughter's basic femininity but at the same time they encouraged and expected them to develop their competencies without any infringement of sex role stereotypes. There was much compatibility between their fathers and mothers and the women developed positive identifications with both parents and comfortable and feminine sex role orientations.

A second group of women that Lozoff described also were very autonomous but were in much personal conflict. Their fathers tended to be aloof, perfectionistic and self-disciplined. They had very high expectations for their daughters but did not provide enough emotional support for them to develop a solid self-confidence. A third group of women who were very low in autonomy also came from economically privileged but highly sex-typed family situations. The father in such families seemed to offer his daughter little encouragement for intellectual competence, leaving her socialization mainly up to his wife.

Block, von der Lippe, and Block (1973) emphasized how difficult it is for a female to get the necessary family support to develop into a well-rounded, secure, and competent adult. It is striking from their data that few fathers tended to be adequately involved with their daughters and to encourage both a positive feminine self-concept and instrumental competence. Again, many of these problems seem associated with our overly rigid sex-typing and negative definitions of feminine behavior. Our gradually increasing flexibility in sex roles should lead to more and more women having a positive feminine self-concept as well as a wide range of competencies and a successful, fulfilling career.

Other data reveal that long-term consequences of the father-daughter relationship can have on marital relationships. In Winch's (1950, 1951) questionnaire study with college students, females who had long-term romantic relationships (who appeared near marriage) reported closer relationships with their fathers than did females who did not have serious heterosexual involvements. Luckey (1960) reported that women who were satisfied with their marriages perceived their husbands as more similar to their fathers than did women who were not satisfied in their marriages. The female's ability to have a successful marriage relationship is increased when she has experienced a warm affectionate relationship with a father who has encouraged her positive feminine development. In questionnaire studies with college and graduate students, I have found a strong association between their perceived relationships with their fathers during childhood and their marital adjustments. Divorce, separation, and unhappy marriages were much higher among women reporting that they had been father absent or had poor or very infrequent interactions with their fathers (Biller 1974d).

Fisher (1973) presented evidence indicating that paternal deprivation in early childhood is associated with infrequent orgasms among married women. He and his coworkers studied the sexual feelings and fantasies of almost 300 middle-class married women. The women were well-educated volunteers primarily married to graduate students and in their early and middle twenties. An extensive array of assessment procedures including interviews, questionnaires, and projective techniques was used. The limited representativeness of Fisher's sample could be questioned, but his findings do seem very consistent with other data concerning the father's general impact on the female's sexual development.

A central theme emerging from low-orgasmic women was their lack of meaningful relationships with their fathers. There was a high incidence of early loss and frequent separation from the father among the low-orgasmic group. Low-orgasmic women were more preoccupied with fear of loss of control than were high-orgasmic women and this was associated with their lack of security and trust of their fathers during childhood. Low-orgasmic women more often saw themselves as lacking dependable relationships with their fathers.

Questionnaire data revealed that the lower a woman's orgasmic capacity, the more likely she was to report that her father treated her in a laissez-faire manner. Low-orgasmic women described uninvolved fathers who did not have well-defined expectations or rules for their daughters. Low-orgasmic women also described much physical and psychological father absence during early childhood. In contrast, high-orgasmic women were more likely to perceive their fathers as having had definite and demanding expectations and a concern for their enforcement. Fisher continually emphasized that his findings reveal that the father is much more important in the development of orgasmic adequacy than is the mother.

Other findings discussed by Fisher also support the notion of the father's importance in the development of the female's sexual responsivity. Fisher presents considerable evidence indicating that a clitorally stimulated orgasm is generally more intense and arouses more total bodily involvement than does a vaginally stimulated orgasm. In turn, he found that women preferring a clitorally stimulated orgasm described their fathers as having shown more affectionate approval of their behavior than did women preferring a vaginally stimulated orgasm. Fisher also notes a supplementary and somewhat obscure analysis from Terman's (1938) study of marital adjustment. Terman compared wives who reported a preference for relatively frequent intercourse (12 or more times a month) and those who preferred infrequent intercourse (less than two times per month). Those who preferred frequent intercourse were found to more often be strongly attached to their fathers and to rate them as above average in attractiveness than were those who preferred infrequent intercourse.

Female Homosexuality

Inappropriate and/or inadequate fathering is a major factor in the development of homosexuality in females as well as in males. Bené (1965) reported that female homosexuals felt their fathers were weak and incompetent. The homosexual women were more hostile toward and afraid of their fathers than were the heterosexual women. Kaye et al. (1967) analyzed background data on homosexual women in psychoanalysis. These investigators found that the fathers of the homosexual woman (as compared to the fathers of women in a heterosexual control group) tended to be puritanical, exploitative, and feared by their daughters, as well as possessive and infantalizing. Kaye et al. also presented evidence that suggests that female homosexuality is associated with rejection of femininity early in life. In another study, lesbians described their fathers as less involved and affectionate than did heterosexual women (Gundlach and Reiss 1968). In general, the lesbians described their fathers as acting like strangers toward them. Other researchers have also found that girls who feel devalued and rejected by their fathers are more likely to become homosexual than are girls whose fathers are warm and accepting (e.g., Hamilton 1929; West 1967).

College-age, well-educated female homosexuals were recruited by their friends in a study by Thompson et al. (1973). Compared to a control group of female heterosexuals, the female homosexuals indicated that they were less accepting of their fathers and their femininity during early childhood. There was also some evidence that they perceived their fathers as more detached, weak and hostile toward them. In general, available research has suggested that inadequate fathering is more of a factor in the development of female homosexuality than is inadequate mothering. It is also relevant to note the general similarity in negative father-child relations among female and male homosexuals. Paternal deprivation makes the individual more vulnerable to difficulties in sexual development, but again it is only one of many factors which determine the type of adjustment an adult will make.

Father Absence

As was emphasized in previous chapters, the specific effects of paternal absence are influenced by such factors as the personality of the mother, sociocultural background, and the presence and sex of siblings. Some data suggest that females are less affected by father absence than are males (e.g., Bach 1946; Lessing, Zagorin, and Nelson 1970; Lynn and Sawrey 1959; Santrock 1972; Winch 1950). However, there is other research which supports the conclusion that girls are at least as much influenced in their social and heterosexual development by father absence as are boys (e.g., Biller 1971a; Biller and Weiss 1970; Hetherington 1972). The extent and direction of the differential impact of father absence on males and females probably varies with respect to which dimensions of personality development are considered.

Father-absence can interfere with the girl's feminine development and her overall heterosexual adjustment. In Seward's (1945) study, women who rejected the feminine role of wife and mother were more likely to come from broken homes than were women who accepted these roles. White (1959) reported similar results. Landy, Rosenberg, and Sutton-Smith's (1967) results suggest that among college females, father-absence during adolescence is sometimes associated with a rejection of feminine interests. Although she studied father-present females, Fish's (1969) data also seem relevant. College females who reported that their fathers spent little time with them during their childhoods had less feminine self-concepts than did those who reported moderate or high father availability. It is also interesting to note anthropological evidence which suggests that low father availability is associated with sex role conflicts for girls as well as boys (Brown 1963; Stephens 1962).

In Jacobson and Ryder's (1969) interview study, many women who had been father absent early in life complained of difficulties in achieving satisfactory sexual relationships with their husbands. Lack of opportunity to observe meaningful male-female relationships in childhood can make it much more difficult for the father-absent female to develop the interpersonal skills necessary for adequate heterosexual adjustment. Case studies of father-absent girls are often filled with details of problems concerning interactions with males, particularly in sexual relationships (e.g., Leonard 1966; Neubauer 1960).

However, other findings suggest that father-absent girls are not inhibited in terms of their development of sex-typed interests or perceptions of the incentive value of the feminine role (Hetherington 1972; Lynn and Sawrey 1959; Santrock 1970). In fact, in a study with disadvantaged black children, Santrock (1970) found a tendency for father-absent girls to be more feminine on a doll-play sex role measure than were father-present girls; a very high level of femininity may be associated with a rigid sex role development which devalues males and masculine activities. In any case, father absence seems to have more effect on the girl's ability to function in interpersonal and heterosexual relationships than it does on her sex role preference.

The father-absent girl often has difficulty in dealing with her aggressive impulses. In their study of doll play behavior, Sears et al. (1946) found "no indication that the girls are more frustrated when the father is present; on the contrary, his absence is associated with greater aggression, especially self-aggression" (p. 240). These investigators speculated that a high degree of aggressive doll play behavior may be a function of the father-absent girl's conflict with her mother. In a clinical study, Heckel (1963) observed frequent school maladjustment, excessive sexual interest, and social acting-out behavior in five fatherless preadolescent girls. Other investigators have also found a high incidence of delinquent behavior among lower-class father-absent girls (Monahan 1957; Toby 1957). Such acting-out behavior may be a manifestation of frustration associated with the girl's unsuccessful attempts to find a meaningful relationship with an adult male. Father absence appears to increase the probability that a girl will experience difficulties in interpersonal adjustment. Many studies referred to in Chapter 5 suggested that father-absent girls are likely to have emotional and social problems. But one difficulty in interpreting many of these studies is that they do not differentiate between boys and girls in data analyses.

The devaluation of maleness and masculinity, so prevalent in paternally deprived, matrifocal families, adversely affects many girls as well as boys. Children in lower-class families often do not have opportunities to interact with adequate adult males. Even in intact lower-class families, father-daughter relationships are generally not very adequate. The father may be very punitive and express little affection towards his daughter (Elder and Bowerman 1963). Many investigators have observed that lower-class black girls, in families in which the father is absent or ineffectual, quickly develop derogatory attitudes toward males (e.g., Pettigrew 1964, Rohrer and Edmonson 1960).

The downgrading of males in terms of their seeming social and economic irresponsibility is common among lower-class black families. Negative attitudes towards males are transmitted by mothers, grandmothers, and other significant females, and, unfortunately, are often strengthened by the child's observation or involvement in destructive male-female relationships. Paternal deprivation, in the rubric of the devaluation of the male role, is a major factor in the lower-class females' frequent difficulties in interacting with their male relatives, boyfriends, husbands, and children. Maternally-based households seem to become like family heirlooms—passed from generation to generation (Rohrer and Edmonson 1960).

Interactions with Males

The most comprehensive and well-controlled study concerning father absence and the girl's development was conducted by Hetherington (1972). Her subjects were white, adolescent, lower-middle-class girls (ages 13 to 17) who regularly attended a community recreation center. Hetherington was particularly interested in the possible differential effects of father absence due to divorce or death of the father. She compared three groups of girls; girls whose fathers were absent because of divorce and who had no contact with their fathers since the divorce, girls whose fathers were absent because of death, and girls with both parents living at home. She was careful to control for sibling variables (all the girls were first borns without brothers) and none of the father-absent children had any adult males living in their homes following separation from the father.

The most striking finding was that both groups of father-absent girls had great difficulty in interacting comfortably with men and male peers. Hetherington discovered that the difficulties were manifested differently for the daughters of divorcees than for the daughters of widows. The daughters of divorcees tended to be quite aggressive and forward with males while daughters of widows tended to be extremely shy and timid in interacting with males. Although their behavior was much different, both of the father-absent groups reported that they were very insecure with males. In contrast, all three groups of girls generally appeared to have appropriate interactions with their mothers and with female adults and peers. One of the exceptions was that the father-absent girls seemed more dependent on women, which is consistent with Lynn and Sawrey's (1959) findings of increased mother dependency among father-separated girls.

Observations at the recreation center revealed that, compared with the other girls, daughters of divorcees sought more attention from men and tried to be near and have physical contacts with male peers. On the other hand, the daughters of widows avoided male areas and much preferred to be with females. Compared to other girls, the daughters of widows reported less heterosexual activity; the daughters of divorcees more heterosexual activity.

With male interviewers, the daughters of widows sat as far away as possible, whereas the daughters of divorcees tended to sit as close as possible. (The girls from intact families generally sat at an intermediate distance.) Daughters of widows also showed avoidance behavior in their postures during interactions with male interviewers; they often sat stiffly upright, leaned backward, kept their legs together, and showed little eye contact. In contrast, the daughters of divorcees tended to sprawl in their chairs, have an open leg posture, lean slightly forward, and exhibit much eye contact and smiling. Nelsen and Vangen (1971) also found that among lower-class eighth-grade black girls, those who were father absent because of divorce or separation were more precocious in their dating behavior and in their knowledge of sex than were father-present girls. Nelsen and Vangen emphasized that when the father is in the home he is an important limit-setter for the girl's sexual behavior and that when he is absent there is a great decrease in parental control.

However, the presence of the father during preadolescence or early adolescence does not appear to be the key factor in preventing the girl's sexual difficulties. As with data reviewed in Chapter 4 concerning boys' development, Hetherington generally found that girls had the most difficulties in their heterosexual interactions when their father absence began before the age of five. Early father separation was usually more associated with inappropriate behavior with males than was father absence after the age of five, although differences were not significant for every measure. Early father absence was also associated with more maternal overprotection than was father absence after the age of five. There is other evidence indicating that early father absence is more associated with maternal overprotection than is father absence beginning later in the child's life (e.g., Biller 1969b; Biller and Bahm 1971).

There were additional findings in Hetherington's study which indicated the importance of taking into account the context of and reason for father absence. Daughters of widows recalled more positive relationships with their fathers and described them as warmer and more competent than did daughters of divorcees. The divorced mothers also painted a very negative picture of their marriages and ex-husbands. Daughters of divorcees were quite low in self-esteem, but daughters of widows did not differ significantly in their self-esteem from daughters from father-present homes. Nevertheless, both groups of father-absent girls had less feelings of control over their lives and more anxiety than did father-present girls.

Inadequate Fathering

The father-mother interaction can have much impact on the child's personality development. Family stability and cohesiveness helps to provide a positive atmosphere for the developing child. An inadequate father is often also an inadequate husband. The father may influence his daughter's personality development indirectly in terms of his relationship with his wife. If the father meets his wife's needs she may, in turn, be able to interact more adequately with her children. Bartemeier (1953) emphasized that the wife's capacity for appropriately nurturing her children, and her general psychological adjustment, is much influenced by her relationship with her husband. A number of investigations have suggested that a warm and nurturant mother-daughter relationship is important in positive feminine development (e.g., Hetherington 1965; Hetherington and Frankie 1967; Mussen and Parker 1965; Mussen and Rutherford 1963).

Inadequate fathering or mothering is frequently a reflection of difficulties in the husband-wife relationship. Such difficulties may be particularly apparent in the husband's and wife's inability to adequately provide one another with affection and sexual satisfaction. The parents' interpersonal problems are usually reflected in their interactions with their children and in their children's adjustment. For example, clinical studies have revealed that difficulties in parental sexual adjustment, combined with overrestrictive parental attitudes, are often associated with incestuous and acting out behavior among adolescent females (e.g., Kaufman, Peck, and Tagiuri 1954; Robey et al. 1964).

Severe marital conflict can have a disorganizing effect on both paternal and maternal behavior. Baruch and Wilcox's (1944) results indicated that marital conflict negatively influences the personality development of both boys and girls. Some of their data suggested that girls can be even more handicapped than boys. Girls may suffer more because of their interpersonal sensitivity. Some research findings suggest that familial factors seem to have more impact on girls' than on boys' personality development (Lynn 1969).

The Becker and Peterson research group reported that conduct problems were generally found in children whose parents showed poor self-control and arbitrary behavior in their interactions with their children (Becker et al. 1959, 1962; Peterson et al. 1959). In many cases, the mother was tense and thwarting while the father showed minimal concern for his family. Fathers whose children had conduct problems were frequently poor enforcers of discipline, especially of rules established by the mother. On the other hand, maladjusted and domineering fathers appeared to contribute to shyness and emotional immaturity in their children. These fathers were likely to make arbitrary power assertions and to lack warmth in dealing with their wives and children. Becker and Krug (1964) found that girls who were overly submissive and fearful often had excessively punitive and overbearing fathers. These findings are in line with those of Rubenstein and Levitt (1957) and Hoffman (1960), who emphasized the adverse effects of arbitrary paternal power assertion on the development of the child's autonomy and interpersonal maturity.

Rosenthal et al. (1962) found that inadequate fathering was associated with a number of psychological problems in children, particularly those of an antisocial nature. These investigators attempted to relate specific patterns of paternal inadequacy with certain types of childhood psychopathology. However, as with many other studies in this area, analyses were not done in terms of the sex of the child. Studies taking into account the sex of the child as well as the type of paternal behavior and type of child maladjustment need to be done.

Father Imitation

Sopchak (1952) and Lazowick (1955) presented findings which support the proposition that inadequate fathering is related to the development of psychological problems. Lazowick (1955) found that lack of identification with the father was related to a high degree of manifest anxiety among undergraduate women. Sopchak (1952) also studied college students and reported that:

Women with tendencies toward abnormality as measured by the MMPI show a lack of identification with their fathers . . . Masculine women identify with their fathers less than feminine women . . . and identification with the father is more important in producing normal adjustment than is identification with the mother (pp. 164-165).

The well-adjusted female's identification with her father involves understanding and empathizing with the father rather than rejecting her basic femininity and wishing she were a male. A positive father identification may also include the sharing of many paternal values and attitudes, as long as there is no interference with the girl's development of a feminine self-concept and an expressive mode of social interaction (Biller 1971a).

Wright and Tuska (1966) compared college women who rated themselves as very feminine with those who rated themselves as only slightly feminine, or masculine. The highly feminine women had more favorable conceptions of their fathers while the unfeminine women seemed to have engaged in more imitation of their fathers' masculine behaviors. Wright and Tuska speculated that the masculine women coped with frustrating relationships with their mothers by imitating their fathers, whereas the feminine women adopted expressive role behavior by imitating their mothers' interactions with their fathers.

Poffenberger (1959) described some of the adverse effects of paternal rejection on the child's self-concept and general attitude toward life. Case studies illustrate how fathers who do not accept their daughters' femininity can have very destructive effects on their daughters' personality development (e.g., Neubauer 1960; West 1967). The father who wants his daughter to be the son he never had, or the father who cannot cope with feminine behavior, may consistently reinforce his daughter's rejection of her femininity. Difficulties in the husband-wife relationship which center around sexual interactions are particularly common in such families.

If she receives adequate fathering, the probability of a girl compulsively imitating the father's behaviors and spurning her femininity seems high *only* if the mother is cold and rejecting or somehow unable to express acceptance, warmth, and nurturance toward her daughter. When the father plays an active and competent masculine role in the family, his daughter is likely to imitate his positive attributes and develop a broad, adaptive behavioral repertoire. If the father is inadequate, his daughter may be generally limited in her social experience and not be able to fully develop her intellectual and interpersonal competence. The above speculations appear to integrate and make more intelligible the results of a number of diverse studies (e.g., Ackerman 1957; Beier and Ratzeburg 1953; Carpenter and Eisenberg 1935; Gray 1959; Mussen and Rutherford 1963; Rychlak and Legerski 1967; Williams 1973).

Much data are reviewed in the next chapter that indicate that the father-daughter relationship is very important for a girl's cognitive and academic functioning. For example, father absent girls have often been found to perform more poorly on intelligence and achievement tests than father-present girls. On the other hand, high paternal expectations in the context of a positive father-daughter relationship has been found to facilitate the girl's development of independence, assertiveness, and other personality characteristics which can help her maximize her intellectual and career success (Biller 1974a, 1974b).

Severe Psychopathology

Paternal inadequacy can be a factor in the development of severe psychopathology in the female child as well as in the male child. Unfortunately, many of the studies examining the influence of paternal deprivation on childhood psychopathology (see Chapter 5) did not include female children or did not take the sex of the child into account in data analyses. However, there is some research which focuses on—or specifically includes—females.

In their extensive studies, Lidz, Parker, and Cornelison (1956) reported a high incidence of inadequate fathering for both male and female schizophrenics. The fathers of the schizophrenic females were frequently observed to be in severe conflict with their wives, to contradict their wives' decisions, and to degrade their wives in front of their daughters. These fathers made rigid and unrealistic demands on their wives. Similarly, such fathers were insensitive to their daughters' needs to develop an independent self-concept. The fathers of the schizophrenic females made attempts to manipulate and mold their daughters in terms of their own unrealistic needs. Females who formed an allegiance with a disturbed father, frequently in reaction to rejection by an unloving mother, seemed most likely to become psychotic.

Hamilton and Wahl (1948) found that almost 75 percent of the hospitalized schizophrenic women they studied had experienced some inadequacy of fathering in childhood. Prolonged father absence, paternal rejection, and paternal abuse were very common. Baker and Holzworth (1961) compared a group of male and female adolescents who were hospitalized because of psychological disturbances with a group who were successful in their interpersonal and school adjustments. The fathers of the hospitalized group were more likely to have had social histories involving court convictions and excessive drinking than were the fathers of the successful adolescents.

However, it is important to emphasize that variations in sociocultural background may be a primary factor contributing to such findings. For example, both criminal convictions and commitment to state hospitals are more frequent for lower-class individuals than for middle-class individuals. The general economic and social deprivation that lower-class children experience seems to exacerbate the effects of paternal deprivation.

Severe psychopathology is also often related to the child's constitutional predispositions and does not usually develop simply as a function of disturbed parent-child relationships. For example, the girl who is temperamentally unresponsive to affection may negatively reinforce her father's attempts to form a positive relationship with her. Similarly, if a little girl is extremely hyperactive and aggressive, it may be very difficult for her father to relate to her.

Summary

Interpersonal sensitivity and the ability to express affection are particularly important facets of the girl's femininity. Fathers more than mothers vary their behavior as a function of the sex of the child, and fathers appear to play an especially significant role in encouraging their daughters' feminine development. The father's acceptance and reinforcement of his daughter's femininity greatly facilitates the development of her self-concept.

Interaction with a masculine and competent father provides a girl with basic experiences which she can generalize to her relationships with other males. Girls who have positive relationships with their fathers are more likely to be able to obtain satisfaction in their heterosexual relationships and to achieve happiness as wives and mothers.

Father absence and paternal deprivation can hamper a girl's personality development. Compared to girls who have had adequate fathering, father-absent girls have more difficulties in their feminine development and in their interpersonal relationships with males. Overdependency on the mother and difficulties in controlling aggressive impulses appear to be more frequent for father-absent females. Females who have experienced inadequate fathering are more likely to be homosexual than are those who have had warm affectionate relationships with their fathers. Paternal inadequacy is also a frequent concomitant of severe psychological disturbance among females.

However, other facets of family functioning, and the child's constitutional and sociocultural background, must be considered if a thorough understanding of the influence of the father-daughter relationship is to be achieved. The father-mother relationship seems to have much impact on the girl's personality development. Chronic marital conflict and inappropriate husband-wife interaction can greatly distort the child's view of heterosexual interactions. The girl may learn very unsatisfactory patterns of interacting with males or to avoid close relationships with males. On the other hand, if the father and mother mutually satisfy and value each other, the child is much better able to learn effective interpersonal skills.

8

Fathering and Cognitive and Academic Functioning

The major purpose of this chapter is to examine the relationship between paternal influence and the young child's cognitive functioning and classroom adjustment. Topics include the influence of paternal deprivation on intellectual competence and academic achievement; the impact of the father-child relationship on creativity, cognitive styles, and sex differences in intellectual development; the interaction of sociocultural and maternal variables in the paternally deprived child's academic adjustment; the effect of the feminized classroom on boys' and girls' academic functioning and sex role stereotypes; and the potential significance of male teachers on children's academic achievement and classroom adjustment. Much of the material in this chapter is based on my presentation (Biller 1974a) at the 1973 *Nebraska Symposium on Motivation* (Cole and Dienstbier 1974) and my contribution (Biller 1974b) to David's (1974) *Child Personality and Psychopathology: Current Topics.*

Paternal Influence and Cognitive Functioning

This section includes a description of research efforts which in some way have explored the relationship between fathering and cognitive functioning. Results from several investigations have revealed an association between inadequate father-son relationships and academic difficulties among boys.

Academic Achievement

Kimball (1952) studied highly intelligent boys enrolled in a residential preparatory school. She compared 20 boys who were failing in school with a group of boys who were selected randomly from the total school population. Interview and psychological test material revealed consistently that the underachieving boys had very inadequate relationships with their fathers. Many of the fathers were reported to work long hours and to be home infrequently, or to attempt to dominate and control their sons by means of excessive discipline.

Using a specifically designed sentence completion technique, Kimball found further evidence that significantly more of the boys in the underachieving group had poor relationships with their fathers. Responses suggesting feelings of paternal rejection and paternal hostility were considerably more frequent among the underachieving boys. Projective test data also suggested that the boys had much hostility towards their fathers because they perceived that their fathers had rejected them. There is other evidence that paternal hostility and lack of acceptance is negatively related to the child's scholastic ability (Hurley 1967).

Through the use of extensive clinical interviews, Grunebaum et al. (1962) examined the family life of elementary school boys who had at least average intelligence, but were one to two years below expectation in their academic achievement (Metropolitan Achievement Test). These boys seemed to have very poor relationships with their fathers. Their fathers were reported to feel generally inadequate and thwarted in their own ambitions and to view themselves as failures. The fathers appeared to be particularly insecure about their masculinity and did not seem to offer their sons adequate models of male competence. Most of the fathers viewed their wives as being far superior to them, and their wives generally shared this perception. Most of the mothers perceived both their husbands and sons as inadequate and incompetent and seemed to be involved in undermining their confidence. This study was of an exploratory, clinical nature but it did suggest some of the ways in which the dynamics of the husband-wife relationship can affect the child's academic functioning.

Shaw and White (1965) conducted an investigation of the familial correlates of high and low academic achievement among high school students with above-average intelligence. Adjective checklist rating scales were administered to the students and their parents, who were instructed to describe themselves and other members of the family. High-achieving boys (B average or better) perceived themselves as more similar to their fathers than did low-achieving boys (below a B average). The high-achieving boys also perceived themselves as more similar to their fathers than their mothers but low-achieving boys did not. Among the high-achieving group, but not among the low-achieving group, father and son self-ratings were positively correlated. Such results suggest that father-son closeness and identification are related to academic achievement.

I worked with a group of high school boys who were involved in a project designed to motivate them to utilize their academic potential (described by Davids 1972). In general, these boys had very superior intelligence, but their academic functioning was below grade level. Most of the boys were alienated from their fathers. Many of their fathers were quite successful, but according to their sons' reports were much more devoted to their work than to their families (Biller 1966b).

Mutimer, Loughlin, and Powell (1966) compared children who were relatively retarded in their reading ability with children who were reading above grade level. Children in both groups were generally well above average intelligence. On a task involving various choice situations, boys who were high achievers in reading more often indicated that they would prefer to be with their fathers than did boys who were poor readers. Although not statistically significant, similar differences were noted among the girls.

Both Katz (1967) and Solomon (1969) reported data that indicated a strong positive association between paternal interest and encouragement and academic achievement among lower-class, black elementary school boys. Katz's findings were based on the boys' perceptions of their parents, whereas Solomon had ratings of parent-child interactions while the boys were performing a series of intellectual tasks. Interestingly, in both studies, the fathers' behavior appeared to be a much more important factor than did the mothers' behavior.

The studies so far discussed have dealt with paternal factors and their association with academic achievement. In addition, there is evidence that the quality of fathering is related to the child's performance on intelligence and aptitude tests.

Radin (1972) found both the quality and quantity of father-son interactions strongly associated with four-year-old boys' intellectual functioning. Father-son interactions during an interview with the father were recorded and later coded for frequency of paternal nurturance and restrictiveness. The overall number of father-son interactions was positively correlated to both Stanford-Binet and Peabody Picture Vocabulary Test Intelligence Test scores. However, the strongest relationship observed was between paternal nurturance (seeking out the child in a positive manner, asking information of the child, meeting the child's needs, etc.) and the intelligence test measures. On the other hand, paternal restrictiveness (demands for obedience, etc.) was negatively correlated with level of intellectual functioning. The quality of the father's behavior, particularly paternal nurturance, appeared to be more important than did the total number of father-son interactions.

In a subsequent study Radin (1973) reported evidence indicating that the amount of paternal nurturance at the time of the initial study was also positively related to the boys' intellectual functioning one year later. In addition, a questionnaire measure of degree of paternal involvement in direct teaching activities (e.g., teaching the boy to count and read) at the time of the initial study was positively associated with the boys' intellectual functioning both at that time and one year later.

Radin (1972, 1973) also found some interesting social class differences. For the middle-class subsample, the relationship between paternal nurturance and intellectual functioning was much more clear-cut. Middle-class fathers were found to interact more with their children and to be more nurturant than lower-class fathers. These findings are consistent with those of Davis and Havighurst (1946), who reported that middle-class fathers spent more time with their children in activities, such as taking walks as well as in educational functions, than did those from the lower class. Boys with nurturant fathers seem to become motivated to imitate their fathers' instrumental behaviors, cognitive skills, and problem-solving abilities.

Individual Differences

Of course, there is more than one path to high level cognitive functioning and some children develop specific areas of intellectual competence even though they are paternally deprived, sometimes as a by-product of coping with a frustrating environment. Also, correlational data do not prove that a positive father-son relationship directly facilitates the boys' intellectual functioning. A father may be much more available, accepting, and nurturant to a son who is bright and performs well in school. On the other hand, disappointment with the son's abilities may lead the father to reject him and/or the son's performance may further weaken an already flimsy father-son relationship. Individual differences in the child's constitutional predispositions and behavior can have much influence on the quality of interactions between father and child (Biller 1971a).

Fathers are reported to be much less tolerant of severely intellectually handicapped children than are mothers (Farber 1962). They seem to develop particularly negative attitudes towards retarded sons (Farber 1962; Tallman 1965). The father who highly values intellectual endeavors is especially likely to reject a retarded child (Downey 1963). Paternal deprivation lessens the probability that the retarded child will maximize his intellectual potential or have adequate sex-role development (Biller 1971a; Biller and Borstelmann 1965).

In addition to being the antecedents of some forms of mental retardation, constitutional predispositions and genetic factors may be related to other types of influences affecting the father-child relationship. Father and son can manifest cognitive abilities in the same area primarily as a function of a similar genetic inheritance. Poffenberger and Norton (1959) found that the attitudes of fathers' and of their college freshman sons toward mathematics were similar, yet were not related to closeness of father-son relationship. These investigators speculated that genetic factors are involved in degree of success in mathematics and can predispose similar father-son attitudes toward mathematics. However, Hill's (1967) findings suggest that more than genetic factors are involved in the child's attitude toward mathematics. In studying the relationship between paternal expectations and upper-middle-class seventh-grade boys' attitudes towards mathematics, Hill found that positive attitudes toward mathematics were more common among boys whose fathers viewed mathematics as a masculine endeavor and expected their sons to behave in a masculine manner.

Paternal Availability

Much of the evidence concerning the father's importance in cognitive development has come indirectly from studies in which father-absent and father-present children have been compared. The first investigator to present data suggesting an intellectual disadvantage among father-absent children was Sutherland (1930). In a rather ambitious study involving Scottish children, he discovered that those who were father absent scored significantly lower than did those who were father present. Unfortunately, specific analyses concerning such variables as length of father absence, sex of child, and socioeconomic status are not included in this report. A number of more recent and better controlled studies are also generally consistent with the supposition that father-absent children, at least those from lower-class backgrounds, are less likely to function well on intelligence and aptitude tests than are father-present children (e.g., Blanchard and Biller 1971; Deutsch and Brown 1964; Lessing, Zagorin, and Nelson 1970; Santrock 1972).

Maxwell (1961) reported some evidence indicating that father absence after the age of five negatively influences children's functioning on certain cognitive tasks. He analyzed the Wechsler Intelligence Test scores of a large group of 8-to-13-year-old children who had been referred to a British psychiatric clinic. He found that children whose fathers had been absent since the children were five performed below the norms for their age on a number of subtests. Children who had become father absent after the age of five had lower scores on tasks tapping social knowledge, perception of details, and verbal skills. Father absence since the age of five was the only family background variable which was consistently related to subtest scores; it seems surprising that there were no findings related to father absence before the age of five.

Sutton-Smith, Rosenberg, and Landy (1968) explored the relationship between father absence and college sophomores' aptitude test scores (American College Entrance Examination). These investigators defined father absence as an absence of the father from the home for at least two consecutive years. Compared to father-present students, those who were father absent performed at a lower level in terms of verbal, language, and total aptitude test scores. Although father absence appeared to affect both males and females, it seemed to have more influence on males. Some interesting variations in the effects of father absence as a function of sex of subject and sex of sibling are also reported; for example, in two-child father-absent families, boys with brothers appeared to be less deficient in academic aptitude than did boys with sisters. On the other hand, the father-present girl who was an only child seemed to be at a particular advantage in terms of her aptitude test scores.

In a related investigation, Landy, Rosenberg, and Sutton-Smith (1969) found that father absence had a particularly disruptive effect on the quantitative aptitudes of college females. Total father absence before the age of ten was highly associated with a deficit in quantitative aptitude. Their findings also suggested that father absence during the age period of three to seven may have an especially negative effect on academic aptitude.

Lessing, Zagorin, and Nelson (1970) conducted one of the most extensive investigations concerning father absence and cognitive functioning. They studied a group of nearly 500 children (ages 9 to 15) who had been seen at a child guidance clinic and explored the relationship between father absence and functioning on the Wechsler Intelligence Test for Children. They defined father absence as separation from the father for two or more years, not necessarily for a consecutive period of time.

Father absence, for both boys and girls, was associated with relatively low ability in perceptual-motor and manipulative-spatial tasks (Block Design and Object Assembly). Father-absent boys also scored lower than did father-present boys on the arithmetic subtest. In terms of our society's standards, such tasks are often considered to require typically male aptitudes. In a study with black elementary school boys, Cortés and Fleming (1968) also reported an association between father absence and poor mathematical functioning.

The results of the Lessing, Zagorin, and Nelson investigation suggest some rather complex interactions between father absence and social class. Among working class children, those who were father absent performed at a generally lower level than did those who were father present. They were less able in their verbal functioning as well as on perceptual-motor and manipulative-spatial tasks. In comparison, middle-class children did not appear to be as handicapped by father absence. They earned lower performance scores (particularly in Block Design and Object Assembly), but they actually scored higher in verbal intelligence than did father-present children.

Lessing, Zagorin, and Nelson also found that previously father-absent children who had a father-surrogate in their home (e.g., a stepfather) did not have intelligence test scores that were significantly different from father-present children. (In general, children with no father figure in the home accounted for most of the differences between father-absent and father-present children.) These findings can be interpreted in terms of a stepfather presenting a masculine model and/or increasing stability in the home.

The Lessing, Zagorin, and Nelson study is very interesting and impressive. In many ways it is a vast improvement over earlier research in which there was an attempt to link father absence and intellectual deficits. For example, there is more detail in the analysis of sex differences, social class, and specific areas of intellectual functioning. In general, the investigators show awareness of potential variables that may interact with father absence. Nevertheless, a number of serious questions can be raised in regard to the methodology of the research. The investigation can be criticized because it is based solely on findings from a clinic population. Of even more direct relevance, the study has a weakness similar to almost all of its predecessors in that the variables of father absence and father presence are not clearly enough defined. Two years of not necessarily consecutive separation from the father was used as the criterion for father absence. An obvious question is whether age at onset of father absence is related to intellectual functioning. There is also no consideration as to the amount of availability of father-present fathers or the quality of father-child interactions within the intact home. Similar inadequacies may account for the lack of clear-cut findings concerning father absence and academic functioning in some studies (e.g., Coleman et al. 1966; Engemoen 1966; Herzog and Sudia 1970).

Early Paternal Deprivation

Blanchard and I attempted to specify different levels of father availability and to ascertain their relationship to the academic functioning of third-grade boys (Blanchard and Biller 1971). We examined both the timing of father absence and the degree of father-son interaction in the father-present home. The boys were of average intelligence and were from working class and lower-middle-class backgrounds. Four groups of boys were studied; early father-absent (beginning before age three), late father-absent (beginning after age five), low father-present (less than six hours per week), and high father-present (more than two hours per day). To control for variables (other than father availability) which might affect academic performance, there was individual subject matching so that each boy in the early father-absent group was matched with a boy from each of the other three groups in terms of essentially identical characteristics of age, IQ, socioeconomic status, and presence or absence of male siblings.

Academic performance was assessed by means of Stanford Achievement Test scores and classroom grades. (The teachers did not have the children's achievement test scores available to them until after final classroom grades had been assigned.) The high father-present group was very superior to the other three groups. With respect to both grades and achievement test scores, the early father-absent boys were generally underachievers, the late father-absent boys and low father-present boys usually functioned somewhat below grade level, and the high father-present group performed above grade level.

The early father-absent boys were consistently handicapped in their academic performance. They scored significantly lower on every achievement test index as well as in their grades. The early father-absent group functioned below grade level in both language and mathematical skills. When compared to the high father-present group, the early father-absent group appeared to be quite inferior in skills relating to reading comprehension. In a study with elementary school boys, Dyl and I also found early father absence to be associated with deficits in reading comprehension (Dyl and Biller 1973).

Santrock (1972) reported additional evidence which indicated that early father absence can have a very significant debilitating effect on cognitive functioning. Among lower-class junior high and high school children, those who became father absent before the age of five, particularly before the age of two, generally scored significantly lower on measures of IQ (Otis Quick Test) and achievement (Stanford Achievement Test) that had been administered when they were in the third and sixth grades than did those from intact homes. The most detrimental effects occurred when father absence was due to divorce, desertion, or separation, rather than to death. The findings of this study also provided some support for the positive remedial effects of a stepfather for boys, especially when the stepfather joined the family before the child was five years of age.

At this point, it is relevant to again emphasize that there is much evidence indicating that early father absence can have a very profound effect on the boy's personality development. The early father-absent boy, especially if he is from a lower-class background, often enters school with much uncertainty about himself and his ability to succeed. On the other hand, evidence reviewed in Chapter 3, relating to factors influencing the infant's attachment to his father, suggests ways in which the father may positively influence his child's early cognitive and personality development. Fathers, when they are involved, are likely to encourage the infant's efforts to explore his environment and develop his physical and intellectual abilities. The child with a strong attachment to both his mother and father may be particularly secure in dealing with new learning experiences.

Boys who have consistently experienced high paternal availability and involvement are much more likely to actualize their cognitive potential. Highly available fathers seem to afford their sons models of perseverance and achievement motivation. The father can provide his son a model of a male functioning successfully outside of the home atmosphere. Frequent opportunity to observe and imitate his father can facilitate the development of the boy's overall instrumental competence and problem-solving skill. But a highly competent father would not seem to facilitate his son's cognitive development if he were not consistently accessible or if the father-son relationship were negative in quality (e.g., the father generally critical and frustrating in his relationship with his son).

When the father has intellectual interests, a positive father-child relationship can greatly stimulate the child's academic achievement. If the father's activity involves reading, writing, or mathematics, it is likely that the child will develop skills in these areas. Frequent observation of a father who enjoys intellectual activities does much to further a child's cognitive development. However, if the father does not enjoy such activities, the child is less likely to excel in school.

Creativity

There may be more controversy concerning the definition and measurement of creativity than any other psychological concept. There are certainly many different types of creativity and creativity can occur in any field of human endeavor.

A major problem is deciding how to measure creativity (Wallach and Kogan 1965). Is creativity just a particular dimension of intelligence, an ability to generate new ideas, or must it be accompanied by some concrete act that has, at least after a certain amount of time, been judged to be creative by others? Further discussion of the meaning of creativity is beyond the scope of this book, but this brief introduction is important before describing available data concerning fathering and creativity.

Fathers of creative individuals have generally been found to be very well-educated and to have high status occupations (Chambers 1964; Dauw 1966). Among parents of creative individuals, there seems to be an inordinate representation of men in professional and scientific fields (Dauw 1966; Helson 1971). Of particular interest is the fact that these fathers are often pictured as being very autonomous and independent in their work (Weisberg and Springer 1961). Even though fathers of creative individuals are well-educated and are in prestigious occupations, many put their independence ahead of financial security (Helson 1971). Fathers may play a critical role in the development of creativity by being models of autonomy and independence.

Weisberg and Springer (1961) administered a wide range of creativity tasks to fourth graders with high scholastic aptitude test scores. The investigators found that children who did very well on creativity tasks (including those tasks relating to originality, ideational fluency, hypothesis development and flexibility of thought) were likely to come from homes where the parents were expressive, undominating, and gave the child much freedom. The fathers of the creative children generally had occupations which allowed them much autonomy.

Cross (1966) found that adolescent males who demonstrated a high level of flexibility and imaginativeness in completing sentences had fathers who were especially warm and accepting and listened to their sons rather than imposing their own opinions. Datta and Parloff (1967) reported that young scientists generally viewed their parents as accepting, moderately affectionate, and encouraging intellectual independence. However, those who were particularly creative were more likely to perceive both their mothers and fathers as having allowed them total freedom as children.

In a study by Helson (1967), creative college women frequently described their fathers as having high principles and integrity. Fathers of the creative women described themselves in ways which suggested that they were more controlled, rational, logical and calmer than fathers of less creative women. There was also evidence that high paternal expectations and values were related to competition between the creative women and their brothers.

There is more than one path towards creativity. Some individuals develop creative talents in an atmosphere facilitating self-actualization while others seem to have their creativity heightened as a result of dealing with their psychological conflicts (Biller, Singer, and Fullerton 1969). In a family background analysis, Albert (1969) discovered a high rate of father loss during childhood among male geniuses. He speculated that the early loss of the father, though causing certain conflicts, may permit the gifted individual to more freely explore his environment and develop more original and creative types of behavior. The intellectual development of some male geniuses has been stimulated by the formation of an intense relationship with an intellectually-oriented mother; the childhood of Leonardo da Vinci seems to be an example (Freud 1947).

There are studies which suggest that creative children come from homes where there is much conflict and dissension. In a study of preschool children, Dreyer and Wells (1966) found that parents of high-creative children had more role tension and were less in agreement in terms of domestic values than were parents of low-creative children. Long, Henderson, and Ziller (1967) reported that elementary school children who manifested creativity in giving novel problem solutions were defiant toward their fathers. Consistent defiance toward the father is certainly a sign of parent-child conflict, but may also be related to the finding reported in other studies that parents of creative children are likely to give them a very high level of autonomy. Of course, both the level of parent-child conflict, and the degree of the child's autonomy, may be very much linked with the child's constitutionally-based precocity.

Long, Henderson, and Ziller also found that the creative children in their study tended to model themselves less after the same sex parent than did non-creative children. There are other data indicating that fathers may be particularly significant in fostering creativity for girls and mothers for sons (Anastasi and Schaefer 1969). Many investigators have presented evidence that creative individuals are likely to have both positive masculine and positive feminine characteristics and to have a broad range of interests (Biller, Singer, and Fullerton 1969).

Cognitive Styles

There is a wealth of evidence documenting sex differences in intellectual functioning (Garai and Scheinfeld 1968; Maccoby 1966). Analytical, mathematical, spatial, and mechanical skills are generally more developed in males, whereas females usually perform at a higher level on most types of tasks requiring verbal fluency, language usage, and perception of details, including reading. The father may greatly influence the acquisition of certain sex-typed intellectual skills in his children (Biller 1971a).

Carlsmith (1964) made an interesting discovery concerning the relationship between father absence and differential intellectual abilities. She examined the College Board Aptitude Test scores of middle-class and upper-middle-class high school males who had experienced early father absence because of their fathers' military service during World War II. Boys who were father absent in early childhood were more likely to have a feminine patterning of aptitude test scores. Compared to the typical male pattern of math score higher than verbal score, males who had experienced early separation from their fathers more frequently had a higher verbal score than math score. She found that the earlier the onset of father absence and the longer the father absence, the more likely was the male to have a higher verbal than math score. The effect was strongest for students whose fathers were absent at birth and/or were away for over 30 months. Higher verbal than math functioning is the usual pattern among females, and Carlsmith speculated that it reflects a feminine-global style of cognitive functioning. Results from other studies have also indicated a relationship between father absence and a feminine patterning of aptitude test scores among males (e.g., Altus 1958; Maccoby and Rau 1962; Nelsen and Maccoby 1966).

A study with adolescent boys by Barclay and Cusumano (1967) supports the supposition that difficulties in analytical functioning are often related to father absence. Using Witkin's rod and frame procedure, Barclay and Cusumano found that father-absent males were more field dependent than those who were father present. Wohlford and Liberman (1970) reported that father separation (after the age of six) was related to field dependency among elementary school children from an urban section of Miami. Their procedure involved an embedded figures test. Field dependent individuals have difficulties in ignoring irrelevant environmental cues in the analysis of certain types of problems (Witkin et al. 1962).

Louden (1973), in a very extensive study with college students, presented evidence indicating that both males and females who had been father absent during childhood were more field dependent than were those who were father present. Father absence was defined as the continuous absence of the father or father-surrogate for at least three years during one of three age periods (0 to 5 years, 6 to 12 years, or 13 to 18 years). Field dependence-independence was measured by a group-administered embedded figures procedure. Father absence during each age period was associated with greater field dependence than was father presence, but, as in Wohlford and Liberman's research, father absence during the 6 to 12 year age period seemed to be most linked with field-dependent behavior. Louden argued that this period is especially important for the development of an ability to adapt to changing environments. Such data suggest that the father may serve different functions at different stages in the child's development.

There is evidence that a close father-son relationship is conducive to the development of analytical thinking and field independence. Bieri (1960) found that boys who perceived themselves as more similar to their fathers and as having a close relationship with their fathers did better on an embedded figures test than did boys who were not close to their fathers. Dyk and Witkin (1965) reported that field-independent boys were more likely to perceive warm father-son relationships in a projective story task (TAT) than were field dependent boys. Dyk and Witkin also described the results of a study by Seder (1957). Fathers of field-independent boys participated more actively with their sons than did fathers of field dependent boys. Father-son participation in sports, outings, and trips was more frequent among the field independent boys. In contrast, fathers of field-dependent boys spent relatively little time with their sons. Boys who have neglecting or passive fathers appear to be more likely to adopt a global rather than an analytical conceptual style (Witkin 1960).

Lynn (1969) hypothesized that there is a curvilinear relationship between paternal closeness and field independence. Low paternal availability, Lynn assumed, makes the boy very dependent on his mother. He speculated that moderate father availability is most conducive for the development of field independence. According to Lynn, when the father is moderately available, the boy has an outline of the masculine role but has to interact actively with his environment to develop his masculinity. However, if the father is highly available to his son, Lynn argued, then the task of becoming masculine will be very easy for the boy, and he will not develop an analytical, independent stance in interacting with his environment.

Lynn reasoned that research with Eskimo children supports his contention that high father availability actually leads to field dependence among boys. Eskimo boys spend a great deal of time with their fathers, and they seem from an early age to engage in much imitation of the father. Nevertheless, among Eskimo children, boys are not more field independent than girls (Berry 1966; MacArthur 1967). Lynn also cited a study by Sherman and Smith (1967) in which orphans who received full-time care from male counselors were less field independent than males from normal families.

Availability of a father or father-surrogate per se is not sufficient to promote independent and analytical behavior. Some data indicate that many fathers who are constantly home play rather unassertive roles in their families (Biller 1968a). Lynn noted that the male caretakers of the orphan boys in the Sherman and Smith (1967) study performed some typically mothering functions. Unless the father's or the father-surrogate's behavior has a clear analytical-independent component, it will not directly facilitate the boy's problem-solving ability. Lynn's analysis is interesting, but available data suggest a generally positive relationship between the adequacy of the boy's analytical ability and the amount of his interaction with a salient, competent father.

It should again be emphasized that a boy can imitate a highly available and nurturant but nonanalytical father. Corah (1965) assessed the congruence between the cognitive styles of parents and their elementary school children. His results suggested that field-dependent fathers generally have field-dependent sons and field-independent fathers generally have field-independent sons.

Mediating Factors

In this section several important variables which may mediate the influence of the father-child relationship on cognitive and academic functioning are discussed. They include persistence and motivation, sex differences, sociocultural background, and the mother-child relationship.

Persistence and Motivation

In addition to certain intellectual skills, other abilities that are important in academic success also appear to be hampered by paternal deprivation. There is evidence that paternally deprived children have difficulty in controlling their impulses. Such difficulties seem to be particularly frequent among children whose fathers are continually absent. Aggressive outbursts and delinquent behavior are reported to be more common among father-absent children, especially those from lower-class backgrounds, than among father-present children. Academic success requires the capacity to concentrate, delay gratification, and plan ahead. These abilities are less likely to be well-developed among paternally deprived children than among well-fathered children (e.g., Biller 1971a; Biller and Davids 1973).

Paternally deprived boys frequently lack a secure masculine self-concept and have difficulties in peer relationships. Such boys are usually much more interested in getting the attention of their peers than in concentrating on schoolwork. Anxiety also seems to be more intense among paternally deprived children than among well-fathered children. Lower-class boys who are paternally deprived and insecure in their underlying sex role orientations, even though they may be quite masculine in other facets of their behavior, are often very anxious and defensive about their intellectual abilities (Biller 1971a).

As stressed in Chapter 5, the quality and quantity of the father-child interactions can influence the child's overall adjustment, responsibility, and motivation for success. Bronfenbrenner (1961) found a positive association between the amount of time fathers spent with their adolescent sons and the degree of leadership and responsibility that the boys displayed in school. Both the quality and quantity of father-son interactions must be taken into account. For example, Reuter and I found that college males who perceived their fathers as both nurturant and available had very adequate scores on personality adjustment measures, whereas those who perceived their fathers as highly available but low in nurturance, or as high in nurturance and low in availability, had very inadequate scores on personality adjustment measures (Reuter and Biller 1973).

Mussen et al. (1963) reported that instrumental achievement striving was more frequent among adolescent males who had warm and close relationships with their fathers than among those who had poor relationships with their fathers. Cervantes' (1965) results revealed an association between the father's inadequacy and the child's not completing high school. Results from other studies have suggested that males who have been father absent during childhood have both lower achievement motivation and less career success than do those who have been father present (McClelland 1961; Terman and Oden 1946; Veroff et al. 1960).

Independence, competence, and achievement motivation can be much stimulated by an involved father. Rosen and D'Andrade (1959) found a high level of paternal encouragement for independence and self-reliance among nine-to-eleven-year-old boys with strong achievement strivings. These investigators assessed achievement motivation in terms of stories the boys told to pictures and then observed the boys perform some difficult tasks in the presence of their parents at home. They found that the parents of boys with high achievement motivation encouraged their independence. The fathers were particularly supportive of their high achievement-motivated sons' ability to work in a self-reliant manner. They gave hints rather than telling them all the details of mastering the tasks, and did not interfere with their sons' decisions. These fathers appeared to be competent men who felt comfortable enough to allow their sons the opportunity to succeed by themselves. Cross and Allen (1969) found that among college men, those who were high academic achievers described their fathers as more accepting and slightly less controlling than did those who were low academic achievers.

The father can facilitate his child's independence and achievement by giving him a model of effective behavior and allowing him to make his own decisions. The quality of the father-mother relationship is also very important. A man who is consistently dominated by his wife is not an effective model for his child. Several research projects have suggested that boys from maternally dominated families are likely to be overly dependent and unsuccessful in their academic performance (e.g., Devereux, Bronfenbrenner, and Suci 1962; Elder 1962; Smelser 1963).

The father who is involved in his family and is viewed as a salient family decisionmaker can do much to facilitate his child's personality development and cognitive functioning. The father's self-confidence, encouragement, and involvement can be significant factors in the development of the child's academic and problem-solving skills. However, in addition to being a competent model, the father must allow his child to function in an independent and assertive manner. Paternal interference and pressure can hamper the child's ability to think flexibly and independently (Busse 1969; Rosen and D'Andrade 1959). Paternal domination as well as maternal domination can undermine the child's competency by denying him sufficient opportunity to solve his own problems. Some research has indicated that rigid paternal subordination of the mother and child by the father stifles the boy's achievement strivings (Strodtbeck 1958). Evidence reviewed in Chapter 5 also indicates that the quality of the mother-father relationship is an important factor in the child's academic and social success at school. For example, father-mother agreement with respect to childrearing practices and education seems related to the child's ability to develop his cognitive and interpersonal skills at school (Medinnus 1963a; van der Veen 1965; Wyer 1965b).

Many other studies have revealed that father-absent children have a high rate of behavior problems relating to school adjustment, both academic and interpersonal (e.g., Crescimbeni 1964; Hardy 1937; Holman 1953; Layman 1960; Palmer 1960; Risen 1939; Rouman 1956; Russell 1957). Unfortunately, methodological limitations make for difficulties in interpreting the findings of most studies linking father absence with maladjustment in school. For example, such studies have usually lacked analyses relating to the potential effects of such variables as age at onset and length of father absence, socioeconomic background, and sex of child (Biller 1971a).

Sex Differences

Most of the research concerning paternal influence and the child's personality development and cognitive functioning has focused on the father-son relationship. However, the quantity and quality of fathering can affect girls as well as boys, as is evident from data reviewed in Chapter 7. Although both boys and girls are influenced, current evidence suggests that paternal deprivation has a somewhat more negative effect on the cognitive functioning of boys (e.g., Lessing, Zagorin, and Nelson 1970; Santrock 1972; Sutton-Smith, Rosenberg, and Landy 1968).

Nevertheless, there is much evidence indicating that fathers can greatly stimulate their daughters' cognitive functioning and intellectual attainment. Plank and Plank (1954) discovered that outstanding female mathematicians were particularly attached to and identified with their fathers. Bieri (1960) also reported that high analytical ability in college women was associated with father identification. Crandall et al. (1964) found that elementary school girls who did well in reading and mathematics had fathers who consistently praised and rewarded their intellectual efforts. In Katkovsky, Crandall, and Good's (1967) study, six-to-twelve-year-old girls taking responsibility for their academic successes and failures was associated with paternal acceptance and praise. The type of model that the father represents to the girl can be very important as is suggested by Bing's (1963) findings of a positive association between the amount of reading fathers do at home and their daughter's verbal ability.

Data from a number of studies, when taken together, indicate that high paternal expectations in the context of a warm father-daughter relationship are conducive to the development of autonomy, independence, achievement, and creativity among girls (Crandall et al. 1964; Helson 1967; Honzik 1967; Lozoff 1974; Nakamura and Rogers 1971).

On the other hand, paternal rejection seems related to deficits in females' functioning in certain types of cognitive tasks (Heilbrun et al. 1967). Findings from a study by Hurley (1967) suggest that paternal hostility can be particularly detrimental to the girl's scholastic functioning. Other types of paternal behavior often interfere with the cognitive development of females. The highly nurturant father who reinforces the "feminine" stereotype of passivity, timidity, and dependency greatly inhibits his daughter's intellectual potential (Biller 1974b; Biller and Meredith 1974).

The degree and direction of sex differences associated with the influence of paternal deprivation probably varies with respect to which age periods and which components of cognitive functioning are considered. As with other issues relating to paternal influence, there is a need for much more research. But we do know that a warm relationship with a competent father is very significant in the personality development of girls as well as boys. Children who have positively involved fathers develop more adequate self-concepts and are more effective in their interpersonal and cognitive functioning than children who have been paternally deprived or inadequately fathered.

Sociocultural Variables

Paternal deprivation is often a major factor contributing to a disadvantaged environment (Bronfenbrenner 1967). Father absence appears to particularly hamper lower-class black children. Some investigators have reported that among lower-class black children, those who are father absent score considerably lower on intelligence and achievement tests than do those who are father present (e.g., Cortés and Fleming 1968; Deutsch 1960; Deutsch and Brown 1964; Mackie et al. 1967).

With respect to such findings, Kohlberg (1966) has suggested that the relatively immature cognitive development of the lower-class, father-absent child is the key factor associated with differences in the sex-role development of father-absent and father-present boys. Kohlberg proposed that sex role development is a dimension of the general process of cognitive development. He reasoned that if father-absent and father-present boys were matched in intelligence, differences in sex role development would not be found or would be very small. He cited the data of one of his students (C. Smith), which suggest that differences in sex role preference are considerably lessened when father-absent and father-present boys are matched in terms of intellectual level. Other research has indicated that there is a generally positive correlation between intelligence and appropriate sex role preferences among young children (Biller and Borstelmann 1965, 1967; Kohlberg and Zigler 1967).

However, there is no clear-cut linear relationship between intelligence and sex role preference. Some data suggest that intelligence, at least as measured by the usual verbal-oriented tests, may even be negatively correlated with masculinity of sex role preference among lower-class boys (Radin 1972). Also, as individuals gain wider experiences and education, there is usually a broadening of interests so that their preferences often become less sex-typed (Biller and Borstelmann 1967). To further complicate the situation, all aspects of sex role are not equally affected by rate of cognitive development (Biller 1968a; Biller and Borstelmann 1967).

General knowledge about social norms is related to age and experience. Father-absent children, at least after they reach elementary school, are not usually deficient with respect to their awareness of cultural values concerning sex typing (e.g., Biller 1968a; Thomes 1968). Nevertheless, such awareness does not appear to be sufficient to promote a positive and secure sex role development. For example, even when matched in terms of intelligence and social class, father-absent boys have been found to have less secure masculine sex role orientations than father-present boys (Biller 1969b, Biller and Dahm 1971). The sex role development process involves much more than the acquisition of social norms.

Socioeconomic and sociocultural variables have to be considered more carefully if there is to be a greater understanding of the effects of paternal deprivation on cognitive development. A problem in some research is the absence of specific comparisons among individuals from different social backgrounds. In particular, culturally disadvantaged groups and members of stable blue-collar occupations (e.g., teamsters, and skilled factory workers) are often both placed under the rubric of lower class. Such generalized groupings seem to obscure possible relationships (Biller 1971a). For example, the incidence of continual father absence is much higher among culturally disadvantaged families than among working-class families.

The classification becomes very difficult to untangle because a family that has been working class may be redefined as disadvantaged or lower class if it becomes father absent (Miller 1958). Herzog and Sudia (1970) pointed out that there have been inadequate controls for income level in research with disadvantaged children. They emphasized that differences in income level between father-absent and father-present families may be more closely related to intellectual disadvantagement than is father absence per se.

In any case, paternal deprivation seems to be associated with much more serious consequences among lower-class children than among middle-class children (Biller 1971a). Some research already discussed in this chapter has suggested that among father-absent children, those who are from working-class backgrounds are consistently more handicapped in their cognitive functioning than are those from middle-class backgrounds (Lessing, Zagorin, and Nelson 1970). A general depression in academic achievement associated with father absence has usually been found with working-class or lower-class children (Blanchard and Biller 1971; Santrock 1972).

On the other hand, middle-class, father-absent children often do well in situations requiring verbal skills. Carlsmith's (1964) middle- and upper-middle-class, father-absent group apparently was equal or superior to her father-present group in verbal aptitude, although inferior in mathematical aptitude. Lessing, Zagorin, and Nelson (1970) found that middle-class, father-absent children had higher verbal scores, although lower performance (e.g., perceptual-manipulative) scores than did father-present children. Dyl and I found that, although lower-class father-absent boys were particularly handicapped in their reading skills, middle-class father-absent boys functioned quite adequately in reading (Dyl and Biller 1973). Because academic achievement, particularly in elementary school, is so heavily dependent on verbal and reading ability, father-absent, middle-class children do not seem to be very handicapped.

Maternal Influence

The middle-class mother seems to strongly influence her father-absent son's intellectual development. In an interview study in a university town, Hilgard, Neuman, and Fisk (1960) found that men who lost their fathers during childhood tended to be highly successful in their academic pursuits despite, or maybe because of, a conspicuous, overdependence on their mothers. Clinical findings presented by Gregory (1965) also suggest that many upper-middle-class students who have been father absent do well in college. Evidence reviewed by Nelsen and Maccoby (1966) reveals that high verbal ability in boys is often associated with a close and restrictive mother-son relationship. Levy (1943) reported that middle-class maternally-overprotected boys did superior work in school, particularly in subjects requiring verbal facility. However, their performance in mathematics was not at such a high level, which seems consistent with Carlsmith's (1964) results.

Middle-class mothers are much more likely to place strong emphasis on academic success than are lower-class mothers (Kohn 1959). Some findings suggest that among lower-class mothers, those without husbands are preoccupied with day-to-day activities and less frequently think of future goals for themselves or for their children (Heckscher 1967; Parker and Kleiner 1956). Compared to the middle-class mother, the lower-class mother usually puts much less emphasis on long-term academic goals and is also generally a much less adequate model for coping with the demands of the middle-class school.

In homes in which the father is absent or relatively unavailable, the mother assumes a more primary role in terms of dispensing reinforcements and emphasizing certain values. A father-absent boy who is strongly identified with an intellectually-oriented mother may be at an advantage in many facets of school adjustment. He may find the transition from home to the typically feminine-oriented classroom quite comfortable. Such father-absent boys might be expected to do particularly well in tasks where verbal skills and conformity are rewarded.

Although they may stimulate the paternally deprived child's acquisition of verbal skills and his adaptation to the typical school environment, middle-class overprotecting mothers often inhibit the development of an active, problem-solving attitude toward the environment. A mother who is excessively overprotective and dominating may interfere with the development of the child's assertiveness and independence (Biller 1971b). As is discussed in Chapter 6, the psychological adjustment of the mother is a crucial factor; a mother who is emotionally disturbed and/or interpersonally handicapped can have a very negative effect on the father-absent child's self-concept and ability to relate to others. On the other hand, mothers who are self-accepting, have high ego strength, and are interpersonally mature can do much to facilitate positive personality development among their paternally deprived children (Biller 1971a, 1971b).

Variations in fathering can influence the child's cognitive development, but it must be emphasized that fathering is only one of many factors which have an impact on the child's intellectual functioning. Sociocultural, maternal, and peer group values are especially important. For example, among children in the lower class, paternal deprivation usually intensifies lack of exposure to experiences linking intellectual activities with masculine interests. Many boys, in their desperate attempts to view themselves as totally masculine, become excessively dependent on their peer group and perceive intellectual tasks as "feminine." The school setting which presents women as authority figures and makes strong demands for obedience and conformity is particularly antithetical to such boys' fervent desires to feel masculine.

The Feminized Classroom

In this section the emphasis is on the academic and interpersonal difficulties encountered by paternally deprived boys in elementary school. Much of the difficulty that many boys encounter in adjusting to the school atmosphere is related to the interaction of their inadequate fathering and the feminized classroom. Many boys enter school with intense motivation to behave in a masculine manner. However, as a result of paternal deprivation, they are very insecure in their basic sex role orientations. Their insecurity is exacerbated because of the omnipresence of female authority figures and a general atmosphere that reinforces behavior antithetical to their expectations of the masculine role. The emphasis is on conformity, neatness, and passivity. In addition, on a maturational level, the boys are often at a disadvantage in relation to girls, and this adds to their feelings of insecurity.

Reading Skills

The superiority of girls as compared to boys in terms of language development is well-documented (e.g., Garai and Scheinfeld 1968; Maccoby 1966). Both earlier maturation and more social reinforcement from the mother (at least in our society) seem to be involved. It is not surprising, given the positive relationship between reading and verbal development, that girls generally do better in reading than do boys. Much concern has been focused on the fact that boys are much more likely to have reading disabilities than are girls. Compared to girls, about four times as many boys are referred to reading clinics (Bentzen 1963; Kopel and Geerded 1933; Marzurkrewicz 1960).

Part of the sex difference in reading ability may be due to less visual maturity among boys (Anderson, Hughes, and Dixon 1962) as well as general verbal maturity of girls (Garai and Scheinfeld 1968). Constitutionally related sex differences stemming from genetic and prenatal factors may, to some extent, account for boys' more frequent problems in impulse control and related academic problems. The situation is very complicated, in that males may be more vulnerable to disadvantaged environments than are females. For example, some evidence suggests that more males than females are neurologically handicapped because of poor nutrition and/or lack of adequate medical assistance during the prenatal period (e.g., Bronfenbrenner 1967).

In terms of many reading criteria relating to motivation, as well as ability, girls seem to far exceed boys. Girls are more interested in reading at all ages and read more than boys (Anderson, Hughes, and Dixon 1962). Among elementary school children, girls attach more social prestige to reading and are more highly motivated to read well in class (Strang 1968). Girls begin to read earlier than boys. By the age of six, more than half of the girls are reading compared to less than 40 percent of the boys (Baker 1948). The sex differences observed in reading ability seem to be manifested throughout the elementary school years (Gates 1961).

Sex differences in reading are reflected in interest areas as well as in amount of time spent reading. Masculine material relating to adventure, exploration, science, technical matters, and sports is preferred by boys, whereas girls are more likely to prefer books concerning family life and romance (Anastasi 1958). A number of studies in the United States and Europe have suggested that with the exception of a strong interest in politics, boys have more circumscribed reading interests than do girls. Usually (as with their general preferences) boys' readings interests tend to be more sex-typed than do girls' (Garai and Scheinfeld 1968).

It is interesting to note that boys in kindergarten seem to learn to read as well as girls do when programmed techniques are used (McNeil 1964). Such techniques may be more consistent with masculine role demands for autonomy and independence. There is some evidence suggesting that boys who have clear-cut, masculine sex role preferences prior to first grade are more mature and develop better reading skills than do boys who have inconsistent sex role preferences (Anastasiow 1965).

In any case, girls do better when taught by teachers in small reading groups, which may be a reflection of their sensitivity to adults, particularly females. It should also be noted that girls are usually much in the majority among "high" reading groups and this factor, too, may work to discourage boys in developing their reading skills. There is evidence that suggests teacher expectations can influence the extent of sex differences in reading. It has been reported that boys with teachers who believe that there is no inherent sex difference in reading skills read better than boys with teachers who believe that girls are naturally more successful readers (Polardy, 1969).

Teacher Bias

Both boys and girls report that female teachers react less favorably to boys during reading instruction (Davis and Slobodian 1967; McNeil 1964). However, research involving ratings of teacher behavior during reading instruction has not confirmed the supposition that female teachers react in a more negative manner with boys than they do with girls (Brophy and Laosa 1971; Davis and Slobodian 1967).

Nevertheless, much evidence indicates that compared to girls, boys are at a general disadvantage in terms of the reactions of female teachers. Certainly, if boys feel that female teachers have negative attitudes toward them, their classroom performance will probably be hampered. Moreover, some studies have suggested that female teachers give girls better grades even when boys have objectively achieved a higher level of performance (Arnold 1968; Carter 1952; Hanson 1959). Boys receive more negative reactions and criticisms and less supportive feedback from their teachers than do girls (Davis and Slobodian 1967; Meyer and Thompson 1956; Lippitt and Gold 1958).

Fagot and Patterson's (1969) data suggest that female teachers direct most of their disapproval toward assertive and aggressive behaviors and toward activities that are usually labeled masculine. In their study of the interactions between female teachers and nursery school children, Fagot and Patterson found that teachers reinforced boys about six times as often as for "feminine" behaviors as they did for masculine behaviors. Boys as well as girls received more teacher reinforcement when they were engaged in quiet, sedentary-type activities, and appeared to be generally ignored and/or criticized for relatively mechanical or rough and tumble activities. Although such teacher reaction per se did not seem to feminize the boys, the fact that teachers reacted in such a nonreinforcing manner toward masculine behavior probably led many boys to the conclusion that boyish behavior and success in school do not go together. Another study with nursery school children suggested that female teachers initiate far fewer contacts with boys than with girls; they seem to make fewer requests for information and give less information to boys (Biber, Miller, and Dyer 1972).

Many boys spend much of their time involved in physically demanding sports activities and acquire considerable knowledge in the process. However, female teachers seldom have much interest in such endeavors, and this widens the gulf between teachers and masculine boys. Sports can also be a constructive outlet for aggressive and competitive feelings which may otherwise come out in a disruptive manner in the classroom. There is little opportunity in most elementary schools for intense physical activity, except for an occasional recess or gym period.

Female teachers often react negatively to assertive behavior in the classroom and seem to feel much more comfortable with girls, who are generally quieter, more obedient, and conforming. Boys perceive that teachers are much more positive in responding to girls and to "feminine" behavior than they are to boys and "masculine" behavior. Unfortunately, the type of "feminine" behavior reinforced in the classroom is often of a very negative quality, if self-actualization is used as a criterion. Timidity, passivity, dependency, obedience, and quietness are usually rewarded. The boy or girl who is independent, assertive, questioning, and challenging is typically at a great disadvantage. Even though girls generally seem to adapt more easily to the early school environment, such an atmosphere is not conducive to their optimal development. Girls need to learn how to be independent and assertive just as much as do boys.

Although female teachers may generally respond more favorably to girls, they also tend to promote restrictive, "feminine" stereotypes. Much of the elementary school reading material also depicts females in a narrow range of endeavors and often presents an image of female inferiority. Girls usually adapt more easily than boys to the feminized elementary school atmosphere, but they may suffer even more in terms of long-term effects on their intellectual development.

Sexton's (1969) essential thesis is that our educational system exerts a very feminizing influence on children and teachers. Sexton labels feminization as inducing very passive, conforming, uncreative types of behavior. According to her, masculine males are turned off by their experiences in the classroom and reject academically related intellectual endeavors. She argues that much of the reason for our high number of male problem children, of both the inhibited and the acting-out variety, is our school system. Women are given too large a role in our school system (and in childrearing) and too small a role in our other institutions. The growing tendency toward suburban living also seems to have increased the salience of a community of women and children with little exposure to competent male models.

Sexton presents extensive data that indicate that our traditional conceptions of masculinity are incompatible with success in school. Her findings suggest that the top scholars in school are all too often feminized boys. (Males who are conforming, polite, obedient, and neat are favored.) She believes that there is no basic incompatibility between a healthy masculinity and academic achievement, but that our present educational system works against such development. She is not arguing for a rigid adherence to masculine standards, but that males (and females) be liberated and be given more flexibility and freedom.

She found that boys with high masculine standards did much more poorly in school than did those with relatively feminine values. Similar to other investigators, she reported that girls generally achieved higher grades than did boys and that more boys were identified as severely, emotionally disturbed (e.g., being sent to see a psychiatrist). In most specific categories of problem behavior, over 70 percent of the children were boys. Almost one out of four boys was either a total failure or did barely passing work (a D or F student).

Sex Role and School Achievement

Many of Sexton's conclusions fit well with other data reported in this chapter. However, a major criticism of her research is that she did not put enough emphasis on how socioeconomic and sociocultural factors interact with sex role development and the educational process. For example, there is no control for socioeconomic status in her analysis of the relationship between sex role behavior and school success. Much of the relationship she finds between femininity and academic achievement seems to be due to the differences in values between working-class and middle-class individuals. It may be that, to some extent, middle-class individuals are generally more feminized (partly as a function of being more "educated") and less concerned with sex role distinctions than are working-class individuals, but is also true that there are social class differences in the definitions of what is appropriate sex role behavior. For example, middle-class adults have been found to stress intellectual competence in their definition of masculine behavior while working-class adults stress physical prowess (Biller 1966a). Sexton's sex role measures essentially assess degree of interest in sports, mechanical, and technical areas. What is needed is a definition of masculinity with no incompatibility among physical, mechanical, and intellectual abilities.

A related criticism of Sexton's and other researchers' work is that overgeneralizations about the relationship between masculinity and academic functioning are often made on the basis of very restricted measures of sex role. For example, many investigators have used measures of sex role preference which force the subject to choose between either a traditionally masculine or a traditionally feminine activity (e.g., being a mechanic or a librarian). On such procedures an individual cannot score both highly masculine and highly feminine; masculinity and femininity are conceived as polar opposites. There is ample evidence that, with increasing education, individuals become more and more interested in many cultural activities traditionally labeled as feminine (Biller and Borstelmann 1967; Kohlberg 1966). However, this does not mean that the highly educated male has to give up his masculine interests; a well-rounded person of either sex has both "masculine" and "feminine" interests. For example, many creative and productive people have a basic sex role security which helps them transcend rigid sex role stereotypes (Biller, Singer, and Fullerton 1969; Helson 1967; Maslow 1960).

There is also considerable evidence that sex role preference (masculinity-femininity of interests) is more subject to variation as a function of increasing experience than are either sex role orientation (masculinity-femininity of self-concept) or sex role adoption (masculinity-femininity of the individual's social and environmental interactions). Sex role preference measures seem more influenced by temporary life situation factors and are less meaningful representations of an individual's sex role functioning than are orientation or adoption measures. In any case, research attempting to relate sex role behavior to other facets of personality functioning should take into account different aspects and patterns of sex role (Biller 1971a, (Biller 1971a, 1972b).

A further criticism of Sexton's research is that it does not deal with the issue of varying academic performance as a function of grade level. Boys who perform the best in sixth grade are not necessarily the ones who do best in high school or college. Sexton seems to make the assumption of a consistent homogeneity in the sex role relatedness of school atmosphere and curriculum across grade level. Such an assumption is open to question (Kagan 1964). For example, many males do better in high school and/or college than they do in the earlier grades. This may be because the curriculum becomes more "masculinized." For these same reasons, females often have a more difficult time in the later stages of their education, particularly in college and graduate school. It is again important to emphasize that females as well as males are restricted in their cognitive development because of the rigidities and sex-role stereotypes associated with our educational process.

Stein's findings serve as an excellent illustration of the way in which sex typing can affect the child's motivation in relation to particular areas of school achievement (Stein 1971; Stein, Pohly, and Muellar 1969; Stein and Smithells 1969). In a particularly well-designed study, Stein and Smithells (1969) found that children perceived reading, artistic, and social skills as feminine, and mathematical, spatial, mechanical, and athletic skills as masculine. Such results are consistent with studies concerning sex differences in abilities (Garai and Scheinfeld 1968).

In the Stein and Smithells (1969) study, there was evidence that sex-typing of academic activities was stronger among older children. Sixth graders expressed higher attainment values and expectancies on tasks that they perceived as sex appropriate (Stein, Pohly, and Mueller 1969). Furthermore, the boys' achievement was clearly related to their expectations. The degree to which boys perceive tasks as sex appropriate influenced the extent of their involvement and achievement. Other evidence suggests that intellectual performance is higher for children when assessment is made in terms of problems that can be considered sex-appropriate (e.g., Epstein and Liverant 1963; Milton 1957). However, sex role preference measures have not been found to be related consistently to specific areas of cognitive functioning (e.g., Maccoby 1966; Stein 1971).

In a study with sixth- and ninth-grade children, Stein (1971) focused on attitudes and expectancies concerning mechanical, athletic, mathematical, reading, artistic, and social skills. Girls tended to rate all the areas as relatively more feminine than did the boys, particularly reading, artistic, and social skills. Both sexes gave athletic, mechanical, and mathematical skills predominantly masculine ratings, while they gave generally feminine ratings to reading, artistic, and social skills.

Stein's prediction that boys would value masculine areas as important, and girls feminine areas, was generally supported. The findings were most clear-cut with the ninth-grade children; mathematics was the only area in which the results were not as predicted. It is interesting to note that lower-class children of both sexes perceived reading as less important and had less expectancy of success than did middle-class children. Lower-class boys seemed to have a particularly negative attitude toward reading. There was also evidence that the more boys tended to perceive reading as feminine, the less likely they were to be motivated to read well. Unfortunately, individual differences were not examined separately in terms of social class. A particularly strong correlation between a view of reading as feminine and a lack of motivation in reading could be predicted for lower-class boys.

Male Teachers

Less than 15 percent of elementary school teachers are men, and the great majority of these teach in the fourth, fifth, and sixth grades. Statistics indicate that less than 2 percent of teachers at third grade or below are men (Lee 1973). The percentage of men teaching in nursery school, kindergarten, and in day care centers is even lower. However, some data suggest that among elementary school teachers, men are more emotionally mature and flexible in the classroom than are women (Sexton 1969). In a national sample, Ryans (1960) reported more emotional stability, permissiveness, and child-centeredness among male teachers. Arnold's (1968) findings indicated that compared to female teachers, male teachers are more objective and unbiased in assigning grades to children of both sexes. Such data could support the notion that male teachers may generally be better models for both boys and girls than are female teachers.

Some studies suggest that boys do better in reading when they have male teachers. In contrast to the sex differences reported in the United States, Preston (1962) found that among fourth and sixth graders, German boys had significantly better reading scores than did German girls. In addition, severe reading retardation was significantly less common among German boys than among German girls. Even at the elementary level, teachers in Germany are usually males. The high frequency of male teachers may be a factor in the seemingly better reading performance of German boys. It may also be very difficult for German girls to optimize their academic skills since intellectual endeavors such as reading are labeled as masculine within their culture (Anderson and Ritscher 1969).

Other evidence which suggests the facilitating influence that male teachers may have on boys comes from a study with Japanese children cited by Kagan (1969). In contrast to the high rates of reading difficulties reported for American boys, there was no differential sex ratio in reading difficulties found for children living in a community of Hokkaido, a Japanese island where about 60 percent of the teachers in the first and second grades were males.

Cascario (1971) found a tendency for male-taught children to earn higher reading achievement scores than female-taught children. Children taught by males perceived teachers as reacting more positively to boys than to girls. Such data are, of course, in direct contrast to findings among children taught by female teachers. Hopefully, we can work toward a situation where all children feel that they are valued and accepted by their teachers, regardless of their sex or of the teacher's sex. Some of Cascario's data suggest that father-absent children score higher in reading achievement when taught by a teacher of the same sex. Father-absent boys may be particularly responsive to an adult male model. Cortés and Fleming (1968) found that father-absent, fourth-grade boys expressed greater preference for male teachers than did father-present boys.

In addition to investigations relating to reading achievement, a number of researchers have attempted to explore the effects of male teachers on various other facets of the child's academic adjustment. Unfortunately, the majority of these studies have particularly serious methodological limitations. Kyselka (1966) studied the performance of four male high school seniors in a nursery school classroom. These "male teachers" were in the classroom for 45 minutes per day for 15 weeks. The high school seniors reported much confusion as to their role in the classroom and emphasized their concern about discipline, and their own ability to deal with young children. It must be emphasized that the type of "male teachers" in this study did not have the level of competence and experience that is typical of the male elementary school teacher.

Triplett (1968) studied kindergarten and first-grade children who were in either all-male classrooms taught by male teachers or in coeducational classes taught by female teachers. Both groups were similar in academic achievement. However, in terms of paper and pencil tests, boys in the all-male sections had more positive self-esteem and attitudes toward school and teachers. Nevertheless, a major problem in interpreting the results of this study is the impossibility of separating out the effects of the male teacher from the effects of the all-male peer group.

McFarland (1969) assigned first-grade children to one of two classes. In one class there was a supervising female teacher with 26 male college juniors who were sequentially scheduled over the school year. In the other class there was a female teacher and a female supervisor. Unfortunately, in this study no male teacher was present throughout the school year. One also has to question the perceived status of younger males in such a transient teaching position. In general, little difference was found between the two classes. The female-taught class did better in arithmetic, but both classes performed similarly in other areas. McFarland did present observations that some children, particularly boys, did well when they had a close and positive relationship with a male teacher, but again the nature of this study makes any conclusions very tenuous.

Brophy and Laosa (1971) compared the behavior of children in a kindergarten conducted by a woman with the behavior of children in a kindergarten conducted by a man and a woman (husband and wife). In general, few differences were observed. The investigators found no consistent relationships between measures of the children's sex typing as a function of whether they were taught by the male teacher. However, children of both sexes who were in the kindergarten with the male teacher performed better on tasks related to spatial skills, and boys in this kindergarten seemed to enjoy a relatively higher peer status. The care with which Brophy and Laosa developed and selected measures of sex typing, the amount of data they collected, and the depth to which they analyzed their results are very impressive. Nevertheless, the fact that their investigation was limited to two comparison groups seems to greatly restrict the generality of their findings.

Lee and Wolinsky (1973) did an excellent observational study focusing on the differential behavior of male and female teachers in classrooms with young children. They studied teachers in eighteen classes ranging from preschool through second grade. All the classes had two teachers, and in twelve of the classes responsibilities were shared by a male and female teacher. Both male and female teachers were more disapproving of boys than of girls but male teachers were generally more approving of boys than were female teachers. Male teachers gave boys much more positive reinforcement than did female teachers. Male teachers seemed to be unbiased in their evaluation of boys, but rather nonevaluative toward girls.

Compared to female teachers, male teachers were more likely to allow the children freedom in choosing activities and in forming their own groups. Male teachers were more responsive to the children's activities, whereas female teachers were more likely to initiate groupings and activities. But male teachers seemed particularly sex-biased in their leadership assignments. They gave boys leadership assignments about four times as often as girls. In contrast, female teachers gave leadership assignments approximately twice as often to girls as to boys. Male teachers were more responsive to male activities in contrast to female teachers, who were most responsive to non-sex-typed activities. The latter finding is in contrast to other data which suggest that female teachers are particularly responsive to feminine activities (e.g., Fagot and Patterson 1969).

Boys clearly preferred male teachers, whereas there was no clear-cut preference regarding sex of teacher among girls. However, girls as well as boys generally perceived that their male teachers liked them better than did their female teachers. The children attributed no sex preference to male teachers, but viewed their female teachers as preferring girls. On the other hand, when asked to name their teachers' favorite child, boys reported that male teachers strongly preferred boys, but did not attribute a sex preference to their female teachers. Girls generally named girls as both male and female teachers' favorite children. When these findings are combined with the observations on teacher behavior, they lend support to the positive student morale value of male teachers, especially for boys. This study is interesting in suggesting the possible advantages of male-female team teaching. However, as with the Brophy and Laosa (1971) study, one cannot draw any conclusions with respect to the advantages or disadvantages of classrooms with *only* male teachers.

Perhaps more important, there has been no systematic investigation of how adequate the teachers in these studies were in terms of their own sex role behavior and what types of personality characteristics they possessed. The studies would have been much improved if several different classes could have been compared; some having a male teacher, some having a female teacher, and some having both a male and a female teacher. In addition, careful personality assessment of the teachers might reveal important interactions among sex of teacher, personality of teacher, sex of child, age of child, and personality of child. For example, assertive male teachers may have the greatest effect on paternally deprived boys with aggressive characteristics but have little effect on well-fathered, moderately aggressive girls.

Previous studies are also limited in that the children studied are from primarily middle- and upper-middle-class backgrounds. The situation gets even more complicated when we consider the importance of sociocultural variables. For example, as emphasized earlier in this chapter, among boys who are father absent, those who come from lower-class backgrounds are particularly likely to perform inadequately on academic tasks. A male teacher, other things being equal, may have a greater effect on lower-class children than on middle-class children. These are obviously simplified examples, but they again point out the need for more research. The systematic evaluation of the effects of sex of teacher on the cognitive functioning and general academic adjustment of children is a little explored but very provocative and promising area of research.

Summary

The quality of the father-child relationship is very important in the cognitive development and academic achievement of children. Inadequate fathering is frequent in the backgrounds of academic underachievers and positive paternal involvement facilitates girls' as well as boys' cognitive development. The early father-child relationship appears to have much impact on the child's ability to fully develop his cognitive potential and motivational and personality characteristics which are associated with high level academic and occupational success. The father seems to have a particularly significant role in the development of persistence, achievement motivation, and assertive, analytical problem-solving behavior.

Father absence has a more negative effect on the lower-class boy's cognitive and academic functioning than it does on the middle-class boy's. The mother-child relationship is an important factor mediating the effects of sociocultural background on the paternally deprived child. Middle-class mothers are more often intellectually and academically oriented than are lower-class mothers. Paternally deprived lower-class boys are especially likely to have difficulty adjusting to the "feminized" elementary school classroom. The development of reading skills often seems to be a focal point of teacher-student conflicts.

Although boys generally have more problems in adjusting to the demands of the female teacher, girls suffer at least as much from the rigidity of expectations for passive and conforming behavior and sex role stereotypes concerning various areas of intellectual endeavor. Competent male teachers appear to offer some advantages, especially in providing a more meaningful academic experience for the paternally deprived child.

Paternal Deprivation: Some Potential Solutions

In dealing with the possible causes and effects of paternal deprivation in this book, a vast array of research has been cited and a great many interpretations and speculations have been put forth. Certain practical implications follow from the related generalizations that paternal deprivation often leads to problems in personality development, and that effective fathering can positively influence many facets of psychological functioning. This final chapter is a brief attempt to look at what is being done, or could be done, to counteract and prevent paternal deprivation. The first section of this chapter concerns some current and potential modes of treating and preventing problems associated with paternal deprivation. A number of guidelines for the effective fathering of the young child are outlined in the second section of this chapter.

Therapy and Prevention

Since paternally deprived individuals are overrepresented among individuals with psychological problems, it is not surprising that they are found in abundance in the case reports of psychotherapists. Despite the lack of controlled research, there are many illuminating descriptions of how psychotherapists have attempted to help father-absent or inadequately fathered children (e.g., Forrest 1966, 1967; Green 1974; Meerloo 1956; Neubauer 1960; Stoller 1968; Wylie and Delgado 1959).

Green (1974) has presented some particularly helpful therapeutic suggestions that are relevant for working with paternally deprived children who have severe sex role conflicts. He gives a detailed description of a promising multifaceted therapy program which includes individual and group sessions for mothers and fathers as well as for children. His depth interview protocols are especially impressive and he demonstrates a creative integration of a number of different methods for increasing the incentive value of masculine behavior and male models for extremely feminine boys.

Unfortunately, the emphasis on the mother-child relationship in most child psychotherapy has usually obscured the father's role. Rubenstein and Levitt (1957) emphasized that the father should be included in treatment considerations, but the father is often ignored or just peripherally involved. Even in the early stages of contacting an agency, the father's participation in getting help for his child seems very significant. Using standardized paper and pencil techniques,

L'Abate (1960) assessed the level of emotional disturbance of mothers and children when they initially made contact with a child guidance clinic. He compared mothers and children who were accompanied by fathers with those who came without fathers. The mothers and children of families in which the father did not come to the clinic were found to be more emotionally disturbed.

Family Therapy

Fathers should be encouraged to participate in the assessment and treatment of the child's problem. In many cases, the father's participation can be made a condition for helping the family. The importance of the father to the family and his potential for positively affecting his child should be stressed in making such demands. Even if the child's problems do not stem from inadequate fathering, the father's active involvement may do much to improve the situation. If a child has been paternally deprived, a family difficulty may provide the opportunity for getting the father more integrated into the family (Biller and Meredith 1974). It is striking how many well-meaning fathers are relatively peripheral members of their families. Many difficulties that children and mothers experience can be quickly remedied or mitigated if ways in which the father can become a more active participant are clearly communicated to the family. Much of the success of family therapy is due to the inclusion of the father (e.g., Ackerman 1966; Forrest 1969; Green 1974; Haley and Hoffman 1967).

A child's problems, if not directly a result of family interactions, can be increased by the family's reaction to them. Treating the father, mother, child, and other relevant family members as a group allows the therapist to observe both strengths and difficulties in family interactions. Valuable time can be saved and a more accurate understanding can be achieved by direct observation of family behavior rather than inferring how the family interacts from comments made separately by the child or his parents.

The application of modeling and related behavior modification techniques such as those described by Bandura (1969) is a particularly meaningful course to explore in individual, group, and family therapy with paternally deprived children. The probability of successful treatment can be greatly increased if knowledge concerning positive fathering is integrated into the psychotherapy process. For example, the therapist can demonstrate appropriate paternal behaviors in his interactions with the family; however, the therapist must be careful to support the father's strengths and not undermine his effectiveness by unwittingly competing with him.

The therapist can explicitly model ways in which a father can communicate to his wife and to his children. Having both a male and female therapist provides even more explicit examples of appropriate male-female interactions for the family to observe. Role-playing procedures for family members are very helpful in teaching and reinforcing effective behavior patterns. Of course, any attempt to modify the family's functioning should take into account their previous modes of interaction and their sociocultural background. It is important that the family's environment is considered in treatment. Observing and modifying the family's behavior is often more meaningful when it is done in their own home rather than in the therapist's office.

Father Substitutes

The availability of father-surrogates is important for father-present children with inadequate fathers, as well as for father-absent children. Many paternally deprived children have potentially effective father-surrogates in their own families or find an adequate role model among teachers or older peers. Older well-adjusted boys can be very salient and influential models for younger paternally deprived children. In cases in which it is impossible or impractical to deal with the child's father, therapists can strengthen their impact on the father-absent or paternally disadvantaged child by also working with the child's actual or potential father surrogate. This could be accomplished by consultation, but engaging the father-surrogate and child in joint sessions (or in groups with other children and father-surrogates) can be even more beneficial.

The Gluecks (1950) reported that many delinquent boys who form a close relationship with a father-surrogate resolve their antisocial tendencies. Similarly, Trenaman (1952) found that young men who had been chronically delinquent while serving in the British army improved as a function of their relationships with father surrogates. A father absent child may be particularly responsive to a male therapist or role model because of his motivation for male companionship. Rexford (1964), in describing the treatment of young antisocial children, noted that therapists are more likely to be successful with father-absent boys than with boys who have strongly identified with an emotionally disturbed, criminal, or generally inadequate father.

There are many organizations, including Big Brothers, Y.M.C.A., Boy Scouts, athletic teams, camps, churches, and settlement houses, which provide paternally deprived children with meaningful father surrogates. Additional professional consultation and more community support (especially more father-surrogates), would allow these organizations to be of even greater benefit to many more children.

Available research indicates that even in the first few years of life the child's personality development can be very much influenced by the degree and type of involvement of a father or father-surrogate. Group settings such as day care centers can be used as vehicles to provide father-surrogates for many children (*both boys and girls*). The facilities of such organizations as Big Brothers and the Y.M.C.A. could also be utilized to help younger children.

Educational Implications

Our educational system could do much to mitigate the effects of paternal deprivation if more male teachers were available, particularly in nursery school, kindergarten, and the early elementary school grades. Competent and interpersonally able male teachers could facilitate the cognitive development of many children as well as contribute to their general social functioning (Biller 1974a, 1974b).

There is much need for greater incentives to encourage more males to become teachers of young children. There has to be more freedom and autonomy to innovate, as well as greater financial rewards. We must make both men and women aware of the impact that males can have in child development and also the importance of male influence in the early years of personality development. Just having more male teachers is not going to be a significant factor. The feminized school atmosphere must become more humanized and teachers must be selected on the basis of interpersonal ability and overall competency. If a man is basically feminized or allows himself to be dominated by a restrictive atmosphere, he may be a particularly poor model for children.

The remedy for the feminized classroom is not just having more male teachers per se, but giving men and women a more equal distribution of the responsibilities and decisions related to education. As Sexton (1969) suggests, both boys and girls might be better off if there were more women in top administrative positions as well as more men in the classroom. As in the family situation, children can profit much from opportunities of seeing males and females interact in a cooperative, creative manner. Men and women in the classroom could help each other better understand the different socialization experiences of males and females and contribute to a lessening of sex role stereotypes.

Even if significantly more male teachers are not immediately available, our school system could better utilize existing personnel. Many of the males who teach in the upper elementary school grades, junior high, and high school could also be very effective with younger children. Again, we need to put emphasis on the importance of males interacting with young children (as well as with older children). Programs could also be planned so that male teachers could spend some of their time with a wider range of children, particularly in tasks where they had much skill and enthusiasm. Perhaps their responsibilities could be concentrated on father-deprived children. In addition, other males such as older students or retired men may be encouraged to participate in the educational process of young children.

There is a general need to make our schools more a part of the community and to invite greater participation especially from fathers (Biller and Meredith 1974). Men in the community could be invited to talk about and demonstrate their work. Participants could include members of various professions, skilled craftsmen and technicians, politicians, and athletes.

Of course, it is also important to have women in various occupations come to the school and describe their activities. Both boys and girls need to become aware that women can be successful in "traditionally masculine" fields.

Sexton (1969) suggests that we provide more flexibility in educational job classifications. She advocates school job classifications such as resource person, group leader, or technical specialist. Such positions could be filled by individuals with skills or knowledge that would have much relevance to children. Electricians, carpenters, mechanics, dentists, politicians, plumbers, and such could fill these jobs. Individuals with various physical or interpersonal skills could also be recruited. In addition, we could recruit more paraprofessional teacher aides from the community. These aides could assist in specific school subjects, but could also instruct both teachers and children in certain areas.

An atmosphere in which older children help younger children, or children help less able peers of the same age, could go a long way toward encouraging males to gain the skills and experiences that are important in being competent fathers. Men from the community could come in during lunch breaks and eat with the children. They could also interact with children on the playground and ride with them on school buses. Hopefully, business and industries could regularly cooperate in giving men the opportunities and incentives to make such contributions. Another function that could be performed by business and industry would be to set up regular visits for children to various settings in their community. Such visits can be very educational and also can provide children with more experiences in interacting with competent adults of both sexes. Some of these and other suggestions have also been made by a number of observers who have criticized the lack of male influence in our educational system (e.g., Biller 1971a; Garai and Scheinfeld 1968; Grambs and Waetjen 1966; Ostrovsky 1959; Sexton 1969).

In a number of different educational and treatment contexts, I have observed some rather dramatic effects of paternally deprived children responding to the attention of an interested male adult. In practicing and supervising psychotherapy with young boys, I have often found an improvement in school work associated with explicit reinforcement from adult males. Some particularly interesting results were achieved by having books about sports and sports' heroes available during therapy. In these cases reading and talking about sports became a major focus of therapy. These boys needed to become aware that there was no incompatibility between intellectual endeavors such as reading and their conception of masculine behavior. It seemed particularly helpful to the boys that the therapist clearly exhibited athletic as well as reading skill, and that, equally as important, he obviously enjoyed both reading and athletics. In therapy the emphasis was on modeling and joint participation in concretely reinforcing activities. Similarly, through the process of family therapy, positive involvement of the father (or father-surrogate) has often been associated with a marked improvement in the child's academic functioning (Biller 1974a, 1974b).

Community Mental Health

Children confined to institutions are especially in need of warm relationships with competent father-surrogates. Institutionalized children, including those who are orphaned or emotionally disturbed, can benefit from a larger proportion of interaction with adult males. For example, Nash's (1965) data suggest that having institutionalized children live in a situation in which they are cared for and supervised by a husband-wife team is beneficial for their sex role development. Keller and Alper (1970) have contributed many guidelines for adult males working with delinquent children in institutional settings and halfway houses. Many of the same variables that are involved in children's social learning and imitation within the family setting are important to consider in an analysis of the impact of child care workers in residential settings (Portnoy, Biller, and Davids 1972).

Prospective fathers and father-surrogates can be made more aware of the significance of the father in child development through education and the mass media (Biller and Meredith 1972, 1974). Potentially, such exposure along with other programs can lessen the number of families which become father absent. Explicit advantages such as financial and other support for fathers remaining with their families in contrast to the current rewarding of father absence by many welfare departments, might do much to keep some families intact and reconstitute other families.

Preventive programs can focus on families which seem to have a high risk of becoming father absent. Systematic techniques can be developed to determine the potential consequences of father absence for a family where separation or divorce is being contemplated. There are many families in which both the parents and the children would be able to function better subsequent to divorce. When the divorce process is taking place, more consideration should be given to whether all or some of the children might benefit from remaining with the fathers (Biller and Meredith 1974). It is usually easier to find mother-surrogates (e.g., grandmothers, housekeepers) than to find father-surrogates. It is also relevant to consider potential paternal effectiveness in placing children with adoptive or foster parents.

Applications of existing knowledge should not be divorced from research endeavors. Treatment and preventive projects can be integrated with research programs. Baker and his coworkers have provided an excellent example of research designed to suggest answers to practical issues concerning paternal deprivation (Baker et al. 1967, 1968; Fagen et al. 1967). They carried out a short-term longitudinal investigation of the families of army professionals. Their findings have clearly detailed some of the complexities of family adjustment to (1) anticipated father absence (first phase of assessment, one to three months before father's departure); (2) temporary father absence (second phase of assessment, six to nine months after father had left), and (3) the father's reunion with his family (third phase of assessment, at least six months after the father had returned).

Although extensive assessment procedures were used, the age of the boys at the time of father absence (six- and seven-years-old), the relatively short duration of father absence, and the seemingly significant pre-father-absent differences among families made it difficult to find any consistent personality differences directly attributable to father absence. However, the Baker et al. research project has made important contributions by delineating individual differences in modes of family adjustment to father absence, and by leading to specific suggestions concerning the use of family and community resources to alleviate crisis situations concerning father absence.

The mother in the paternally deprived family must not be neglected. For example, the mother's reaction to husband absence may greatly influence the extent to which father absence or lack of father availability affects her children. She is often in need of psychological as well as social and economic support. Mental health professionals have outlined many useful techniques for helping mothers and children in fatherless families (e.g., Baker et al. 1968; Despert 1953; Hill 1949; Jones 1963; Klein 1973; Lerner 1954; McDermott 1968; Wylie and Delgado 1959).

In a pilot project one of the central goals of a welfare mothers' group was to help husbandless mothers constructively deal with their social and familial problems (Biller and Smith 1972). Pollak (1970) discussed the frequent interpersonal and sexual problems of parents without partners and gave some excellent suggestions for helping such parents cope with their concerns. Education and therapeutic groups such as "Parents without Partners" can be very meaningful for the wifeless father as well as the husbandless mother (e.g., Egelson and Frank 1961; Freudenthal 1959; Schlesinger 1966).

A significant dimension of community mental health efforts, both in terms of prevention and treatment, should be supplying father surrogates to groups of paternally deprived children; far-reaching community, state, and government programs are needed. A vast number of children do not have consistent and meaningful contact with adult males. This very serious situation must be remedied if all our children are to take full advantage of their growing social and educational opportunities.

Some Guidelines for Effective Fathering

A critical dimension in the battle against paternal deprivation can be in terms of educational and training programs for parents and prospective parents. Gordon's (1970) *Parent Effectiveness Training* is probably the best example of a successful program to improve parent-child relationships. However, there have not been systematic programs especially designed for fathers. Unfortunately most parent education programs focus on mothers, and relatively few fathers participate. Meredith and I have written a book, *Fathers and Children*, which we hope will stimulate parent education programs focusing on issues relating to the father-child and father-mother relationships (Biller and Meredith 1974).

The remainder of this chapter includes some general guidelines for the effective fathering of the young child based on my article in *The London Sunday Times Magazine* (Biller 1973a). These and additional guidelines, and other practical issues concerning fathering, are discussed in much more depth in *Fathers and Children* (Biller and Meredith 1974).

Where To Begin

At a very basic level, learning how to become an effective father begins in childhood. Perhaps the best way to develop the abilities of being a good father is the experience of having had one. A realistic evaluation by a man of the strengths and weaknesses of his relationship with his father can be a helpful ingredient in developing his ability to become an effective father. Some fathers are unthinkingly trapped in patterns of behavior evolving out of inadequate interactions with their own fathers.

Boys usually do not get many opportunities to interact with young children in a positive supportive manner. They usually perceive taking care of young children more as a restriction than as a gratifying experience. If we can creatively remedy this situation by allowing older boys to demonstrate their skills, knowledge, and experiences to younger children, we may do much to promote a basic foundation for fatherhood. Setting up nursery schools as a part of the family life education curricula of high schools may be one way of giving adolescent males more of an opportunity to constructively interact with young children.

The New Father

Having a child should be a well-thought out decision for both the father and mother. Even before the child is conceived it is advisable for the prospective parents to feel a joint commitment to their future family. The positive influence of the father is greatly increased when it takes place in a context of father-mother mutuality. The expectant father should not be ignored. Often all the attention is focused on the expectant mother and the expectant father is left out in the cold. Many expectant fathers have feelings of alienation and their psychological and physical health can be adversely affected. Husbands can be involved in visits to obstetricians and, if agreeable with the physician, can be with their wives during labor and in the delivery room. The new father should be encouraged to spend considerable time with his wife and infant. The earlier the father can feel involved with the infant, the more likely will a strong father-child attachment develop.

A father can be very important to his child's development even in the first year of life. The father's involvement in various activities with the infant can build a strong foundation for a growing relationship. Whether or not a father changes diapers, dresses or feeds the infant is not the key factor—what is important is that the father and infant find some mutually satisfying activities, and also that the father and mother can develop the view that they both have definite day-to-day responsibilities for the infant's welfare. Many fathers enjoy holding and snuggling their babies, watching their reactions to new objects and situations, and tossing and crawling with them as they get older. Infants and fathers can provide each other with much mutual stimulation. Babies can be fascinating when fathers feel comfortable and relaxed with them. New fathers are often anxious about holding infants some have never held an infant before and react as if it were a "time-bomb," and the wife's support and encouragement can be very helpful.

It is never too early for the father to get involved, and the sharing of responsibilities for the child can also do much to strengthen the husband-wife bond and overall family cohesiveness. The father who gets a good start with his first child can play a very significant role with the arrival of additional children. For example, a young child who can spend much time with an involved father is less likely to feel depressed or jealous when his mother is out of the home giving birth to his new brother or sister, or to express severe sibling rivalry when the mother and infant return home.

Father and Work

A very frequent problem that gets in the way of father-child interaction is the father's work schedule. In some cases, modifications in the father's work schedule are possible to insure his fuller participation in the family. Some fathers spend great amounts of time at work as a means of avoiding family responsibilities and not because of economic necessity. Many fathers are very competent and active at work but feel quite inexperienced and ineffectual when at home with their children. Of course, each family has to assess its priorities—but it is important that both the husband and wife share in such decisions as to how much money is necessary, the degree to which each contributes, and the amount of time they spend with their children. Many fathers, because of long-term goals, "sacrifice" time with their families only to find that they have lost their children, at least psychologically, in the process. They may end up with much financial security but a very empty family.

In some cases, the father has to be away from home a great deal. Whether this is a temporary or a relatively permanent situation, adjustments in family schedules can be made to maximize the father's involvement. For example, if the father works until late in the evening, the child can take naps and spend time with him when he comes home, or they can regularly have a special time in the mornings. Also, in many cases, children may be able to accompany their fathers to work or the mother and child can go and visit the father during the lunch hour. Each family may have a unique situation but there are ways to schedule maximal opportunity for father-child interaction.

Learning With Father

Father-child interaction, even for the young child, does not have to be limited to the home and neighborhood. Many fathers enjoy taking their children on errands (e.g., to the local garage, flower shop, or grocery store) and including them in various recreational activities. For the young child, what may seem beyond his comprehension to the adult may be very intriguing. Seeing new faces, new buildings, new machinery can be very engrossing, especially when he's with someone he loves and respects. The two year old may not comprehend the meaning of a movie, or sporting event, but he may be very stimulated and engrossed in the action and feel very happy sharing something with his father (provided it does not last too long). On the other hand, a father may get much added enjoyment by seeing his child's reaction to what is a rather mundane experience solely from an adult perspective. Similarly, even though a child may not fully understand the intricacies of his father's job, he may be very excited by seeing where his father works and by meeting the people his father works with.

Doing things with his father offers the child many new learning experiences and stimulates his curiosity. A father does not have to be a scholar to whet his child's appetite for new knowledge. A child may greatly enjoy hearing about jobs his father has had, places he's visited, and people he's known. Answering the child's questions can be a learning experience for both the father and child. A child's academic success and, more importantly, the degree to which he manifests his creative potential may have much to do with his interactions with his father, especially if they have a close relationship. For example, a father who enjoys reading and reads to his child (and also when his child is ready, encourages his child to read to him) can have a much more positive impact than a father who continually tells his child that school is important but does not engage in an intellectual activity in a way that his child can observe.

However, the specific activities that father and child engage in are not the key—the quality of their interaction is most crucial. Open communication and the sharing of mutually gratifying experiences are important. Young children learn most by observing and imitating their parents. The best way for a father to instill positive qualities in a child is by demonstrating these qualities in his relationship with him. A father may be very skillful in understanding people and in solving problems, but if a child only sees his father occasionally he is not going to learn much from him. Similarly, a child is not going to learn respect and tolerance from a father who constantly criticizes him, even if the father is considered a wonderful person by his fellow workers and friends.

Special Times

Respect and understanding work two ways. A father must give if he expects to receive. A good father-child relationship may be particularly fostered when the father and child can have some "special times" together. That is when the father and child can spend time just with each other. Such occasions are very important in focusing on each other's needs and interests. It is usually much easier to listen to a child when you are alone with him, and listening is an essential in being a good parent. We usually attend very carefully to our children's material needs, but their needs for individual expression are often neglected. When it comes to taking attitudes and feelings into consideration, our children frequently get less consideration than our friends and quite often even strangers.

Attention to "special times" can become crucial especially in families with many children where it may be very difficult for family members to know one another as individuals. The ability of parents to relate to each of their children is at least as important as their ability to economically provide for them. This consideration should be taken into account in family planning.

Hopefully, the father and child can develop many mutual interests and awareness of each others' activities. Often the father can take the initiative by giving attention to what the child is doing. There is nothing immature about a father getting down on the floor and playing with his child, building with blocks, moving dolls and toy animals around, etc. Such activities can be fun for both participants. Some fathers do not have much patience for the typical children's games, but may be able to teach children activities they enjoy such as checkers or various card games. The child can happily participate with his father in typical adult activities including washing the car, fixing furniture, or working in the garden, if the father takes into account the child's developmental level. Such activities may also provide the beginnings of his sharing responsibilities at home. A child needs to feel that his father values him as an individual and appreciates his skills. It is easy for a father to be critical of the way his child plays a game or hammers a nail but the father's capacity to remember, or imagine, his level of performance when he was a young child can be helpful. A child will usually respond positively to his father's comment that the child is doing as well, or better, than the father did at a similar age.

Fathers can enjoy frolicking with their children and wrestling with them.

Physical contact between father and child can be a very healthy experience particularly when love and tender feelings are expressed. Hugging, tickling, cuddling, and tossing are very meaningful expressions of caring and closeness between father and child. The child can also sense his father's strength and power and yet feel secure rather than being frightened. It is important for both father and child to feel comfortable in expressing warmth and tenderness towards one another. Too many fathers and consequently too many children often become inhibited in expressing positive emotions.

The consequences of paternal deprivation include disadvantages for fathers as well as children. The uninvolved father does not experience the gratification of actively facilitating the successful development of his children. He misses an important opportunity to learn to deal in a sensitive way with many interpersonal situations. Widespread paternal inadequacy contributes to the existence of large numbers of interpersonally insensitive men. Many of these men are in positions of authority and their alienation as fathers has limited their ability to interact with young people. Inadequate paternal involvement is a factor in the problems of communication between individuals of different ages—contributing to the generation gap.

Discipline and Responsibility

Discipline is a chronic problem in many families. Traditionally this was often the scope of the father's role and "wait till your father gets home" is still a very frequent cry from frustrated mothers. But making the father's role center on discipline can lead to a very frustrating and unsatisfactory father-child relationship. If the mother is alone with the child, she should take the responsibility, as should the father when he is alone with the child. Hopefully the child will feel that his mother and father generally are supportive of one another's actions. If the parents are together with the child, setting limits should be a joint responsibility. Again it should be emphasized that the best way to teach a child appropriate behavior is by exposing him to effective models—the behavior of the mother and father is most significant. If parents are continually yelling at each other, if they don't listen or trust one another, it is difficult to expect their child to respect the feelings of others.

The child can learn much from resolving disagreements with his parents. The father is wise to have clear-cut standards, but he should be responsive to his child's rational arguments, and needs to express himself. Children have to learn constructive ways of influencing others and asserting their rights. Inattention to a child's reasoning is no better than giving in to immature temper tantrums. The father does not always have to have the last word. The father who must always win an argument is not allowing his child to develop independence and the ability to assert himself. A child should be encouraged to respect his father, but he should not be burdened with the image of an all-perfect father. If he is to learn to objectively assess his own capabilities, a child must learn that his father has his limitations and can make mistakes. The father who can occasionally admit that he is wrong and that his child is right may do much to facilitate his child's sense of competence. A father who "never" makes a mistake can be too frustrating to emulate.

Father-Mother Relationship

The opportunities the child has to spend together with both his mother and father are of crucial importance. A child forms much of his attitude toward male-female relationships by watching his mother and father interact. The effective father values his wife's competencies and respects her opinions. The child's sex role adjustment is much influenced by the quality of the father-mother relationship. A father who feels certain about his basic masculinity is more likely to positively accept his wife than one who rejects his masculinity or must constantly prove that he is a man. The effective father encourages his daughter to feel positively about being a female and his son about being a male. He communicates his pride in their developing bodies and biological potential-ities. However, this does not mean that he expects his children to rigidly adhere to cultural stereotypes. For example, he fosters the development of assertiveness and independence in his daughters as well as his sons; and the development of nurturance and sensitivity in his sons as well as his daughters.

The parents' respect for one another and their ability to communicate openly and honestly foster the child's development. Parental consistency and agreement give the child a feeling of security. It is helpful to the child to know that his parents have discussed issues concerning his welfare and that they are in general agreement. Of course, parents are not always going to agree and the child is fortunate if he can observe parental disagreements as long as they usually result in mutually satisfactory outcomes. Children have to learn how to resolve conflicts and father-mother interactions can provide important lessons.

The purpose of this book has not been to argue that the father is more important than the mother. The child who experiences *both positive fathering and positive mothering* is more likely to achieve effective personality functioning than the child who has only one adequate parent. Childrearing can be a very demanding process, but can be much more rewarding when the husband and wife function as a cooperative team. Together, parents often react in a more creative and responsible manner. They can be more secure in allowing their children autonomy and freedom, as well as maintaining firmness in setting necessary limits.

References

References

Aberle, D.F. and Naegele, F.D. "Middle-class fathers' occupational role and attitude toward children." *American Journal of Orthopsychiatry*, 1952, *22*, 366-378.

Ackerman, N.W. "The principle of shared responsibility of child rearing." *International Journal of Sociology*, 1957, *12*, 280-291.

Ackerman, N.W. *Treating the troubled family*. New York: Basic Books, 1966.

Aichorn, A. *Wayward youth*. New York: Viking Press, 1935.

Albert R.S. "Early cognitive development among the gifted." Paper presented at the meeting of the Western Psychological Association, Vancouver, British Columbia, Canada, June, 1969.

Aldous, J. "Children's perceptions of adult roles as affected by class, father absence, and race." *DARCEL Papers and Reports*, 1969, *4*, No. 3.

Alkire, A.A. "Social power and communication within families of disturbed and nondisturbed preadolescents." *Journal of Personality and Social Psychology*, 1969, *13*, 335-349.

Altucher, N. "Conflict in sex identification in boys." Unpublished doctoral dissertation, University of Michigan, 1957.

Altus, W.D. "The broken home and factors of adjustment." *Psychological Reports*, 1958, *4*, 477.

Anastasi, A. *Differential psychology: Individual and group differences in behavior*. New York: Macmillan, 1958.

Anastasi, A. and Schaefer, C.E. "Biographical correlates of artistic and literary creativity in adolescent girls." *Journal of Applied Psychology*, 1969, *53*, 267-273.

Anastasiow, N.S. "Success in school and boys' sex-role patterns." *Child Development*, 1965, *36*, 1053-1066.

Ancona, L.; Cesa-Bianchi, M.; and Bocquet, C. "Identification with the father in the absence of the paternal model. Research applied to children of Navy officers." *Archivo di Psicologia Neurologia e Psichiatria*, 1964, *24*, 339-361.

Anderson, I.H.; Hughes, B.O.; and Dixon, W.R. "The rate of reading development and its relation to age of learning to read, sex, and intelligence." *Journal of Educational Research*, 1962, *65*, 132-135.

Anderson, L.M. "Personality characteristics of parents of neurotic, aggressive, and normal preadolescent boys." *Journal of Consulting and Clinical Psychology*, 1969, *33*, 575-581.

Anderson, R. and Ritscher, C. "Pupil progress." in R. Ebel (ed.), *Encyclopedia of educational research*. London: Macmillan, 1969.

Anderson, R.E. "Where's Dad? Paternal deprivation and delinquency." *Archives of General Psychiatry*, 1968, *18*, 641-649.

Andrews, R.O. and Christensen, H.T. "Relationship of absence of a parent to courtship status: A repeat study." *American Sociological Review*, 1951, *16*, 541-544.

Andry, R.G. "Paternal and maternal roles in delinquency." In *Deprivation of maternal care.* Public Health Paper No. 14. Geneva: World Health Organization, 1962, 31-43.

Angrilli, A.F. "The psychosexual identification of preschool boys." *Journal of Genetic Psychology*, 1960, *97*, 329-340.

Apperson, L.B. and McAdoo, W.G. Jr. "Parental factors in the childhood of homosexuals." *Journal of Abnormal Psychology*, 1968, *73*, 201-206.

Arnold, R.D. "The achievement of boys and girls taught by men and women teachers." *Elementary School Journal*, 1968, *68*, 367-372.

Arnstein, H. "The crisis of becoming a father." *Sexual Behavior*, 1972, *2* (4), 42-48.

Bach, G.R. "Father-fantasies and father typing in father-separated children." *Child Development*, 1946, *17*, 63-80.

Bach, G.R. and Bremer, G. "Projective father fantasies of preadolescent, delinquent children." *Journal of Psychology*, 1947, *24*, 3-17.

Bacon, M.K.; Child, I.L.; and Barry, H. III. "A cross-cultural study of correlates of crime." *Journal of Abnormal and Social Psychology*, 1963, *66*, 291-300.

Baer, D.J. and Ragosta, R.A. "Relationship between perceived child-rearing practices and verbal and mathematical ability." *Journal of Genetic Psychology*, 1966, *108*, 106-108.

Baggett, A.T. "The effect of early loss of father upon the personality of boys and girls in late adolescence." *Dissertation Abstracts*, 1967, *28* (1-B), 356-357.

Baker, E. "Reading problems are caused." *Elementary English*, 1948, *25*, 360.

Baker, J.W. and Holzworth, A. "Social histories of successful and unsuccessful children." *Child Development*, 1961, *32*, 135-149.

Baker, S.L.; Cove, L.A.; Fagen, S.A.; Fischer, E.G.; and Janda, E.J. "Impact of father-absence: III. Problems of family reintegration following prolonged father-absence." Paper presented at the meeting of the American Orthopsychiatric Association, Washington, D.C., March 1968.

Baker, S.L.; Fagen, S.A.; Fischer, E.G.; Janda, E.J.; and Cove, L.A. "Impact of father-absence on personality factors of boys: I. An evaluation of the military family's adjustment." Paper presented at the meeting of the American Orthopsychiatric Association, Washington, D.C., March 1967.

Baldwin, A.L.; Kalhorn, J.; and Breese, F.A. "The appraisal of parent behavior." *Psychological Monographs*, 1949, *63*, No. 1 (Whole No. 299).

Ban, P.L. and Lewis, M. "Mothers and fathers, girls and boys: Attachment behavior in the one-year-old." Paper presented at the meeting of the Eastern Psychological Association, New York, April 1971.

Bandura, A. *Principles of behavior modification.* New York: Holt, Rinehart and Winston, 1969.

Bandura, A.; Ross, D.; and Ross, S.A. "A comparative test of the status envy, social power, and secondary reinforcement theories of identificatory learning." *Journal of Abnormal and Social Psychology*, 1963, *67*, 527-534.

Bandura, A. and Walters, R.H. "Dependency conflicts in aggressive delinquents." *Journal of Social Issues*, 1958, *14*, 52-65.

Bandura, A. and Walters, R.H. *Adolescent aggression: A study of the influence of child-rearing practices and family interrelationships.* New York: Ronald Press, 1959.

Bandura, A. and Walters, R.H. *Social learning and personality development.* New York: Holt, Rinehart, and Winston, 1963.

Barclay, A.G. and Cusumano, D. "Father-absence, cross-sex identity, and field-dependent behavior in male adolescents." *Child Development*, 1967, *38*, 243-250.

Bardwick, J.M. *Psychology of women*, New York: Harper and Row, 1971.

Barry, H. III; Bacon, M.K.; and Child, I.L. "A cross-cultural survey of some sex differences in socialization." *Journal of Abnormal and Social Psychology*, 1957, *55*, 327-332.

Barry, W.A. "Marriage research and conflict: An integrative review." *Psychological Bulletin*, 1970, *73*, 41-55.

Bartemeir, L. "The contribution of the father to the mental health of the family." *American Journal of Psychiatry*, 1953, *110*, 277-280.

Baruch, D.W. and Wilcox, J.A. "A study of sex differences in preschool children's adjustment coexistent with interparental tensions." *Journal of Genetic Psychology*, 1944, *61*, 281-303.

Baumrind, D. "Child rearing practices anteceding three patterns of preschool behavior." *Genetic Psychology Monographs*, 1967, *75*, 43-88.

Baumrind, D. and Black, A.E. "Socialization practices associated with dimensions of competence in preschool boys and girls." *Child Development*, 1967, *38* 291-327.

Baxter, J.C.; Horton, D.L.; and Wiley, R.E. "Father identification as a function of the mother-father relationship." *Journal of Individual Psychology*, 1964, *20*, 167-171.

Beck, A.T.; Sehti, B.B.; and Tuthill, R.W. "Childhood bereavement and adult depression." *Archives of General Psychiatry*, 1963, *9*, 295-302.

Becker, W.C. "Consequences of different kinds of parental discipline." In M.L. Hoffman and L.W. Hoffman (eds.), *Review of child development research: Vol. I.* New York: Russell Sage Foundation, 1964, 169-208.

Becker, W.C. and Krug, R.S. "A circumplex model for social behavior in children." *Child Development*, 1964, *35*, 371-396.

Becker, W.C.; Peterson, D.R.; Hellmer, L.A.; Shoemaker, D.J.; and Quay, H.C. "Factors in parental behavior and personality as related to problem behavior in children." *Journal of Consulting Psychology*, 1959, *23*, 107-118.

Becker, W.C.; Peterson, D.R.; Luria, Z.; Shoemaker, D.S.; and Hellmer, L.A.

"Relations of factors derived from parent interview ratings to behavior problems of five-year-olds." *Child Development*, 1962, *33*, 509-535.

Bee, H.; Van Egeren, L.; Streissguth, A.; Nyman B.; and Leckie, M. "Social class differences in maternal teaching strategies and speech patterns." *Developmental Psychology*, 1969, *1*, 724-734.

Beier, E.G. and Ratzeburg, F. "The parental identifications of male and female college students." *Journal of Abnormal and Social Psychology*, 1953, *48*, 569-572.

Bell, A.P. "Role modeling of fathers in adolescence and young adulthood." *Journal of Counseling Psychology*, 1969, *16*, 30-35.

Bell, R.Q. "A reinterpretation of the direction of effects of studies of socialization." *Psychological Review*, 1968, *75*, 81-95.

Beller, E.K. "Maternal behaviors in lower-class Negro mothers." Paper presented at the meeting of the Eastern Psychological Association, Boston, April 1967.

Bené, E. "On the genesis of female homosexuality." *British Journal of Psychiatry*, 1965, *3*, 815-821.

Benjamin, H. "Age and sex differences in the toy preferences of young children." *Journal of Genetic Psychology*, 1932, *41*, 417-429.

Bennett, I. *Delinquent and neurotic children: A comparative study.* New York: Basic Books, 1959.

Benson, L. *Fatherhood: A sociological perspective.* New York: Random House, 1968.

Bentzen, F. "Sex ratios in learning and behavior disorders." *American Journal of Orthopsychiatry*, 1963, *33*, 92-98.

Berry, J.W. "Temne and Eskimo perceptual skills." *International Journal of Psychology*, 1966, *1*, 207-229.

Biber, H.; Miller, L.B.; and Dyer, J.L. "Feminization in preschool." *Developmental Psychology*, 1972, *7*, 86.

Bieber, I. et al. *Homosexuality: A psychoanalytic study.* New York: Basic Books, 1962.

Bieliauskas, V. "Recent advances in the psychology of masculinity and femininity." *Journal of Psychology*, 1965, *60*, 255-263.

Bieri, J. "Parental identification, acceptability, and authority, and within sex-differences in cognitive behavior." *Journal of Abnormal and Social Psychology*, 1960, *60*, 76-79.

Bieri, J. and Lobeck, R. "Acceptance of authority and parental identification." *Journal of Personality*, 1959, *27*, 74-87.

Bigner, J.J. "Fathering: Research and practical implications." *The Family Coordinator*, 1970, *19*, 357-362.

Biller, H.B. "Adult's conceptions of masculinity and femininity in children." Unpublished study, Emma Pendleton Bradley Hospital, Riverside, Rhode Island, 1966(a).

Biller, H.B. "Experiences with underachieving adolescents enrolled in an academic potential project." Unpublished manuscript, Emma Pendleton Bradley Hospital, Riverside, Rhode Island, 1966(b).

Biller, H.B. "A multiaspect investigation of masculine development in kindergarten-age boys." *Genetic Psychology Monographs*, 1968(a), *76*, 89-139.

Biller, H.B. "A note on father-absence and masculine development in young lower-class Negro and white boys." *Child Development*, 1968(b), *39*, 1003-1006.

Biller, H.B. "Father dominance and sex-role development in kindergarten-age boys." *Developmental Psychology*, 1969(a), *1*, 87-94. Reprinted in slightly abridged form in D.R. Heise (ed.), *Personality and socialization*. New York: Rand McNally, 1972, 73-85.

Biller, H.B. "Father-absence, maternal encouragement, and sex-role development in kindergarten-age boys." *Child Development*, 1969(b), *40*, 539-546. Reprinted in R.C. Smart and M.S. Smart (eds.), *Readings in child development and relationships*. New York: Macmillan, 1972, 239-254.

Biller, H.B. "Maternal salience and feminine development in young girls." *Proceedings of the 77th Annual Convention of the American Psychological Association*, 1969(c), *4*, 259-260.

Biller, H.B. "Father-absence and the personality development of the male child." *Developmental Psychology*, 1970, *2*, 181-201. Reprinted in S. Chess and A. Thomas (eds.), *Annual progress in child psychiatry and child development*. New York: Brunner-Mazel, 1971, 120-152. Reprinted in slightly abridged form in D.R. Heise (ed.), *Personality and socialization*. New York: Rand McNally, 1972, 407-433.

Biller, H.B. *Father, child, and sex role*, Lexington, Mass.: Lexington Books, D.C. Heath and Company, 1971(a).

Biller, H.B. "The mother-child relationship and the father-absent boy's personality development." *Merrill-Palmer Quarterly*, 1971(b), *17*, 227-241. Reprinted in slightly abridged form in U. Bronfenbrenner (ed.), *Influences on human development*. Hinsdale, Ill.: Dryden, 1972, 306-319.

Biller, H.B. "Fathering and female sexual development." *Medical Aspects of Human Sexuality*, 1971(c), *5*, 116-138.

Biller, H.B. "Syndromes resulting from paternal deprivation in man." Paper presented at the Medical Research Council of Ireland's Symposium on the Experimental Behavior Basis of Mental Disturbance, Galway, Ireland, April 1972(a).

Biller, H.B. "Sex-role learning: Some comments and complexities from a multidimensional perspective." Paper presented at the Annual Meeting of the American Association for the Advancement of Science (Sec. 1). Symposium on Sex-role Learning in Childhood and Adolescence, Washington, D.C., December 1972(b).

Biller, H.B. "The father's role." *The London Sunday Times Magazine*, 1973(a), (Feb. 25), 48-50.

Biller, H.B. "Sex-role uncertainty and psychopathology." *Journal of Individual Psychology*, 1973(b), *29*, 24-25.

Biller, H.B. "Paternal and sex-role factors in cognitive and academic functioning." In J.K. Cole and R. Dienstbier (eds.), *Nebraska symposium on motivation*, Lincoln: University of Nebraska Press, 1974(a), 83-123.

Biller, H.B. "Paternal deprivation, cognitive functioning, and the feminized classroom." In A. Davids (ed.), *Child personality and psychopathology: current topics*. New York: Wiley, 1974(b), 11-52.

Biller, H.B. "The father-infant relationship: Some naturalistic observations." Unpublished study, University of Rhode Island, 1974(c).

Biller, H.B. "Paternal deprivation and marriage relationships among females." Unpublished study, University of Rhode Island, 1974(d).

Biller, H.B. and Bahm, R.M. "Father-absence, perceived maternal behavior, and masculinity of self-concept among junior high school boys." *Developmental Psychology*, 1971, *4*, 178-181.

Biller, H.B. and Barry, W. "Sex-role patterns, paternal similarity, and personality adjustment in college males." *Developmental Psychology*, 1971, *4*, 107.

Biller, H.B. and Borstelmann, L.J. "Intellectual level and sex-role development in mentally retarded children." *American Journal of Mental Deficiency*, 1965, *70*, 443-447.

Biller, H.B. and Borstelmann, L.J. "Masculine development: An integrative review." *Merrill-Palmer Quarterly*, 1967, *13*, 253-294.

Biller, H.B. and Davids, A. "Parent-child relations, personality development and psychopathology." In A. Davids (ed.), *Issues in abnormal child psychology*. Belmont, California: Brooks/Cole, 1973, 48-77.

Biller, H.B. and Liebman, D.A. "Body build, sex-role preference, and sex-role adoption in junior high school boys." *Journal of Genetic Psychology*, 1971, *118*, 81-86.

Biller, H.B. and Meredith, D.L. "The invisible American father." *Sexual Behavior*, 1972, *2*, (7), 16-22.

Biller, H.B. and Meredith, D.L. *Fathers and children*. New York: David McKay, 1974, in press.

Biller, H.B. and Poey, K. "An exploratory comparison of sex-role related behavior in schizophrenics and nonschizophrenics." *Developmental Psychology*, 1969, *1*, 629.

Biller, H.B.; Singer, D.L.; and Fullerton, M. "Sex-role development and creative potential in kindergarten-age boys." *Developmental Psychology*, 1969, *1*, 291-296.

Biller, H.B. and Smith, A.E. "An AFDC mothers group: An exploratory effort in community mental health." *Family Coordinator*, 1972, *21*, 287-290.

Biller, H.B. and Weiss, S. "The father-daughter relationship and the personality development of the female." *Journal of Genetic Psychology*, 1970, *114*, 79-93. Reprinted in D. Rogers (ed.), *Issues in adolescent psychology*. New York: Appleton Century Crofts, 1972, 106-116.

Biller, H.B. and Zung, B. "Perceived maternal control, anxiety, and opposite sex-role preference among elementary school girls." *Journal of Psychology*, 1972, *81*, 85-88.

Bing, E. "Effect of child-rearing practices on development of differential cognitive abilities." *Child Development*, 1963, *34*, 631-648.

Blanchard, R.W. and Biller, H.B. "Father availability and academic performance among third-grade boys." *Developmental Psychology*, 1971, *4*, 301-305.

Block, J. "Parents of schizophrenic, neurotic, asthmatic, and congenitally ill children: A comparative study." *Archives of General Psychiatry*, 1969, *20*, 659-674.

Block, J. *Lives through time*. Berkeley: Bancroft Books, 1971.

Block, J. "Generational continuity and discontinuity in the understanding of societal rejection." *Journal of Personality and Social Psychology*, 1972, *12*, 333-345.

Block, J.; von der Lippe, A.; and Block, J.H. "Sex-role and socialization: Some personality concomitants and environmental antecedents." *Journal of Consulting and Clinical Psychology*, 1973, *41*, 321-341.

Block, J.H. "Conceptions of sex role: Some cross-cultural and longitudinal perspectives." *American Psychologist*, 1973, *28*, 512-526.

Blood, R O., Jr. and Wolfe, D.M. *Husbands and wives: The dynamics of married living*. New York: Free Press, 1960.

Bloom, B. and Arkoff, A. "Role-playing in acute and chronic schizophrenia." *Journal of Consulting Psychology*, 1961, *25*, 24-28.

Bodin, A.M. "Family interaction: A social-clinical study of synthetic, normal, and problem family triads." In W.D. Winter and A.J. Ferreira (eds.), *Research in family interaction: Readings and commentary*. Palo Alto, Calif.: Science and Behavior Books, 1969, 125-127.

Bowerman, C.E. and Elder, G.H., Jr. "Variations in adolescent perception of family power structure." *American Sociological Review*, 1964, *29*, 551-567.

Bowlby, J. *Maternal care and mental health*. Geneva: World Health Organization, 1951.

Brenton, M. *The American male*. New York: Coward-McCann, 1966.

Brigham, J.C.; Ricketts, J.L.; and Johnson, R.C. "Reported maternal and paternal behaviors of solitary and social delinquents." *Journal of Consulting Psychology*, 1967, *31*, 420-422.

Brill, N.Q. and Liston, E.H., Jr. "Parental loss in adults with emotional disorders." *Archives of General Psychiatry*, 1966, *14*, 307-314.

Brim, O.G. "Family structure and sex-role learning by children: A further analysis of Helen Koch's data." *Sociometry*, 1958, *21*, 1-16.

Bronfenbrenner, U. "The study of identification through interpersonal perception." In R. Tagiuri and L. Petrullo (eds.), *Person perception and interpersonal behavior*. Stanford: Stanford University Press, 1958, 110-130.

Bronfenbrenner, U. "Freudian theories of identification and their derivatives." *Child Development*, 1960, *31*, 15-40.

Bronfenbrenner, U. "Some familial antecedents of responsibility and leadership in adolescents." In L. Petrullo and B.M. Bass (eds.), *Leadership and interpersonal behavior.* New York: Holt, Rinehart, and Winston, 1961, 239-272.

Bronfenbrenner, U. "The psychological costs of quality and equality in education." *Child Development*, 1967, *38*, 909-925.

Bronson, W.C. "Dimensions of ego and infantile identification." *Journal of Personality*, 1959, *27*, 532-545.

Brophy, J.E. and Laosa, L.M. "The effect of a male teacher on the sex-typing of kindergarten children." *Proceedings of the 79th Annual Meeting of the American Psychological Association*, 1971, *6*, 169-170.

Brown, D.G. "Sex-role preference in young children." *Psychological Monographs*, 1956, *70*, No. 14 (Whole No. 421).

Brown, D.G. "Masculinity-feminity development in children." *Journal of Consulting Psychology*, 1957, *21*, 197-202.

Brown, D.G. "Sex-role development in a changing culture." *Psychological Bulletin*, 1958, *55*, 232-241.

Brown, D.G. "Sex-role preference in children: Methodological problems." *Psychological Reports*, 1962, *11*, 477-478.

Brown, D.G. and Tolor, A. "Human figure drawings as indicators of sexual identification and inversion." *Perceptual and Motor Skills*, 1957, *7*, 199-211.

Brown, F. "Depression and childhood bereavement." *Journal of Mental Science*, 1961, *107*, 754-777.

Brown, J.K. "A cross-cultural study of female initiation rites." *American Anthropologist*, 1963, *65*, 837-853.

Brunkan, R.J. "Perceived parental attitudes and parental identification in relation to field of vocational choice." *Journal of Counseling Psychology*, 1965, *12*, 39-47.

Burlingham, D. "The pre-oedipal infant-father relationship." *The Psychoanalytic Study of the Child*, 1973, *29*, 23-47.

Burton, R.V. "Cross-sex identity in Barbados." *Developmental Psychology*, 1972, *6*, 365-374.

Burton, R.V. and Whiting, J.W.M. "The absent father and cross-sex identity." *Merrill-Palmer Quarterly*, 1961, *7*, 85-95.

Busse, T.W. "Child-rearing antecedents of flexible thinking." *Developmental Psychology*, 1969, *1*, 585-591.

Byers, A.P.; Forrest, G.G.; and Zaccaria, J.S. "Recalled early parent-child relations, adult needs, and occupational choice: A test of Roe's theory." *Journal of Counseling Psychology*, 1968, *15* 324-328.

Carlsmith, L. "Effect of early father-absence on scholastic aptitude." *Harvard Educational Review*, 1964, *34*, 3-21.

Carpenter, J. and Eisenberg, P. "Some relations between family background and personality." *Journal of Psychology*, 1935, *6*, 115-136.

Carter, E.S. "How invalid are marks assigned by teachers?" *Journal of Educational Psychology*, 1952, *43*, 218-228.

Cascario, E.F. "The male teacher and reading achievement of first-grade boys and girls." Unpublished doctoral dissertation, Lehigh University, 1971.

Cava, E.L. and Rausch, H.L. "Identification and the adolescent boy's perception of his father." *Journal of Abnormal and Social Psychology*, 1952, *47*, 855-856.

Cervantes, L.F. "Family background, primary relationships, and the high school dropout." *Journal of Marriage and The Family*, 1965, *27*, 218-223.

Chambers, J.A. "Relating personality and biographical factors to scientific creativity." *Psychological Monographs*, 1964, *78*, No. 7 (Whole No. 584).

Chang, J. and Block, J. "A study of identification in male homosexuals." *Journal of Consulting Psychology*, 1960, *24*, 307-310.

Cheek, F.E. "A serendipitous finding: Sex roles and schizophrenia." *Journal of Abnormal and Social Psychology*, 1964, *69*, 392-400.

Chein, I.; Gerrard, D.L.; Lee, B.S.; and Rosenfeld, E. *The road to H.* New York: Basic Books, 1964.

Christopher, S.A. "Parental relationship and value orientation as factors in academic achievement." *Personnel and Guidance Journal*, 1967, *45*, 921-925.

Clausen, J.A. "Family structure, socialization, and personality." In L.W. Hoffman and M.L. Hoffman (eds.), *Review of child development research*, *Vol. 2.* New York: Russell Sage Foundation, 1966, 1-53.

Cobliner, W.G. "Social factors in mental disorders: A contribution to the etiology of mental illness." *Genetic Psychology Monographs*, 1963, *67*, 151-215.

Cole, J.K. and Dienstbier (eds.), *Nebraska symposium on motivation.* Lincoln: University of Nebraska Press, 1974.

Coleman, J.S.; Campbell, E.Q.; McPartland, J.; Mood, A.M.; Weinfeld, F.D.; and York, R.L. *Equality of educational opportunity.* Washington: Office of Education, 1966.

Colley, T. "The nature and origin of psychological sexual identity." *Psychological Review*, 1959, *66*, 165-177.

Cooper, J.B. and Lewis, J.H. "Parent evaluation as related to social ideology and academic achievement." *Journal of Genetic Psychology*, 1962, *101*, 135-143.

Coopersmith, S. *The antecedents of self-esteem.* San Francisco: W.H. Freeman, 1967.

Corah, N.L. "Differentiation in children and their parents." *Journal of Personality*, 1965, *33*, 300-308.

Cortés, C.F. and Fleming, E. "The effects of father absence on the adjustment of culturally disadvantaged boys." *Journal of Special Education*, 1968, *2*, 413-420.

Cottrell, L.S. "The adjustment of the individual to his age and sex roles." *American Sociological Review*, 1942, *7*, 617-620.

Cox, F.N. "An assessment of children's attitudes towards parent figures." *Child Development*, 1962, *33*, 821-830.

Crain, A.J. and Stamm, C.S. "Intermittent absence of fathers and children's perceptions of parents." *Journal of Marriage and the Family*, 1965, *27*, 344-347.

Crandall, V.J.; Dewey, R.; Katkovsky, W.; and Preston, A. "Parents' attitudes and behaviors and grade-school children's academic achievements." *Journal of Genetic Psychology*, 1964, *104*, 53-66.

Crane, A.R. "A note on preadolescent gangs." *Australian Journal of Psychology*, 1951, *3*, 43-46.

Crane, A.R. "Preadolescent gangs: a sociopsychological interpretation." *Journal of Genetic Psychology*, 1955, *86*, 275-279.

Crescimbeni, J. "Broken homes affect academic achievement." *Education*, 1964, *84*, 440-441.

Crites, J.O. "Parental identification in relation to vocational interest development." *Journal of Educational Psychology*, 1962, *53*, 262-270.

Cross, H.J. "The relation of parental training conditions to conceptual level in adolescent boys." *Journal of Personality*, 1966, *34*, 348-365.

Cross, H.J. and Allen, J. "Relationship between memories of parental behavior and academic achievement motivation." *Proceedings, 77th Annual Convention of the American Psychological Association*, 1969, *4*, 285-286.

Cross, H.J. and Aron, R.D. "The relationship of unobtrusive measures of marital conflict to remembered differences between parents." Paper presented at the meeting of the American Psychological Association, Washington, D.C., September 1971.

Dai, B. "Some problems of personality development among Negro children." In C. Kluckhohn, H.A. Murray, and D.M. Schneider (eds.), *Personality in nature, society, and culture*. New York: Knopf, 1953, 545-566.

D'Andrade, R.G. "Father-absence and cross-sex identification." Unpublished doctoral dissertation, Harvard University, 1962.

D'Andrade, R.G. "Sex differences and cultural institutions." In E.E. Maccoby (ed.), *The Development of sex differences*. Stanford: Stanford University Press, 1966, 174-204.

Da Silva, G. "The role of the father with chronic schizophrenic patients." *Journal of the Canadian Psychiatric Association*, 1963, *8*, 190-203.

Datta, L.E. and Parloff, M.B. "Parent-child relationships and early scientific creativity." *Proceedings of the 75th Annual Convention of the APA*, 1967, *2*, 149-150.

Dauw, D.C. "Life experiences of original thinkers and good elaborators." *Exceptional Children*, 1966, *32*, 433-440.

David, K.H. "Ego-strength, sex differences, and description of self, ideal, and parents." *Journal of General Psychology*, 1968, *79*, 79-81.

Davids, A. *Abnormal children and youth*. New York: Wylie, 1972.

Davids, A. (ed.), *Child personality and psychopathology: Current topics*. New York: Wiley, 1974.

Davids, A.; Joelson, M.; and McArthur, C. Rorschach and TAT indices of homosexuality in overt homosexuals, neurotics, and normal males. *Journal of Abnormal and Social Psychology*, 1956, *53*, 161-172.

Davis, A. and Havighurst, R.J. "Social class and color differences in child rearing." *American Sociological Review*, 1946, *11*, 698-710.

Davis, O. and Slobodian, J. "Teacher behavior toward boys and girls in first grade reading instruction." *American Educational Research Journal*, 1967, *4*, 261-269.

Davis, W.C. and Phares, E. "Parental antecedents of internal-external control of reinforcement." *Psychological Reports*, 1969, *24*, 427-436.

DeLucia, L.A. "The toy preference test: A measure of sex-role identification." *Child Development*, 1963, *34*, 107-117.

Dennehy, C. "Childhood bereavement and psychiatric illness." *British Journal of Psychiatry*, 1966, *112*, 1049-1069.

Despert, L.J. "The fatherless family." *Child Study*, 1957, *34*, 22-28.

Deutsch, H. *The psychology of women, Vol. I.*, New York: Grune & Stratton, 1944.

Deutsch, M. "Minority group and class status as related to social and personality factors in scholastic achievement." *Monograph of the Society for Applied Anthropology*, 1960, *2*, 1-32.

Deutsch, M. and Brown, B. "Social influences in Negro-white intelligence differences." *Journal of Social Issues*, 1964, *20*, 24-35.

Devereux, E.C., Jr.; Bronfenbrenner, U.; and Suci, G.J. "Patterns of parent behavior in the United States and the Federal Republic of Germany: A cross-national comparison." *International Social Science Journal*, 1962, *14*, 488-506.

Diamond, S. *Personality and temperament.* New York: Harper and Row, 1957.

Dinitz, S.; Dynes, R.R.; and Clarke, A.C. "Preferences for male or female children: traditional or affectional." *Marriage and Family Living*, 1954, *16*, 128-130.

Distler, L.S. "Patterns of parental identification: An examination of three theories." Unpublished doctoral dissertation, University of California, Berkeley, 1964.

Donini, G.P. "An evaluation of sex-role identification among father-absent and father-present boys." *Psychology*, 1967, *4*, 13-16.

Douvan, E. "Employment and the adolescent." In F.I. Nye and L.W. Hoffman (eds.), *The employed mother in America.* Chicago: Rand McNally, 1963.

Douvan, E. and Adelson, J. *The adolescent experience.* New York, Wiley, 1966.

Downey, K.J. "Parental interest in the institutionalized, severely mentally retarded child." *Social Problems*, 1963, *11*, 186-193.

Dreyer, A. and Wells, M. "Parental values, parental control, and creativity in young children." *Journal of Marriage and the Family*, 1966, *28*, 83-88.

DuHamel, T.R. and Biller, H.B. "Parental imitation and nonimitation in young children." *Developmental Psychology*, 1969, *1*, 772.

Dyk, R.B. and Witkin, H.A. "Family experiences related to the development of differentiation in children." *Child Development*, 1965, *36*, 21-55.

Dyl, A.S. and Biller, H.B. "Paternal absence, social class, and reading achievement." Unpublished study, University of Rhode Island, 1973.

Egelson, J. and Frank, J.F. *Parents without partners.* New York: Dutton, 1961.

Eisenberg, L. "The fathers of autistic children." *American Journal of Orthopsychiatry*, 1957, *27*, 715-725.

Elder, G.H., Jr. *Adolescent achievement and mobility aspirations.* Chapel Hill, N.C.: Institute for Research in Social Science, 1962(a).

Elder, G.H., Jr. "Structural variations in the child-rearing relationship." *Sociometry*, 1962(b), *25*, 241-262.

Elder, G.H., Jr. and Bowerman, C.E. "Family structure and child-rearing patterns: The effect of family size and sex composition." *American Sociological Review*, 1963, *28*, 891-905.

Emmerich, W. "Parental identification in young children." *Genetic Psychology Monographs*, 1959, *60*, 257-308.

Emmerich, W. "Variations in the parent role as a function of the parent's sex and the child's sex and age." *Merrill-Palmer Quarterly*, 1962, *8*, 3-11.

Engel, I.M. "A factor-analytic study of five masculinity-femininity tests." *Journal of Consulting Psychology*, 1966, *30*, 565.

Engemoen, B.L. "The influence of membership in a broken home on test performance of first grade children." Unpublished doctoral dissertation, North Texas University, 1966.

Epstein, R. and Liverant, S. "Verbal conditioning and sex-role identification in children." *Child Development*, 1963, *34*, 99-106.

Erikson, E.H. "Identity and the life cycle." *Psychological Issues*, 1959, *1* (Whole No. 1).

Eron, L.D.; Walder, L.O.; Toigo, R.; and Lefkowitz, M.M. "Social class, parental punishment for aggression, and child aggression." *Child Development*, 1963, *34*, 849-867.

Etaugh, C. "Effects of maternal employment on children: A review of recent research." *Merrill-Palmer Quarterly*, 1974, *20*, 71-98.

Evans, R.B. "Childhood parental relationships of homosexual men." *Journal of Consulting and Clinical Psychology*, 1969, *33*, 129-135.

Fagen, S.A.; Janda, E.J.; Baker, S.L.; Fischer, E.G.; and Cove, L.A. "Impact of father-absence in military families: II. Factors relating to success of coping with crisis." Paper presented at the meeting of the American Psychological Association, Washington, D.C., September 1967.

Fagot, B.I. and Patterson, G. "An in vivo analysis of reinforcing contingencies for sex-role behaviors in the preschool child." *Developmental Psychology*, 1969, *1*, 563-568.

Farber, B. "Effects of a severely mentally retarded child on the family." In E.P. Trapp and P. Himelstein (eds.), *Readings on the exceptional child.* New York: Appleton-Century Crofts, 1962, 227-246.

Farber, B. "Marital integration as a factor in parent-child relations." *Child Development*, 1962, *33*, 1-14.

Farina, A. "Patterns of role-dominance and conflict in parents of schizophrenic patients." *Journal of Abnormal and Social Psychology*, 1960, *61*, 31-38.

Fauls, L.B. and Smith, W.P. "Sex-role learning of five-year-olds." *Journal of Genetic Psychology*, 1956, *89*, 105-117.

Fenichel, O. *The psychoanalytic theory of neurosis.* New York: Norton, 1945.

Ferreira, A.J.; Winter, W.D.; and Poindexter, E.J. "Some interactional variables in normal and abnormal families." *Family Process*, 1966, *5*, 60-75.

Fish, K.D. "Paternal availability, family role-structure, maternal employment, and personality development in late adolescent females." Unpublished doctoral dissertation, University of Massachusetts, 1969.

Fish, K.D. and Biller, H.B. "Perceived childhood paternal relationships and college females' personal adjustment." *Adolescence*, 1973, *8*, 415-420.

Fisher, S.F. *The female organism: Psychology, physiology, fantasy.* New York: Basic Books, 1973.

Flacks, R. "The liberated generation: An exploration of the roots of student protest." *Journal of Social Issues*, 1967, *22*, 52-75.

Fleck, S.; Lidz, T.; and Cornelison, A. "A comparison of parent-child relationships of male and female schizophrenic patients." *Archives of General Psychiatry*, 1963, *8*, 1-7.

Forrest, T. "Paternal roots of female character development." *Contemporary Psychoanalyst*, 1966, *3*, 21-28.

Forrest, T. "The paternal roots of male character development." *The Psychoanalytic Review*, 1967, *54*, 81-99.

Forrest, T. "Treatment of the father in family therapy." *Family Process*, 1969, *8*, 106-117.

Foster, J.E. "Father images: Television and ideal." *Journal of Marriage and the Family*, 1964, *26*, 353-355.

Franck, K. and Rosen, E.A. "A projective test of masculinity-femininity." *Journal of Consulting Psychology*, 1949, *13*, 247-256.

Frazier, E.F. *The Negro family in the United States.* Chicago: University of Chicago Press, 1939.

Freedheim, D.K. "An investigation of masculinity and parental role patterns." Unpublished doctoral dissertation, Duke University, 1960.

Freedheim, D.K. and Borstelmann, L.J. "An investigation of masculinity and parental role-patterns." *American Psychologist*, 1963, *18*, 339. (Abstract)

Freedman, M. *Homosexuality and psychological functioning.* Belmont, Calif.: Brooks/Cole, 1971.

Freud, A. and Burlingham, D.T. *Infants without families.* New York: International University Press, 1944.

Freud, S. "The passing of the Oedipus complex." *Collected papers, Vol. II.* London: Hogarth Press, 1924.

Freud, S. *New introductory lectures in psychoanalysis.* New York: Norton, 1933.

Freud, S. *Leonardo Da Vinci: A study in psychosexuality.* New York: Random House, 1947.

Freud, S. "Some psychological consequences of the anatomical distinction between the sexes." In *Collected papers, Vol. V.* London: Hogarth Press, 1950, 186-197.

Freud, S. "Group psychology and the analysis of the ego." In J. Strachey (ed.), *The complete psychological works of Sigmund Freud Vol 1.* London: Hogarth Press, 1955, 69-143.

Freudenthal, K. "Problems of the one-parent family." *Social Work,* 1959, *4,* 44-48.

Friedman, A.S. "The family and the female delinquent: An overview." In O. Pollak and A.S. Friedman (eds.), *Family dynamics and female sexual delinquency.* Science and Behavior Books, 1969, 113-126.

Garai, J.E. and Scheinfeld, A. "Sex differences in mental and behavioral traits." *Genetic Psychology Monographs,* 1968, *77,* 169-299.

Garbower, G. *Behavior problems of children in Navy officers' families: As related to social conditions of Navy family life.* Washington, D.C.: Catholic University Press, 1959.

Gardiner, G.E. "Separation of the parents and the emotional life of the child." In S. Blueck (ed.), *The problems of delinquency.* Boston: Houghton-Mifflin, 1959, 138-143.

Gardner, G.G. "The relationship between childhood neurotic symptomatology and later schizophrenia in males and females." *Journal of Nervous and Mental Disease,* 1967, *144,* 97-100.

Gassner, S. and Murray, E.J. "Dominance and conflict in the interactions between parents of normal and neurotic children." *Journal of Abnormal Psychology,* 1969, *74,* 33-41.

Gates, A. "Sex differences in reading ability." *Elementary School Journal,* 1961, *61,* 431-434.

Gay, M.J. and Tonge, W.L. "The late effects of loss of parents in childhood." *British Journal of Psychiatry,* 1967, *113,* 753-759.

Glasser, P. and Navarre, E. "Structural problems of the one-parent family." *Journal of Social Issues,* 1965, *21,* 98-109.

Glueck, S. and Glueck, E. *Unravelling juvenile delinquency.* New York: Commonwealth Fund, 1950.

Glueck, S. and Glueck, E. *Physique and delinquency.* New York: Harper and Row, 1956.

Gold, M. and Slater, C. "Office, factory, store-and family: A study of integration setting." *American Sociological Review,* 1958, *23,* 64-74.

Goldberg, E.M. *Family influences and psychosomatic illness.* London: Tavistock Publications, 1958.

Goldberg, S. and Lewis, M. "Play behavior in the year-old infant: Early sex differences." *Child Development*, 1969, *40*, 21-31.

Goldfarb, W. Emotional and intellectual consequences of psychologic deprivation during infancy: A reevaluation. In P. Hoch and J. Zubin (eds.), *Psychopathology of childhood.* New York: Grune and Stratton, 1955, 449-457.

Goldin, P.C. "A review of children's reports of parent behaviors." *Psychological Bulletin*, 1969, *71*, 222-236.

Goode, W. "Family disorganization." In R.K. Merton and R.A. Nisbet (eds.), *Contemporary social problems.* New York: Harcourt, Brace, and World, 1961.

Goodenough, E.W. "Interest in persons as an aspect of sex differences in the early years." *Genetic Psychology Monographs*, 1957, *55*, 287-323.

Gordon, T. *Parent effectiveness training.* New York: Peter Wyden, 1970.

Gorer, G. *The American People: A study of national character.* New York: Norton, 1948.

Gover, D.A. "Socioeconomic differential in the relationship between marital adjustment and wife's employment status." *Marriage and Family Living*, 1963, *25*, 452-458.

Grambs, J.D. and Waetjen, W.B. "Being equally different: A new right for boys and girls." *National Elementary School Principal*, 1966, *46*, 59-67.

Gray, S.W. "Masculinity-femininity in relation to anxiety and social acceptance." *Child Development*, 1957, *28*, 203-214.

Gray, S.W. "Perceived similarity to parents and adjustment." *Child Development*, 1959, *30*, 91-107.

Gray, W.W. and Klaus, R. "The assessment of parental identification." *Genetic Psychology Monographs*, 1956, *54*, 87-114.

Green, A.W. "The middle-class child and neurosis." *American Sociological Review*, 1946, *11*, 31-41.

Green, L. and Parker, H. "Parental influences upon adolescents' occupational choice: A test of an aspect of Roe's theory." *Journal of Consulting Psychology*, 1965, *12*, 379-383.

Green, R. *Sexual identity conflict in children and adults.* New York: Basic Books, 1974.

Greenstein, J.F. "Father characteristics and sex-typing." *Journal of Personality and Social Psychology*, 1966, *3*, 271-277.

Gregory, I. "Studies of parental deprivation in psychiatric patients." *American Journal of Psychiatry*, 1958, *115*, 432-442.

Gregory, I. "Anterospective data following childhood loss of a parent: I. Delinquency and high school dropout." *Archives of General Psychiatry*, 1965(a), *13*, 99-109.

Gregory, I. "Anterospective data following childhood loss of a parent: II. Pathology, performance, and potential among college students." *Archives of General Psychiatry*, 1965(b), *13*, 110-120.

Grønseth, E. "The impact of father-absence in sailor families upon the personality structure and social adjustment of adult sailor sons, part I." In N. Anderson (ed.), *Studies of the family, Vol. 2.* Gottingen: Vandenhoeck and Ruprecht, 1957, 97-114.

Grunebaum, M.G.; Hurwitz, I.; Prentice, N.M.; and Sperry, B.M. "Fathers of sons with primary neurotic learning inhibition." *American Journal of Orthopsychiatry*, 1962, *32*, 462-473.

Gundlach, R.H. "Childhood parental relationships and the establishment of gender roles of homosexuals." *Journal of Consulting and Clinical Psychology*, 1969, *33*, 136-139.

Gundlach, R.H. and Riess, B.F. "Self and sexual identity in the female: A study of female homosexuals." In B.F. Riess (ed.), *New directions in mental health.* New York: Grune and Stratton, 1968.

Haley, J. and Hoffman, L. *Techniques of family therapy.* New York: Basic Books, 1967.

Hall, M. and Keith, R.A. "Sex-role preference among children of upper and lower-social class." *Journal of Social Psychology*, 1964, *62*, 101-110.

Hall, P. and Tonge, W.L. "Long-standing continuous unemployment in male patients with psychiatric symptoms." *British Journal of Preventive and Social Medicine*, 1963, *17*, 191-196.

Hamilton, C.V. *A research in marriage.* New York: Boni, 1929.

Hamilton, D.M. and Wahl, J.G. "The hospital treatment of dementia praecox." *American Journal of Psychiatry*, 1948, *105*, 346-352.

Hampson, J.L. "Determinants of psychosexual orientation." In F.A. Beach (ed.), *Sex and behavior.* New York: Wiley, 1965, 108-132.

Hanson, E.H. "Do boys get a square deal in school." *Education*, 1959, *79*, 597-598.

Hardy, M.C. "Aspects of home environment in relation to behavior at the elementary school age." *Journal of Juvenile Research*, 1937, *21*, 206-225.

Harlow, R.G. "Masculine inadequacy and compensatory development of physique." *Journal of Personality*, 1951, *19*, 312-333.

Hartley, R.E. "Sex-role pressures and socialization of the male child." *Psychological Reports*, 1959, *5*, 457-468.

Hartley, R.E. "The one-parent family." In *Reference papers on children and youth.* 1960 White House Conference on Children and Youth.

Hartley, R.E. "A developmental view of female sex-role definition and identification." *Merrill-Palmer Quarterly*, 1964, *10*, 3-16.

Hartley, R.E. and Klein, A. "Sex-role concepts among elementary-school-age girls." *Marriage and Family Living*, 1959, *21*, 59-64.

Hartup, W.W. "Some correlates of parental imitation in young children." *Child Development*, 1962, *33*, 85-96.

Hartup, W.W. and Zook, E.A. "Sex-role preference in three- and four-year-old children." *Journal of Consulting Psychology*, 1960, *24*, 420-426.

Haworth, M.R. "Parental loss in children as reflected in projective responses." *Journal of Projective Techniques*, 1964, *28*, 31-35.

Heckel, R.V. "The effects of fatherlessness on the preadolescent female." *Mental Hygiene*, 1963, *47*, 69-73.

Heckscher, B.T. "Household structure and achievement orientation in lower-class Barbadian families." *Journal of Marriage and the Family*, 1967, *29*, 521-526.

Heilbrun, A.B. "Parental identification and college adjustment." *Psychological Reports*, 1962, *10*, 853-854.

Heilbrun, A.B. "The measurement of identification." *Child Development*, 1965(a), *36*, 111-127.

Heilbrun, A.B. "An empirical test of the modeling theory of sex-role learning." *Child Development*, 1965(b), *36*, 789-799.

Heilbrun, A.B. and Fromme, D.K. "Parental identification of late adolescents and level of adjustment: the importance of parent-model attributes, ordinal position, and sex of child." *Journal of Genetic Psychology*, 1965, *107*, 49-59.

Heilbrun, A.B.; Harrell, S.N.; and Gillard, B.J. "Perceived childrearing attitudes of fathers and cognitive control in daughters." *Journal of Genetic Psychology*, 1967, *111*, 29-40.

Helper, M.M. "Learning theory and the self-concept." *Journal of Abnormal and Social Psychology*, 1955, *51*, 184-194.

Helson, R. "Personality characteristics and developmental history of creative college women." *Genetic Psychology Monographs*, 1967, *76*, 205-256.

Helson, R. "Women mathematicians and the creative personality." *Journal of Consulting and Clinical Psychology*, 1971, *36*, 210-220.

Herzog, E. and Sudia, C.E. *Boys in fatherless families*. Washington: Office of Child Development, 1970.

Hetherington, E.M. "A developmental study of the effects of sex of the dominant parent on sex-role preference, identification, and imitation in children." *Journal of Personality and Social Psychology*, 1965, *2*, 188-194.

Hetherington, E.M. "Effects of paternal absence on sex-typed behaviors in Negro and white preadolescent males." *Journal of Personality and Social Psychology*, 1966, *4*, 87-91.

Hetherington, E.M. "Effects of father-absence on personality development in adolescent daughters." *Developmental Psychology*, 1972, *7*, 313-326.

Hetherington, E.M. and Brackbill, Y. "Etiology and covariation of obstinacy, orderliness, and parsimony in young children." *Child Development*, 1963, *34*, 919-943.

Hetherington, E.M. and Frankie, G. "Effects of parental dominance, warmth, and conflict on imitation in children." *Journal of Personality and Social Psychology*, 1967, *6*, 119-125.

Hilgard, J.R.; Neuman, M.F.; and Fisk, F. "Strength of adult ego following bereavement." *American Journal of Orthopsychiatry*, 1960, *30*, 788-798.

Hill, J.P. "Similarity and accordance between parents and sons in attitudes towards mathematics." *Child Development*, 1967, *38*, 777-791.

Hill, O.W. and Price, J.S. "Childhood bereavement and adult depression." *British Journal of Psychiatry*, 1967, *113*, 743-751.

Hill, R. *Families under stress.* New York: Harper, 1949.

Hoffman, L.W. "The father's role in the family and the child's peer-group adjustment." *Merrill-Palmer Quarterly*, 1961, *7*, 97-105.

Hoffman, L.W. "Early childhood experiences and women's achievement motives." *Journal of Social Issues*, 1972, *28* (2), 129-155.

Hoffman, L.W. "Effects of maternal employment on the child—a review of research." *Developmental Psychology*, 1974, *10*, 204-228.

Hoffman, M.L. "Power assertion by the parent and its impact on the child." *Child Development*, 1960, *31*, 129-143.

Hoffman, M.L. "Father absence and conscience development." *Developmental Psychology*, 1971(a), *4*, 400-406.

Hoffman, M.L. "Identification and conscience development." *Child Development*, 1971(b), *42*, 1071-1082.

Holman, P. "Some factors in the etiology of maladjustment in children." *Journal of Mental Science*, 1953, *99*, 654-688.

Holstein, C.E. "The relation of children's moral judgement level to that of their parents and to communication patterns in the family." In R.C. Smart and M.S. Smart (eds.), *Readings in child development and relationships.* New York: Macmillan, 1972, 484-494.

Honzik, M.P. "Environmental correlates of mental growth: Prediction from the family setting at 21 months." *Child Development*, 1967, *38*, 338-364.

Hooker, E. "Parental relations and male homosexuality in patient and non-patient samples." *Journal of Consulting and Clinical Psychology*, 1969, *33*, 140-142.

Horney, K. "The denial of the vagina." *International Journal of Psychoanalysis*, 1933, *14*, 57-70.

Hurley, J.R. "Parental malevolence and children's intelligence." *Journal of Consulting Psychology*, 1967, *31*, 199-204.

Hurvitz, N. "Control roles, marital strain, role deviation, and marital adjustment." *Journal of Marriage and the Family*, 1965, *27*, 29-31.

Hutchison, J.G. "Family interaction patterns and the emotionally disturbed child." In W.D. Winter and A.J. Ferreira (eds.), *Research in family interaction: Readings and commentary.* Palo Alto, California: Science and Behavior Books, 1969, 187-191.

Ingham, H.V. "A statistical study of family relationships in psychoneurosis." *American Journal of Orthopsychiatry*, 1949, *106*, 91-98.

Jacobson, G. and Ryder, R.G. "Parental loss and some characteristics of the early marriage relationship." *American Journal of Orthopsychiatry*, 1969, *39*, 779-787.

Jenkins, R.L. "The varieties of children's behavioral problems and family dynamics." *American Journal of Psychiatry*, 1968, *124*, 1440-1445.

Jenson, P.G. and Kirchner, W.K. "A national answer to the question, 'Do sons follow their fathers' occupations?' " *Journal of Applied Psychology*, 1955, *39*, 419-421.

Johnson, M.A. and Meadow, A. "Parental identification among male schizophrenics." *Journal of Personality*, 1966, *34*, 300-309.

Johnson, M.M. "Sex-role learning in the nuclear family." *Child Development*, 1963, *34*, 319-333.

Jolly, A. *The evolution of primate behavior.* New York: Macmillan, 1972.

Jones, E. *Raising your child in a fatherless home.* New York: Macmillan, 1963.

Kagan, J. "Socialization of aggression and the perception of parents in fantasy." *Child Development*, 1958(a), *29*, 311-320.

Kagan, J. "The concept of identification." *Psychological Review*, 1958(b), *65*, 296-305.

Kagan, J. "Acquisition and significance of sex typing and sex-role identity." In M.L. Hoffman and L.W. Hoffman (eds.), *Review of child development research, Vol. 1.* New York: Russell Sage Foundation, 1964, 137-167.

Kagan, J. "Sex typing during the preschool and early school years." In I. Janis, G. Mahl, J. Kagan, and R. Holt (eds.), *Personality: Dynamics, development, and assessment.* New York: Harcourt, Brace and World, 1969.

Kagan, J. and Moss, H. *Birth to Maturity.* New York: Wiley, 1962.

Kardiner, A. and Ovesey, L. *The mark of oppression.* New York: Norton, 1951.

Katkovsky, W.; Crandall, V.C.; and Good, S. "Parental antecedents of children's beliefs in internal-external control of reinforcements in intellectual achievement situations." *Child Development*, 1967, *38*, 765-776.

Katz, I. "Socialization of academic motivation in minority group children." In D. Levine (ed.), *Nebraska symposium on motivation.* Lincoln, University of Nebraska Press, 1967, 133-191.

Kaufman, I.; Peck, A.I.; and Tagiuri, C.K. "The family constellation and overt incestuous relations between father and daughter." *American Journal of Orthopsychiatry*, 1954, *24*, 266-277.

Kaye, H.E. et al. "Homosexuality in women." *Archives of General Psychiatry*, 1967, *17*, 626-634.

Kayton, R. and Biller, H.B. "Perception of parental sex-role behavior and psychopathology in adult males." *Journal of Consulting and Clinical Psychology*, 1971, *36*, 235-237.

Kayton, R. and Biller, H.B. "Sex-role development and psychopathology in adult males." *Journal of Consulting and Clinical Psychology*, 1972, *38*, 308-310.

Keeler, W.R. "Children's reaction to the death of a parent." In P.H. Hoch and J. Zubin (eds.), *Depression.* New York: Grune, 1954, 109-120.

Keller, O.J., Jr. and Alper, B.S. *Halfway houses: Community-centered correction and treatment.* Lexington, Mass.: Lexington Books, D.C. Heath and Company, 1970.

Kelly, F.J. and Baer, D.J. "Age of male delinquents when father left home and recidivism." *Psychological Reports*, 1969, *25*, 1010.

Kimball, B. "The Sentence Completion Technique in a study of scholastic underachievement." *Journal of Consulting Psychology*, 1952, *16*, 353-358.

King, C.E. "The Negro maternal family: A product of an economic and culture system." *Social Forces*, 1945, *24*, 100-104.

King, K.; McIntyre, J.; and Axelson, L.J. "Adolescents' views of maternal employment as a threat to the marital relationship." *Journal of Marriage and the Family*, 1968, *30*, 633-637.

Kleeman, J. "The establishment of core gender identity in normal girls, I." *Archives of Sexual Behavior*, 1971(a), *1*, 103-116.

Kleeman, J. "The establishment of core gender identity in normal girls, II." *Archives of Sexual Behavior*, 1971(b), *1*, 117-129.

Klein, C. *The single parent experience.* New York: Avon, 1973.

Kluckhohn, C. *Mirror for man.* New York: McGraw-Hill, 1949.

Koch, H.L. "Sissiness and tomboyishness in relation to sibling characteristics." *Journal of Genetic Psychology*, 1956, *88*, 231-244.

Koch, M.B. "Anxiety in preschool children from broken homes." *Merrill-Palmer Quarterly*, 1961, *1*, 225-231.

Kohlberg, L. "A cognitive-developmental analysis of children's sex-role concepts and attitudes." In E.E. Maccoby (ed.), *The development of sex differences.* Stanford: Stanford University Press, 1966, 82-173.

Kohlberg, L. and Zigler, E. "The impact of cognitive maturity on the development of sex-role attitudes in the years four-eight." *Genetic Psychology Monographs*, 1967, *75*, 89-165.

Kohn, H.L. "Social class and parental values." *American Journal of Sociology*, 1959, *64*, 337-351.

Kohn, M.L. and Clausen, J.A. "Parental authority behavior and schizophrenia." *American Journal of Orthopsychiatry*, 1956, *26*, 297-313.

Kopel, D. and Geerded, H. "A survey of clinical services for poor readers." *Journal of Educational Psychology Monograph*, 1933, *13*, 209-224.

Kopf, K.E. "Family variables and school adjustment of eighth grade father-absent boys." *Family Coordinator*, 1970, *19*, 145-150.

Kotelchuck, M. "The nature of the child's tie to his father." Unpublished doctoral dissertation, Harvard University, 1972.

Kriesberg, L. "Rearing children for educational achievement in fatherless families." *Journal of Marriage and the Family*, 1967, *29*, 288-301.

Kriesberg, L. *Mothers in poverty: A study of fatherless families.* Chicago: Aldine, 1970.

Kyselka, W. "Young men in nursery school." *Childhood Education*, 1966, *42*, 293-299.

L'Abate, L. "The effect of paternal failure to participate during the referral of child psychiatric patients." *Journal of Clinical Psychology*, 1960, *16*, 407-408.

La Barre, W. *The human animal.* Chicago: University of Chicago Press, 1954.

Landis, J.T. "The trauma of children when parents divorce." *Marriage and Family Living*, 1960, *22*, 7-13.

Landis, J.T. "A reexamination of the role of the father as an index of family integration." *Marriage and Family Living*, 1962, *24*, 122-128.

Landis, P.H. *Making the most of marriage.* New York: Appleton-Century-Crofts, 1965.

Landy, F.; Rosenberg, B.G.; and Sutton-Smith, B. "The effect of limited father-absence on the cognitive and emotional development of children." Paper presented at the meeting of the Midwestern Psychological Ascociation, Chicago, May 1967.

Landy, F.; Rosenberg, B.G.; and Sutton-Smith, B. "The effect of limited father-absence on cognitive development." *Child Development*, 1969, *40*, 941-944.

Lane, R.E. "Fathers and sons: Foundations of political belief." *American Sociological Review*, 1959, *24*, 502 511.

Langner, T.S. and Michael, S.T. *Life stress and mental health.* New York: Free Press, 1963.

Lansky, L.M. "Patterns of defense against conflict." Unpublished doctoral dissertation. University of Michigan, 1956.

Lansky, L.M. "The family structure also affects the model: Sex-role attitudes in parents of preschool children." *Merrill-Palmer Quarterly*, 1967, *13*, 139-150.

Lansky, L.M. and McKay, G. "Sex-role preferences of kindergarten boys and girls: Some contradictory results." *Psychological Reports*, 1963, *13*, 415-421.

Lawton, M.J. and Sechrest, L. "Figure drawings by young boys from father-present and father-absent homes." *Journal of Clinical Psychology*, 1962, *18*, 304-305.

Layman, E.M. Discussion. In D.G. Applezweig (Chm.) "Childhood and mental health: The influence of the father in the family setting." Symposium presented at the American Psychological Association, Chicago, September, 1960 (Reprinted in *Merrill-Palmer Quarterly*, 1961, *1*, 107-111).

Lazowick, L.M. "On the nature of identification." *Journal of Abnormal and Social Psychology*, 1955, *51*, 175-183.

Lederer, W. "Dragons, delinquents, and destiny." *Psychological Issues*, 1964, *4*, (Whole No. 3).

Lee, P.C. "Male and female teachers in elementary schools: An ecological analysis." *Teachers College Record*, 1973, *75*, 79-98.

Lee, P.C. and Wolinsky, A.L. "Male teachers of young children: A preliminary empirical study." *Young Children*, 1973, *28*, 342-352.

Lefkowitz, M.M. "Some relationships between sex-role preference of children and other parent and child variables." *Psychological Reports*, 1962, *10*, 43-53.

Leichty, M.M. "The effect of father-absence during early childhood upon the Oedipal situation as reflected in young adults." *Merrill-Palmer Quarterly*, 1960, *6*, 212-217.

Leiderman, G.F. "Effect of family experiences on boys' peer relationships." Unpublished doctoral dissertation, Harvard University, 1953.

Leiderman, G.F. "Effect of parental relationships and child-training practices on boys' interactions with peers." *Acta Psychologica*, 1959, *15*, 469.

Leighton, L.A.; Stollak, G.E.; and Ferguson, L.R. "Patterns of communication in normal and clinic families." *Journal of Consulting and Clinical Psychology*, 1971, *36*, 252-256.

LeMasters, E.E. *Parents in modern America: A sociological perspective*. Homewood, Ill.: Dorsey, 1970.

Leonard, M.R. "Fathers and daughters." *International Journal of Psychoanalysis*, 1966, *47*, 325-333.

Lerner, S.H. "Effect of desertion on family life." *Social Casework*, 1954, *35*, 3-8.

Lessing, E.E.; Zagorin, S.W.; and Nelson, D. "WISC subtest and IQ score correlates of father absence." *Journal of Genetic Psychology*, 1970, *67*, 181-195.

Levin, H. and Sears, R.R. "Identification with parents as a determinant of doll play aggression." *Child Development*, 1956, *37*, 135-153.

Levin, R.B. "An empirical test of the female castration complex." *Journal of Abnormal Psychology*, 1966, *71*, 181-188.

Levy, D.M. *Maternal overprotection*. New York: Columbia University Press, 1943.

Lidz, T.; Parker, N.; and Cornelison, A.R. "The role of the father in the family environment of the schizophrenic patient." *American Journal of Psychiatry*, 1956, *13*, 126-132.

Liebenberg, B. "Expectant fathers." *American Journal of Orthopsychiatry*, 1967, *37*, 359-359.

Linton, R. *The study of man*. New York: Appleton-Century Crofts, 1936.

Lippitt, R. and Gold, M. "Classroom social structure as a mental health problem." *Journal of Social Issues*, 1959, *15*, 40-58.

Lipsitt, P.D. and Strodtbeck, F.L. "Defensiveness in decision-making as a function of sex-role identification." *Journal of Personality and Social Psychology*, 1967, *6*, 10-15.

Lipton, E.L.; Steinschneider, A.; and Richmond, J.B. "Psychophysiologic disorders in children." In L.W. Hoffman and M.L. Hoffman (eds.), *Review of child development research, Vol. 2*. New York: Russell Sage Foundation, 1966, 169-220.

Liverant, S. "MMPI differences between parents of disturbed children and nondisturbed children." *Journal of Consulting Psychology*, 1959, *23*, 256-260.

Lockwood, D.H. and Guerney, B. "Identification and empathy in relation to self-dissatisfaction and adjustment." *Journal of Abnormal and Social Psychology*, 1962, *65*, 343-347.

Loeb, J. "The personality factor in divorce." *Journal of Consulting Psychology*, 1966, *30*, 562.

Loeb, J. and Price, J.R. "Mother and child personality characteristics related to parental marital status in child guidance cases." *Journal of Consulting Psychology*, 1966, *30*, 112-117.

Long, B.H.; Henderson, E.H.; and Ziller, R.C. "Self-social correlates of originality in children." *Journal of Genetic Psychology*, 1967, *111*, 47-54.

Louden, K.H. "Field dependence in college students as related to father absence during the latency period." Unpublished doctoral dissertation, Graduate School of Psychology, Fuller Theological Seminary, 1973.

Lozoff, M.M. "Fathers and autonomy in women." In R.B. Kundsin (ed.), *Women and success.* New York: Morrow, 1974, 103-109.

Luckey, E.B. "Marital satisfaction and parental concept." *Journal of Consulting Psychology*, 1960, *24*, 195-204.

Lynn, D.B. "A note on sex differences in the development of masculine and feminine identification." *Psychological Review*, 1959, *66*, 126-135.

Lynn, D.B. "Sex differences in identification development." *Sociometry*, 1961, *24*, 372-383.

Lynn, D.B. "Sex-role and parental identification." *Child Development*, 1962, *33*, 555-564.

Lynn, D.B. *Parental and sex-role identification.* Berkeley: McCutchan, 1969.

Lynn, D.B. *The father: His role in child development.* Belmont, Calif.: Brooks/Cole, 1974.

Lynn, D.B. and Sawrey, W.L. "The effects of father-absence on Norwegian boys and girls." *Journal of Abnormal and Social Psychology*, 1959, 258-262.

MacArthur, R. "Sex differences in field dependence for the Eskimo: replication of Berry's findings." *International Journal of Psychology*, 1967, *2*, 139-140.

MacDonald, A.P., Jr. "Internal-external locus of control: Parental antecedents." *Journal of Consulting and Clinical Psychology*, 1971, *37*, 141-147.

MacDonald, M.W. "Criminal behavior in passive, effeminate boys." *American Journal of Orthopsychiatry*, 1938, *8*, 70-78.

McCandless, B.R. *Children: Behavior and development* Rinehart, and Winston, 1967.

McClelland, D.C. *The achieving society.* Princeton: Van Nostrand, 1961.

McClelland, D.C.; Atkinson, J.W.; Clark, R.A.; and Lowell, E.L. *The achievement motive.* New York: Appleton-Century-Crofts, 1953.

McClelland, D.C. and Watt, N.F. "Sex-role alienation in schizophrenia." *Journal of Abnormal Psychology*, 1968, *73*, 226-239.

Maccoby, E.E. *Sex differences in intellectual functioning.* In E.E. Maccoby (ed.), *The development of sex differences.* Stanford: Stanford University Press, 1966, 25-55.

Maccoby, E.E. and Rau, L. "Differential cognitive abilities." Final report, U.S. Office of Education, Cooperative Research Project No. 1040, 1962.

McCord, J.; McCord, W.; and Howard, A. "Family interaction as an antecedent to the direction of male aggressiveness." *Journal of Abnormal and Social Psychology*, 1963, *66*, 239-242.

McCord, J.; McCord, W.; and Thurber, E. "Some effects of paternal absence on male children." *Journal of Abnormal and Social Psychology*, 1962, *64*, 361-369.

McDermott, J.F. "Parental divorce in early childhood." *American Journal of Psychiatry*, 1968, *124*, 1424-1432.

McFarland, W.J. "Are girls really smarter?" *Elementary School Journal*, 1969, *70*, 14-19.

Machover, K. *Personality projection in the drawing of the human figure.* Springfield, Illinois: Charles C. Thomas, 1949.

Mackie, J.B.; Maxwell, A.D.; and Rafferty, F.T. "Psychological development of culturally disadvantaged Negro kindergarten children: A study of the selective influence of family and school variables." Paper presented at the meeting of the American Orthopsychiatric Association, Washington, D.C. March 1967.

McKinley, D.G. *Social class and family life.* New York: Free Press, 1964.

McNeil, J.D. "Programmed instruction versus usual classroom procedures in teaching boys to read." *American Education Research Journal*, 1964, *1*, 113-119.

McPherson, S. "Communication of intents among parents and their distrubed adolescent child." *Journal of Abnormal Psychology*, 1970, *76*, 98-105.

Madow, L. and Hardy, S.E. "Incidence and analysis of the broken family in the background of neurosis." *American Journal of Orthopsychiatry*, 1947, *17*, 521-528.

Manis, M. "Personal adjustment, assumed similarity to parents, and inferred parental-evaluations of the self." *Journal of Consulting Psychology*, 1958, *22*, 481-485.

Marzurkrewicz, A.J. "Social-cultural influences and reading." *Journal of Developmental Reading*, 1960, *3*, 254-263.

Maslow, A.H. "Creativity in self-actualizing people." In H.H. Anderson (ed.), *Creativity and its cultivation.* New York: Harper, 1960.

Masters, W.H. and Johnson, V.E. *Human sexual inadequacy.* Boston: Little Brown, 1970.

Maxwell, A.E. "Discrepancies between the pattern of abilities for normal and neurotic children." *Journal of Mental Science*, 1961, *107*, 300-307.

May, R. "Deprivation-enhancement fantasy patterns in men and women." *Journal of Projective Techniques and Personality Assessment*, 1969, *33*, 464-469.

Mead, M. *Male and female.* New York: Morrow, 1949.

Mead, M. "Changing patterns of parent-child relations in an urban culture." *International Journal of Psychoanalysis*, 1957, *38*, 369-378.

Medinnus, G.R. "The relation between inter-parent agreement and several child measures." *Journal of Genetic Psychology*, 1963(a), *102*, 139-144.

Medinnus, G.N. "Delinquents' perception of their parents." *Journal of Consulting Psychology*, 1965, *29*, 5-19.

Meerloo, J.A.M. "The father cuts the cord: The role of the father as initial transference figure." *American Journal of Psychotherapy*, 1956, *10*, 471-480.

Meyer, W. and Thompson, G. "Sex differences in the distribution of teacher approval and disapproval among sixth grade children." *Journal of Educational Psychology*, 1956, *47*, 385-396.

Miller, B. "Effects of father-absence and mother's evaluation of father on the socialization of adolescent boys." Unpublished doctoral dissertation, Columbia University, 1961.

Miller, D.R. and Swanson, G.E. et al. *Inner conflict and defense.* New York: Holt, 1960.

Miller, W.B. "Lower-class culture as a generating milieu of gang delinquency." *Journal of Social Issues*, 1958, *14*, 5-19.

Milton, G.A. "The effects of sex-role identification upon problem solving skill." *Journal of Abnormal and Social Psychology*, 1957, *55*, 208-212.

Mischel, W. "Preference for delayed reinforcement: An experimental study of cultural observation." *Journal of Abnormal and Social Psychology*, 1958, *56*, 57-61.

Mischel, W. "Preference for delayed reward and social responsibility." *Journal of Abnormal and Social Psychology*, 1961(a), *62*, 1-7.

Mischel, W. "Father-absence and delay of gratification." *Journal of Abnormal and Social Psychology*, 1961(b), *62*, 116-124.

Mischel, W. "Delay of gratification, need for achievement, and acquiescence in another culture." *Journal of Abnormal and Social Psychology*, 1961(c), *62*, 543-552.

Mischel, W. "A social learning view of sex differences in behavior." In E.E. Maccoby (ed.), *The development of sex differences.* Stanford: Stanford University Press, 1966, 56-81.

Mishler, E.G. and Waxler, N.E. *Interaction in families.* New York: Wiley, 1968.

Mitchell, D. and Wilson, W. "Relationship of father-absence to masculinity and popularity of delinquent boys." *Psychological Reports*, 1967, *20*, 1173-1174.

Mitchell, G.D. "Paternalistic behavior in primates." *Psychological Bulletin*, 1969, *71*, 399-417.

Mitscherlich, A. *Society without the father.* New York: Harcourt, Brace, 1969.

Monahan, T.P. "Family status and the delinquent child." *Social Forces*, 1957, *35*, 250-258.

Money, J. and Ehrhardt, A. *Man and woman: Boy and girl.* Baltimore: Johns Hopkins Press, 1972.

Moulton, P.W.; Burnstein, E.; Liberty, D.; and Altucher, N. "The patterning of parental affection and dominance as a determinant of guilt and sex-typing." *Journal of Personality and Social Psychology*, 1966, *4* 363-365.

Mowrer, O.H. "Identification: A link between learning theory and psychotherapy." In *Learning theory and personality dynamics*. New York: Ronald Press, 1950, 573-616.

Moynihan, D.P. *The Negro family: The case for national action.* Washington, D.C.: United States Department of Labor, 1965.

Mumbauer, C.C. Resistance to temptation in young Negro children in relation to sex of the subject, sex of the experimenter, and father-absence or presence. *DARCEE Papers and Reports*, 1969, *3*, No. 2.

Murdock, G.P. "Comparative data on the division of labor by sex." *Social Forces*, 1936, *15*, 551-553.

Murrell, S.A. and Stachowiak, J.G. "Consistency, rigidity, and power in the interaction of clinic and non-clinic families." *Journal of Abnormal Psychology*, 1967, *72*, 265-272.

Mussen, P.H. "Some antecedents and consequences of masculine sex-typing in adolescent boys." *Psychological Monographs*, 1961, *75*, No. 2 (Whole No. 506).

Mussen, P.H. "Long-term consequents of masculinity of interests in adolescence." *Journal of Consulting Psychology*, 1962, *26*, 435-440.

Mussen, P.H.; Conger, J.J.; and Kagan, J. *Child development and personality*. New York: Harper and Row, 1974.

Mussen, P.H. and Distler, L. "Masculinity, identification, and father-son relationships." *Journal of Abnormal and Social Psychology*, 1959, *59*, 350-356.

Mussen, P.H. and Distler, L. "Child-rearing antecedents of masculine identification in kindergarten boys." *Child Development*, 1960, *31*, 89-100.

Mussen, P.H. and Jones, M.C. "The behavior-inferred motivation of late and early maturing boys." *Child Development*, 1957, *28*, 243-256.

Mussen, P.H. and Parker, A.L. "Mother nurturance and the girls' incidental imitative learning." *Journal of Personality and Social Psychology*, 1965, *2*, 94-97.

Mussen, P.H. and Rutherford, E.F. "Parent-child relationships and parental personality in relation to young children's sex-role preferences." *Child Development*, 1963, *34*, 589-607.

Mussen, P.H.; Young, H.B.; Gaddini, R.; and Morante, L. "The influence of father-son relationships on adolescent personality and attitudes." *Journal of Child Psychology and Psychiatry*, 1963, *4*, 3-16.

Mutimer, D.; Loughlin, L.; and Powell, M. "Some differences in the family relationships of achieving and underachieving readers." *Journal of Genetic Psychology*, 1966, *109*, 67-74.

Nakamura, C.V. and Rogers, M.M. "Parents' expectations of autonomous behavior and children's autonomy." *Developmental Psychology*, 1969, *1*, 613-617.

Nash, J. "The father in contemporary culture and current psychological literature." *Child Development*, 1965, *36*, 261-297.

Nash, J. and Hayes, T. "The parental relationships of male homosexuals: Some theoretical issues and a pilot study." *Australian Journal of Psychology*, 1965, *17*, 35-43.

Nelsen, E.A. and Maccoby, E.E. "The relationship between social development and differential abilities on the scholastic aptitude test." *Merrill-Palmer Quarterly*, 1966, *12*, 269-289.

Nelsen, E.A. and Vangen, P.M. "The impact of father absence upon heterosexual behaviors and social development of preadolescent girls in a ghetto environment." *Proceedings of the 79th Annual Convention of the American Psychological Association*, 1971, *6*, 165-166.

Neubauer, P.B. "The one-parent child and his Oedipal development." *The Psychoanalytic Study of the Child*, 1960, *15*, 286-309.

Norton, A. "Incidence of neurosis related to maternal age and birth order." *British Journal of Social Medicine*, 1952, *6*, 253-258.

Nowicki, S., Jr. and Segal, W. "Perceived parental characteristics, locus of control orientation, and behavioral correlates of locus of control." *Developmental Psychology*, 1974, *10*, 33-37.

Nye, F.I. "Child adjustment in broken and unhappy unbroken homes." *Marriage and Family Living*, 1957, *19*, 356-361.

Nye, F.I. *Family relationships and delinquent behavior.* New York: Wiley, 1958.

Nye, F.I. "Employment status of mothers and adjustment of adolescent children." *Marriage and Family Living*, 1959, *21*, 240-244.

O'Connor, P.J. "Aetiological factors in homosexuality as seen in R.A.F. psychiatric practice." *British Journal of Psychiatry*, 1964, *110*, 381-391.

Oltman, J.E., and Friedman, S. "Parental deprivation in psychiatric conditions: III. In personality disorders and other conditions." *Diseases of the Nervous System*, 1967, *28*, 298-303.

Oltman, J.E.; McGarry, J.J.; and Friedman, S. "Parental deprivation and the 'broken home' in dementia praecox and other mental disorders." *American Journal of Psychiatry*, 1952, *108*, 685-694.

Ostrovsky, E.S. *Father to the child: Case studies of the experiences of a male teacher.* New York: Putnam, 1959.

Palmer, R.C. "Behavior problems of children in Navy officers' families." *Social Casework*, 1960, *41*, 177-184.

Papenek, M.L. "Authority and sex roles in the family." *Journal of Marriage and the Family*, 1969, *31*, 88-96.

Parker, S. and Kleiner, R.J. "Characteristics of Negro mothers in single-headed households." *Journal of Marriage and the Family*, 1966, *28*, 507-513.

Parsons, T. "Family structure and the socialization of the child." In T. Parsons and R.F. Bales (eds.), *Family, socialization and interaction process.* Glencoe, Illinois: Free Press, 1955, 25-131.

Parsons, T. "Social structure and the development of personality: Freud's contribution to the integration of psychology and sociology." *Psychiatry*, 1958, *21*, 321-340.

Payne, D.E. and Mussen, P.H. "Parent-child relations and father-identification among adolescent boys." *Journal of Abnormal and Social Psychology*, 1956, *52*, 358-362.

Pedersen, F.A. "Relationships between father-absence and emotional disturbance in male military dependents." *Merrill-Palmer Quarterly*, 1966, *12*, 321-331.

Pedersen, F.A. and Robson, K.S. "Father participation in infancy." *American Journal of Orthopsychiatry*, 1969, *39*, 466-472.

Peterson, D.R.; Becker, W.C.; Hellmer, L.A.; Shoemaker, D.J.; and Quay, H.C. "Parental attitudes and child adjustment." *Child Development*, 1959, *30*, 119-130.

Pettigrew, T.F. *A profile of the Negro American.* Princeton: Van Nostrand, 1964.

Phelan, H.M. "The incidence and possible significance of the drawing of female figures by sixth-grade boys in response to the Draw-A-Person Test." *Psychiatric Quarterly*, 1964, *38*, 1-16.

Phillips, J. "Performance of father-present and father-absent southern Negro boys on a simple operant task as a function of race and sex of the experimenter and the type of social reinforcement." Unpublished doctoral dissertation, University of Minnesota, 1966.

Piety, K.R. "Patterns of parent perceptions among neuropsychiatric patients and normal controls." *Journal of Clinical Psychology*, 1967, *23*, 428-433.

Pinter, R. and Fortano, G. "Some measures of dominance in college women." *Journal of Social Psychology*, 1944, *19*, 303-315.

Plank, E.H. and Plank, R. "Emotional components in arithmetic learning as seen through autobiographies." *The Psychoanalytic Study of the Child*, 1954, *9*, 274-293.

Podolsky, E. "The emotional problems of the stepchild."*Mental Hygiene*, 1955, *39*, 43-53.

Poffenberger, T.A. "A research note on father-child relations and father viewed as a negative figure." *Child Development*, 1959, *30*, 489-492.

Poffenberger, T.A. and Norton, D. "Factors in the formation of attitudes towards mathematics." *Journal of Educational Research*, 1959, *52*, 171-176.

Polardy, J.N. "What teachers believe, what children achieve." *Elementary School Journal*, 1969, *69*, 370-374.

Pollak, G.K. "Sexual dynamics of parents without partners." *Social Work*, 1970, *15*, 79-85.

Pope, B. "Socioeconomic contrasts in children's peer culture prestige values," *Genetic Psychology Monographs*, 1953, *48*, 157-200.

Portnoy, S.M.; Biller, H.B.; and Davids, A. "The influence of the child care worker in residential treatment." *American Journal of Orthopsychiatry*, 1972, *42*, 719-722.

Preston, R. "Reading achievement of German and American children." *School and Society*, 1962, *90*, 350-354.

Propper, A.M. "The relationship of maternal employment to adolescent roles, activities, and parental relationships." *Journal of Marriage and the Family*, 1972, *34*, 417-421.

Rabban, M. "Sex-role identification in young children in two diverse social groups." *Genetic Psychology Monographs*, 1950, *42*, 81-158.

Rabin, A.I. "Some psychosexual differences between Kibbutz and non-Kibbutz Israeli boys." *Journal of Projective Techniques*, 1958, *22*, 328-332.

Radin, N. "Father-child interaction and the intellectual functioning of four-year-old boys." *Developmental Psychology*, 1972, *6*, 353-361.

Radin, N. "Observed paternal behaviors as antecedents of intellectual functioning in young boys." *Developmental Psychology*, 1973, *8*, 369-376.

Rainwater, L. "Crucible of identity." *Daedalus*, 1966, *95*, 172-216.

Rainwater, L. and Yancey, W.L. *The Moynihan Report and the politics of controversy*. Cambridge, Mass.: M.I.T. Press, 1967.

Rebelsky, F. and Hanks, C. "Fathers' verbal interaction with infants in the first three months of life." *Child Development*, 1971, *42*, 63-68.

Redican, W.K. and Mitchell, G. "The social behavior of adult male-infant pairs of rhesus monkeys in a laboratory environment." *American Journal of Physical Anthropology*, 1973, *38*, 523-526.

Reuter, M.W. and Biller, H.B. "Perceived paternal nurturance-availability and personality adjustment among college males." *Journal of Consulting and Clinical Psychology*, 1973, *40*, 339-342.

Rexford, E.N. "Antisocial young children and their families." In M.R. Haworth (ed.), *Child psychotherapy*. New York: Basic Books, 1964, 58-63.

Ringness, T.A. "Identifying figures, their achievement values, and children's values as related to actual and predicted achievement." *Journal of Educational Psychology*, 1970, *61*, 174-185.

Risen, M.L. "Relation of lack of one or both parents to school progress." *Elementary School Journal*, 1939, *39*, 528-531.

Robey, A.; Rosenwald, R.J.; Snell, J.E.; and Lee, R.E. "The runaway girl: A reaction to family stress." *American Journal of Orthopsychiatry*, 1964, *34*, 762-767.

Robins, E.; Schmidt, E.H.; and O'Neal, P. "Some interrelations of social factors and clinical diagnosis in attempted suicide." *American Journal of Psychiatry*, 1957, *114*, 221-231.

Rogers, W.B. and Long, J.M. "Male models and sexual identification: A case from the Out Island Bahamas." *Human Organization*, 1968, *27*, 326-331.

Rohrer, H.H. and Edmonson, M.S. *The eighth generation*. New York: Harper, 1960.

Romney, A.K. "Variations in household structure as determinants of sex-typed behavior." In F. Beach (ed.), *Sex and behavior*. New York: Wiley, 1965, 208-220.

Rosen, B.C. and D'Andrade, R. "The psychosocial origins of achievement motivation." *Sociometry*, 1959, *22*, 185-218.

Rosen, L. "Matriarchy and lower-class, Negro-male delinquency." *Social Problems*, 1969, *17*, 175-189.

Rosenberg, B.G. and Sutton-Smith, B. "The measurement of masculinity and femininity in children." *Child Development*, 1959, *30*, 373-380.

Rosenberg, B.G. and Sutton-Smith, B. "The measurement of masculine-feminine differences in play activities." *Journal of Genetic Psychology*, 1960, *96*, 165-170.

Rosenberg, B.G. and Sutton-Smith, B. "Ordinal position and sex-role identification." *Genetic Psychology Monographs*, 1964, *70*, 297-328.

Rosenberg, B.G. and Sutton-Smith, B. "Sibling association, family size, and cognitive abilities." *Journal of Genetic Psychology*, 1966, *107*, 271-279.

Rosenberg, B.G.; Sutton-Smith, B.; and Morgan, E. "The use of opposite-sex scales as a measure of psychosexual deviancy." *Journal of Consulting Psychology*, 1961, *25*, 221-225.

Rosenberg, C.M. "Determinants of psychiatric illness in young people." *British Journal of Psychiatry*, 1969, *115*, 907-915.

Rosenberg, M. *Society and the adolescent self-image.* Princeton: Princeton University Press, 1965.

Rosenkrantz, P.; Vogel, S.; Bee, J.; Broverman, I.; and Broverman, D.M. "Sex-role stereotypes and self-concepts in college students." *Journal of Consulting and Clinical Psychology*, 1968, *32*, 287-295.

Rosenthal, M.S.; Ni, E.; Finkelstein, M.; and Berkwits, G.K. "Father-child relationships and children's problems." *Archives of General Psychiatry*, 1962, *7*, 360-373.

Roth, J., and Peck, R.F. "Social class and social mobility factors related to marital adjustment." *American Sociological Review*, 1951, *16*, 478-487.

Rothbart, M.K. and Maccoby, E.E. "Parents' differential reactions to sons and daughters." *Journal of Personality and Social Psychology*, 1966, *4*, 237-243.

Rouman, J. "School children's problems as related to parental factors." *Journal of Educational Research*, 1956, *50*, 105-112.

Rowntree, G. "Early childhood in broken families." *Population Studies*, 1955, *8*, 247-253.

Rubenstein, B.O. and Levitt, M. "Some observations regarding the role of fathers in child psychotherapy." *Bulletin of the Menninger Clinic*, 1957, *21*, 16-27.

Rushing, W.A. "Adolescent-parent relationships and mobility aspirations." *Social Forces*, 1964, *43*, 157-166.

Russell, I.L. "Behavior problems of children from broken and intact homes." *Journal of Educational Sociology*, 1957, *31*, 124-129.

Rutherford, E.E. "A note on the relation of parental dominance to children's ability to make sex-role discriminations." *Journal of Genetic Psychology*, 1969, *114*, 185-191.

Rutherford, E.E. and Mussen, P.H. "Generosity in nursery school boys." *Child Development*, 1968, *39*, 755-765.

Rutter, M. *Maternal deprivation: Reassessed.* New York: Penguin Books, 1972.

Ryans, D.G. *Characteristics of teachers.* Washington, D.C.: American Council on Education, 1960.

Rychlak, J. and Legerski, A. "A sociocultural theory of appropriate sexual role identification and level of personality adjustment." *Journal of Personality*, 1967, *35* (1), 31-49.

Ryder, R.G. and Goodrich, D.W. "Married couples' responses to disagreement." *Family Process*, 1966, *5*, 30-42.

Saghir, M.T. and Robbins, F. *Male and female homosexuality*, Baltimore: Williams and Wilkins, 1973.

Salzman, L. "Psychology of the female: A new look." *Archives of General Psychiatry*, 1967, *17*, 195-203.

Sanford, N. "The dynamics of identification." *Psychological Review*, 1955, *62*, 106-118.

Santrock, J.W. "Paternal absence, sex-typing, and identification." *Developmental Psychology*, 1970(a), *2*, 264-272.

Santrock, J.W. "Influence of onset and type of paternal absence on the first four Eriksonian developmental crises." *Developmental Psychology*, 1970(b), *3*, 273-274.

Santrock, J.W. "Relation of type and onset of father-absence to cognitive development." *Child Development*, 1972, *43*, 455-469.

Santrock, J.W. and Wohlford, P. Effects of father absence: influences of, reason for, and onset of absence. *Proceedings of the 78th Annual Convention of the American Psychological Association*, 1970, *5*, 265-266.

Schaefer, E.S. "Children's reports of parental behavior: An inventory." *Child Development*, 1965, *36*, 413-424.

Schaffer, H.R. and Emerson, P.E. The development of social attachments in infancy. *Monographs of the Society for Research in Child Development*, 1964, *29*,(No. 2).

Schlesinger, B. "The one-parent family: An overview." *Family Life Coordinator*, 1966, *15*, 133-137.

Schoeppe, A.; Haggard, E.A.; and Havighurst, R.J. "Some factors affecting sixteen-year-olds' success in five developmental tasks." *Journal of Abnormal and Social Psychology*, 1953, *48*, 42-52.

Schuham, A.I. "Power relations in emotionally disturbed and normal family triads." *Journal of Abnormal Psychology*, 1970, *75*, 30-37.

Sears, P.S. "Doll-play aggression in normal young children: Influence of sex, age, sibling status, father's absence." *Psychological Monographs*, 1951, *65*, (No. 6).

Sears, P.S. "Child-rearing factors related to playing of sex-typed roles." *American Psychologist*, 1953, *8*, 431 (Abstract).

Sears, R.R. "Identification as a form of behavior development." In D.B. Harris (ed.), *The concept of development*. Minneapolis: University of Minnesota Press, 1957, 149-161.

Sears, R.R. "Relation of early socialization experiences to self-concepts and gender role in middle childhood." *Child Development*, 1970, *41*, 267-289.

Sears, R.R.; Pintler, M.H.; and Sears, P.S. "Effect of father-separation on preschool children's doll-play aggression." *Child Development*, 1946, *17*, 219-243.

Sears, R.R.; Rau, L.; and Alpert, R. *Identification and child rearing.* Stanford: Stanford University Press, 1965.

Seder, J.A. "The origin of differences in extent of independence in children: Developmental factors in perceptual field dependence." Unpublished doctoral dissertation, Radcliffe College, 1957.

Seplin, C.D. "A study of the influence of the father's absence for military service." *Smith College Studies in Social Work* 1952, *22*, 123-124.

Seward, G.H. "Cultural conflict and the feminine role: An experimental study." *Journal of Social Psychology*, 1945, *22*, 177-194.

Seward, G.H. *Sex and the social order.* New York: McGraw-Hill, 1946.

Sexton, P.C. *The feminized male: Classrooms, white collars, and the decline of manliness.* New York: Random House, 1969.

Shaw, M.C. and White, D.L. "The relationship between child-parent identification and academic underachievement." *Journal of Clinical Psychology*, 1965, *21*, 10-13.

Sheldon, W.H. "Constitutional factors in personality." In J. McV. Hunt (ed.), *Personality and the behavior disorders.* New York: Ronald Press, 1944, 526-549.

Sherman, R.C. and Smith, F. "Sex differences in cue-dependency as a function of socialization environment." *Perceptual and Motor Skills*, 1967, *24*, 599-602.

Shortell, J.R. and Biller, H.B. "Aggression in children as a function of sex of subject and sex of opponent." *Development Psychology*, 1970, *3*, 143-144.

Siegelman, M. "College student personality correlates of early parent-child relationship." *Journal of Consulting Psychology*, 1965, *29*, 558-564.

Siegman, A.W. "Father-absence during childhood and antisocial behavior." *Journal of Abnormal Psychology*, 1966, *71*, 71-74.

Slater, P.E. "Parental behavior and the personality of the child." *Journal of Genetic Psychology*, 1962, *101*, 53-68.

Slocum, W.L. and Stone, C.L. "Family culture patterns and delinquent-type behavior." *Marriage and Family Living*, 1963, *25*, 202-208.

Smelser, W.T. "Adolescent and adult occupational choice as a function of family socioeconomic history." *Sociometry*, 1963, *4*, 393-409.

Solomon, D. "The generality of children's achievement-related behavior." *Journal of Genetic Psychology*, 1969, *114*, 109-125.

Sopchak, A.L. "Parental 'identification' and tendency toward disorder as measured by the MMPI." *Journal of Abnormal and Social Psychology*, 1952, *47*, 159-165.

Spelke, E.; Zelazo, P.; Kagan, J.; and Kotelchuck, M. "Father interaction and separation protest." *Developmental Psychology*, 1973, *9*, 83-90.

Stanfield, R.E. "The interaction of family variables and gang variables in the aetiology of delinquency." *Social Problems*, 1966, *13*, 411-417.

Steimel, R.J. "Childhood experiences and masculinity-femininity scores." *Journal of Consulting Psychology*, 1960, 7, 212-217.

Stein, A.H. "The effects of sex-role standards for achievement and sex-role preference on three determinants of achievement motivation." *Developmental Psychology*, 1971, *4*, 219-231.

Stein, A.H.; Pohly, S.R.; and Muellar, E. "Sex-typing of achievement areas as a determinant of children's motivation and effort." Paper presented at the meeting of the Society for Research in Child Development, Santa Monica, California, March 1969.

Stein, A.H. and Smithells, J. "Age and sex differences in children's sex-role standards about achievement." *Developmental Psychology*, 1969, *1*, 252-259.

Stendler, C.B. "Critical periods in socialization and overdependency." *Child Development*, 1952, *23*, 3-12.

Stendler, C.B. "Possible causes of overdependency in young children." *Child Development*, 1954, *25*, 125-146.

Stephens, W.N. "Judgments by social workers on boys and mothers in fatherless families." *Journal of Genetic Psychology*, 1961, *99*, 59-64.

Stephens, W.N. *The Oedipus complex: Cross-cultural evidence*. Glencoe, Illinois: Free Press, 1962.

Stoke, S.M. "An inquiry into the concept of identification." *Journal of Genetic Psychology*, 1950, *76*, 164-184.

Stoller, R.J. *Sex and gender*. New York: Science House, 1968.

Stolz, L.M., et al. *Father relations of war-born children*. Stanford: Stanford University Press, 1954.

Strang, J.B. "Students' reasons for becoming better readers." *Education*, 1968, *89*, 127-131.

Straus, M.A. "Conjugal power structure and adolescent personality." *Marriage and Family Living*, 1962, *24*, 17-25.

Strodtbeck, F.L. "Family interaction, values, and achievement." In D.C. McClelland et al. (eds.), *Talent and society*, New York: Van Nostrand, 1958, 135-194.

Suedfield, P. "Paternal absence and overseas success of Peace Corps volunteers." *Journal of Consulting Psychology*, 1967, *31*, 424-425.

Sunley, R. Early nineteenth-century American literature on childrearing. In M. Mead and M. Wolfenstein (eds.), *Childhood in contemporary cultures*. Chicago: University of Chicago Press, 1955.

Sutherland, H.E.G. "The relationship between I.Q. and size of family in the case of fatherless children." *Journal of Genetic Psychology*, 1930, *38*, 161-170.

Sutton-Smith, B.; Roberts, J.M.; and Rosenberg, B.G. "Sibling associations and role involvement." *Merrill-Palmer Quarterly*, 1964, *10*, 25-38.

Sutton-Smith, B. and Rosenberg, B.G. "Age changes in the effects of ordinal position on sex-role identification." *Journal of Genetic Psychology*, 1965, *107*, 61-73.

Sutton-Smith, B. and Rosenberg, B.G. *The sibling*. New York: Holt, Rinehart and Winston, 1970.

Sutton-Smith, B.; Rosenberg, B.G.; and Landy, F. "Father-absence effects in families of different sibling compositions." *Child Development*, 1968, *38*, 1213-1221.

Swenson, C.H. and Newton, K.R. "The development of sexual differentiation on the Draw-A-Person Test." *Journal of Clinical Psychology*, 1955, *11*, 417-419.

Switzer, D.K.; Grigg, A.E.; Miller, J.S.; and Young, R.K. "Early experiences and occupational choice: A test of Roe's hypothesis." *Journal of Counseling Psychology*, 1962, *9*, 45-48.

Tallman, I. "Spousal role differentiation and the socialization of severely retarded children." *Journal of Marriage and the Family*, 1965, *27*, 37-42.

Tasch, R.J. "The role of the father in the family." *Journal of Experimental Education*, 1952, *20*, 319-361.

Tasch, R.J. "Interpersonal perceptions of fathers and mothers." *Journal of Genetic Psychology*, 1955, *87*, 59-65.

Terman, L.M. *Psychological factors in marital happiness*. New York: McGraw-Hill, 1938.

Terman, L.M. and Miles, C.C. *Sex and personality*. New York: McGraw-Hill, 1936.

Terman, L.M. and Oden, M.H. *The gifted child grows up*. Stanford: Stanford University Press, 1947.

Thomas, A.; Chess, S.; and Birch, H.G. *Temperament and behavior disorders in children*. New York: New York University Press, 1968.

Thomas, A; Chess, S.; Birch, H.G.; Hertzig, M.E.; and Korn, S. *Behavioral individuality in early childhood*. New York: New York University Press, 1963.

Thomes, N.M. "Children with absent fathers." *Journal of Marriage and the Family*, 1968, *30*, 89-96.

Thompson, N.L.; Schwartz, D.M.; McCandless, B.R.; and Edwards, D.A. "Parent-child relationships and sexual identity in male and female homosexuals and heterosexuals." *Journal of Consulting and Clinical Psychology*, 1973, *41*, 120-127.

Thrasher, F.M. *The gang*. Chicago: University of Chicago Press, 1927.

Tiller, P.O. "Father-absence and personality development of children in sailor families." *Nordisk Psyckologi's Monograph Series*, 1958, *9*, 1-48.

Tiller, P.O. *Father separation and adolescence*. Oslo, Norway: Institute for Social Research, 1961.

Toby, J. "The differential impact of family disorganization." *American Sociological Review*, 1957, *22*, 505-512.

Tolor, A.; Brannigan, G.G.; and Murphy, V.M. "Psychological distance, future time perspective, and internal-external expectancy." *Journal of Projective Techniques and Personality Assessment*, 1970, *34*, 283-294.

Torgoff, I. and Dreyer, A.S. "Achievement inducing and independence granting-synergistic parental role components: Relation to daughter's 'parental' role orientation and level of aspiration." *American Psychologist*, 1961, *16*, 345 (Abstract).

Trapp, E.P. and Kausler, D.H. "Dominance attitudes in parents and adult avoidance behavior in young children." *Child Development*, 1958, *29*, 507-513.

Travis, J. "Precipitating factors in manic-depressive psychoses." *Psychiatric Quarterly*, 1933, *8*, 411-418.

Trenaman, J. *Out of step*. London: Methuen, 1952.

Triplett, L. "Elementary education—A man's world?" *The Instructor*, 1968, *78* (3), 50-52.

Trunnell, T.L. "The absent father's children's emotional disturbances." *Archives of General Psychiatry*, 1968, *19*, 180-188.

Tuckman, J. and Regan, R.A. "Intactness of the home and behavioral problems in children." *Journal of Child Psychology and Psychiatry*, 1966 *7*, 225-233.

Tuddenham, R.D. "Studies in reputation: III. Correlates of popularity among elementary school children." *Journal of Educational Psychology*, 1951, *42*, 257-276.

Tuddenham, R.D. "Studies in reputation: I. Sex and grade differences in school children's evaluations of their peers. II. The diagnosis of social adjustment." *Psychological Monographs*, 1952, *66*, (Whole No. 333).

Tyler, L.E. "The relationship of interests to abilities and reputation among first-grade children." *Educational Psychology Measurement*, 1951, *11*, 255-264.

van der Veen, F. "The parent's concept of the family unit and child adjustment." *Journal of Counseling Psychology*, 1965, *12*, 196-200.

Veroff, J.; Atkinson, J.; Feld, S.; and Gurin, G. "The use of thematic apperception to assess motivation in a nationwide interview study." *Psychological Monographs*, 1960, *74*, (Whole No. 499).

Vogel, S.R., et al. "Maternal employment and perception of sex roles among college students." *Developmental Psychology*, 1970, *3*, 384-391.

Vroegh, K.; Jenkin, N.; Black, M.; and Hendrick, M. "Discriminant analysis of preschool masculinity and femininity." *Multivariate Behavioral Research*, 1967, *2*, 299-313.

Wahl, C.W. "Antecedent factors in family histories of 392 schizophrenics." *American Journal of Psychiatry*, 1954, *110*, 668-676.

Wahl, C.W. "Some antecedent factors in the family histories of 568 male schizophrenics of the U.S. Navy." *American Journal of Psychiatry*, 1956, *113*, 201-210.

Walker, R.N. "Body-build and behavior in young children: I. Body-build and nursery school teachers' ratings." *Monograph of the Society for Research in Child Development*, 1962, *27*, No. 3 (Serial No. 84).

Wallach, M.A. and Kogan, N. *Modes of thinking in young children.* New York: Holt, Rinehart and Winston, 1965.

Walters, J. and Stinnett, N. "Parent-Child Relationships: A Decade Review of Research." *Journal of Marriage and The Family*, 1971, *33*, 70-111.

Warren, W. and Cameron, K. "Reactive psychosis in adolescence." *Journal of Mental Science*, 1950, *96*, 448-457.

Washburn, W.C. "The effects of physique and intrafamily tension on self-concept in adolescent males." *Journal of Consulting Psychology*, 1962, *26*, 460-466.

Webb, A.P. "Sex-role preferences and adjustment in early adolescents." *Child Development*, 1963, *34*, 609-618.

Weisberg, P.S. and Springer, K.J. "Environment factors in creative function: A study of gifted children." *Archives of General Psychiatry*, 1961, *5*, 554-564.

Werts, C.E. Paternal influence on career choice. *Journal of Counseling Psychology*, 1968, *15*, 48-52.

West, D.J. "Parental relationships in male homosexuality." *International Journal of Social Psychiatry*, 1959, *5*, 85-97.

West, D.J. *Homosexuality.* Chicago: Aldine, 1967.

Westley, W.A. and Epstein, N.B. *Silent majority.* San Francisco: Jossey-Bass, 1970.

White, B. "The relationship of self-concept and parental identification to women's vocational interests." *Journal of Consulting Psychology*, 1959, *6*, 202-206.

White, R.W. "Competence and the psychosexual stages of development." In M.R. Jones (ed.), *Nebraska symposium on motivation.* Lincoln: University of Nebraska Press, 1960, 97-141.

Whiting, J.W.M. "Sorcery, sin, and the superego: A cross-cultural study of some mechanisms of social control." In M.R. Jones (ed.), *Nebraska symposium on motivation*, Lincoln: University of Nebraska Press, 1959, 174-195.

Whiting, J.W.M. "Research mediation and learning by identification." In I. Iscoe and H.W. Stevenson (eds.), *Personality development in children.* Austin, Texas: University of Texas Press, 1960.

Whiting, J.W.M.; Kluckhohn, R.; and Anthony, A. "The function of male initiation ceremonies at puberty." In E.E. Maccoby, T.M. Newcomb, and E.L. Hartley (eds.), *Readings in social psychology.* New York: Holt, 1958, 359-370.

Williams, D. "Sexual role identification and personality functioning in girls: A theory revisited." *Journal of Personality*, 1973, *41*, 1-8.

Winch, R.F. "The relation between loss of a parent and progress in courtship." *Journal of Social Psychology*, 1949, *29*, 51-56.

Winch, R.F. "Some data bearing on the Oedipus hypothesis." *Journal of Abnormal and Social Psychology*, 1950, *45*, 481-489.

Winch, R.F. "Further data and observations on the Oedipus hypothesis: The consequences of an inadequate hypothesis." *American Sociological Review*, 1951, *16*, 784-795.

Winch, R.F. *Identification and its familial determinants*. New York: Bobbs-Merrill, 1962.

Witkin, H.A., "The problem of individuality in development." In B. Kaplan and S. Wapner (eds.), *Perspectives in psychological theory*. New York: International Universities Press, 1960, 335-361.

Witkin, H.A.; Dyk, R.B.; Faterson, H.F.; Goodenough, D.R.; and Karp, S.A. *Psychological differentiation*. New York: Wiley, 1962.

Wohlford, P. and Liberman, D. "Effects of father absence on personal time, field independence, and anxiety." *Proceedings of the 78th Annual Convention of the American Psychological Association*, 1970, *5*, 263-264.

Wohlford, P.; Santrock, J.W.; Berger, S.E.; and Liberman, D. "Older brothers' influence on sex-typed, aggressive, and dependent behavior in father-absent children." *Developmental Psychology*, 1971, *4*, 124-134.

Wood, H.P. and Duffy, E.L. Psychological factors in alcoholic women. *American Journal of Psychiatry*, 1966, *123*, 341-345.

Wright, B. and Tuska, S. "The nature and origin of feeling feminine." *British Journal of Social Psychology*, 1966, *5*, 140-149.

Wyer, R.S., Jr. "Effect of child-rearing attitudes and behavior on children's responses to hypothetical social situations." *Journal of Personality and Social Psychology*, 1965(a), *2*, 480-486.

Wyer, R.S., Jr. "Self-acceptance, discrepancy between parents' perceptions of their children, and goal-seeking effectiveness." *Journal of Personality and Social Psychology*, 1965(b), *2*, 311-316.

Wylie, H.L. and Delgado, R.A. "A pattern of mother-son relationship involving the absence of the father." *American Journal of Orthopsychiatry*, 1959, *29*, 644-649.

Wynn, M. *Fatherless families*. London: Michael Joseph, 1964.

Yarrow, L.J. "Separation from parents during early childhood." In M.L. Hoffman and L.W. Hoffman (eds.), *Review of child development research*, *Vol. 1*. New York: Russell Sage Foundation, 1964, 89-136.

Zeichner, A. "Psychosexual identification in paranoid schizophrenia." *Journal of Projective Techniques*, 1955, *19*, 67-77.

Zeichner, A. "Conception of masculine and feminine roles in paranoid schizophrenics." *Journal of Projective Techniques*, 1956, *20*, 348-354.

Zelditch, M., Jr. "Role differentiation in the nuclear family: A comparative study." In T. Parsons and R.F. Bales (eds.), *Family, socialization and interaction process*. New York: Free Press, 1955, 307-352.

Author Index

Subject Index

Abusive fathers, 35, 69

Academic adjustment. *See* Classroom adjustment

Academic skills. *See* Cognitive functioning

Achievement, 61, 73, 111, 125-127, 131, 137, 138, 139, 140-152. *See also* Cognitive functioning, Vocational adjustment

Achievement motivation, 61, 110, 112, 132, 137-139, 153

Activity level. *See* Constitutional factors

Adaptation, 28-29, 135. *See also* Interpersonal relations, Psychopathology

Adjective check list, 19, 37, 45, 102, 110, 126

Adjustment. *See* Interpersonal relations, Psychopathology

Adolescence, 6, 17, 30, 34, 45, 47-48, 52, 55-56, 57, 70, 71, 79, 82, 106, 115, 117-118, 119, 133, 162. *See also* Developmental stages

Adoption, 89, 160. *See also* Sex role adoption

Affiliation. *See* Interpersonal relations

Age periods. *See* Developmental stages

Aggression, 30, 35, 41, 42, 48, 52, 65, 66, 88, 91, 94, 101, 102, 105, 111, 116, 117, 137, 145, 146, 152

Alcoholism, 69, 80, 92, 122

American College Entrance Examination, 129

Anaclitic identification, 12, 105

Analytical functioning. *See* Cognitive styles

Anatomical factors. *See* Physique

Animal studies, 2

Antisocial behavior. *See* Delinquency

Anxiety, 23, 34, 57-59, 71, 73, 77, 80, 85, 95, 101, 110, 111, 117, 118, 120, 137. *See also* Sexual anxiety, Sex role conflict

Aptitude. *See* Cognitive functioning

Assertiveness, 8, 96, 101, 108, 110, 111, 121, 143, 145, 146, 152, 153, 166, 167

Athletics, 19, 135, 144, 145-146, 147, 148, 149, 159

Attachment, 5, 6, 25-30, 78, 83, 94, 132, 139, 163. *See also* Identification

Attitudes. *See* Sex role preference, Sex role stereotypes

Australian aborigines, 3

Authority figures, 66-67, 68, 74, 84, 143. *See also* Feminized classroom, Limit setting

Autism, 83

Autonomy. *See* Independence

Baboons, 2

Bahamas, 43

Behavior modification, 156. *See also* Psychotherapy

Big Brothers, 157

Biological perspective, 2-3. *See also* Constitutional factors

Birth order, 50-52, 96. *See also* Siblings

Bisexuality, 11

Black children, 41, 42, 48, 64, 76, 89, 93, 116, 117, 127, 130, 140

Blacky Test, 42-43

Body image. *See* Physique

Body type. *See* Physique

Boy Scouts, 157

Broken homes. *See* Divorce, Death of father, Father absence

California Psychological Inventory, 20, 34, 56, 63, 70, 111

Career. *See* Vocational adjustment

Caribbean children, 44, 45, 64

Castration anxiety, 11, 57, 58, 105

Child custody, 160

Childhood schizophrenia, 83. *See also* Psychopathology, Psychosis

Child Personality and Psychopathology: Current Topics, xiii, 125

Chimpanzees, 2

Class differences. *See* Socioeconomic status

Classroom adjustment, 60, 72, 80, 88, 116, 122, 137-138, 142, 143-152

Cognitive-developmental theory, 15-16, 140

About the Author

Henry B. Biller is an associate professor of psychology at the University of Rhode Island. He was a Phi Beta Kappa, Magna Cum Laude graduate from Brown University, 1962; a United States Public Health Service predoctoral fellow at Duke University, 1962-1965; a clinical psychology intern at the Emma Pendleton Bradley Hospital, 1965-1966; and a United States Public Health predoctoral research fellow at Duke, 1966-1967. After receiving the Ph.D. from Duke in 1967 he was a faculty member at the University of Massachusetts (1967-1969) and at George Peabody College (1969-1970). His academic positions have all included participation in University-affiliated mental health facilities (University of Massachusetts Child Guidance Clinic; George Peabody College Child Study Center; University of Rhode Island Psychology Clinic). He is a consultant at the Emma Pendleton Bradley Hospital and the Providence Veterans Administration Hospital, and is a Fellow of the American Psychological Association. In addition to *Paternal Deprivation* and numerous scientific articles, he is the author of *Father, Child and Sex Role* (Lexington Books, D.C. Heath, 1971) and coauthor with Dennis Meredith of *Fathers and Children* (David McKay, in press).